T0205535

Signals and Communication Technology

This series is devoted to fundamentals and applications of modern methods of signal processing and cutting-edge communication technologies. The main topics are information and signal theory, acoustical signal processing, image processing and multimedia systems, mobile and wireless communications, and computer and communication networks. Volumes in the series address researchers in academia and industrial R&D departments. The series is application-oriented. The level of presentation of each individual volume, however, depends on the subject and can range from practical to scientific.

Indexing: All books in "Signals and Communication Technology" are indexed by Scopus and zbMATH

For general information about this book series, comments or suggestions, please contact Mary James at mary.james@springer.com or Ramesh Nath Premnath at ramesh.premnath@springer.com.

More information about this series at https://link.springer.com/bookseries/4748

Aaisha Makkar · Neeraj Kumar
Editors

Deep Learning for Security and Privacy Preservation in IoT

 Springer

Editors
Aaisha Makkar
University of Derby
Derby, UK

Neeraj Kumar
Thapar Institute of Engineering
and Technology
Patiala, Punjab, India

King Abdul Aziz University
Jeddah, Saudi Arabia

ISSN 1860-4862   ISSN 1860-4870 (electronic)
Signals and Communication Technology
ISBN 978-981-16-6188-4   ISBN 978-981-16-6186-0 (eBook)
https://doi.org/10.1007/978-981-16-6186-0

This Springer imprint is published by the registered company Springer Nature Singapore Pte Ltd.
The registered company address is: 152 Beach Road, #21-01/04 Gateway East, Singapore 189721,
Singapore

Contents

About the Editors

Dr. Aaisha Makkar is serving as a Lecturer in Computer Science in College of Science and Engineering at the University of Derby, UK. For a year (2020/21), she served at Department of Computer Science, Seoul National University of Science & Technology (South Korea) as a postdoctoral (Research) Professor. Prior to that, she worked as a research fellow at Thapar University and awarded with the degree of Doctorate of Philosophy (Ph.D.). Her doctorate objectives were focused towards Cyber Security using techniques of Artificial Intelligence. During her research career, She worked for various research projects like research scientist in NRF project. She also have received many travel grants from reputed organisations such as SERB DST, IEEE CIS. She believes to conduct research on industry oriented techniques such as Federated Learning, although her interests include Machine Learning, Deep Learning, and Active Learning. Dr. Aaisha has demonstrated expertise in these research domains in terms of research publications, book chapters and Book. She is the author of Book, entitled, 'Machine Learning in Cognitive IoT' with the CRC (Taylor & Francis) publisher. As of now (March 2022), she published more than 20 SCI journals (first author) in reputed journals such as IEEE (TII, IoT) Elsevier (FGCS, SCSI, IPM). She is actively participating in editorial services as an Associate Editor, Guest editor, and Program chair.

Prof. Neeraj Kumar is the 2019, 2020 highly-cited researcher from WoS and published more than 400 technical research papers (DBLP: https://dblp.org/pers/hd/k/Kumar_0001:Neeraj) in top-cited journals and conferences which are cited more than 26930 from well-known researchers across the globe with current h-index of 88 and i-10 index as 446 (Google scholar: https://scholar.google.com/citations?hl=en&user=gL9gR-4AAAAJ). He is highly cited researcher in 2019, 2020 in the list released by Web of Science (WoS).

He has guided many research scholars leading to Ph.D. and M.E./M.Tech. His research is supported by funding from various competitive agencies across the globe. His broad research areas are Green computing and Network management, IoT, Big Data Analytics, Deep learning and cyber-security. He has also edited/authored 10 books with International/National Publishers like IET, Springer, Elsevier, CRC.

Security and Privacy of Electronic Healthcare Records: Concepts, paradigms and solutions (ISBN-13: 978-1-78561-898-7), Machine Learning for cognitive IoT, CRC Press, Blockchain, Big Data and Machine learning, CRC Press, Blockchain Technologies across industrial vertical, Elsevier, Multimedia Big Data Computing for IoT Applications: Concepts, Paradigms and Solutions (ISBN: 978-981-13-8759-3), Proceedings of First International Conference on Computing, Communications, and Cyber-Security (IC4S 2019) (ISBN 978-981-15-3369-3). Probabilistic Data Structures for Blockchain based IoT Applications, CRC Press. One of the edited textbook entitled, *"Multimedia Big Data Computing for IoT Applications: Concepts, Paradigms, and Solutions"* published in Springer in 2019 is having **3.5 million downloads till 06 June 2020**. It attracts attention of the researchers across the globe. (https://www.springer.com/in/book/9789811387586).

He is serving as editors of *ACM Computing Survey, IEEE Transactions on Sustainable Computing, IEEE Systems Journal, IEEE Network Magazine, Elsevier Journal of Networks and Computer Applications, Elsevier Computer Communication, Wiley International Journal of Communication Systems.* Also, he has organized various special issues of journals of repute from IEEE, Elsevier, Springer. He has been a workshop chair at IEEE Globecom 2018, IEEE Infocom 2020 (https://infocom2020.ieee-infocom.org/workshopblockchain-secure-software-defined-networking-smart-communities) and IEEE ICC 2020 (https://icc2020.ieee-icc.org/workshop/ws-06-secsdn-secure-and-dependable-software-defined-networking-sustainable-smart) and track chair of Security and privacy of IEEE MSN 2020 (https://conference.cs.cityu.edu.hk/msn2020/cf-wkpaper.php). I am also TPC Chair and member for various International conferences such as IEEE MASS 2020, IEEE MSN2020. He has won the best papers award from **IEEE Systems Journal in 2018, 2020** and **IEEE ICC 2018**, Kansas-city in 2018. I won the best researcher award from parent organization every year from last eight consecutive years. I also won best papers award from JNCA 2021, IEEE Trustcom 2021. I also won Mid-Career Research award from IEEE Technical Committee on Scalable Computing.

Chapter 1
Metamorphosis of Industrial IoT using Deep Leaning

Asmita Biswas and Deepsubhra Guha Roy

1.1 Introduction

The Internet of Things invented as an aggregation of independent devices powerfully communicating and interconnected to achieve a diverse range of purposes, frequently collaboratively. As a developing technology, the IoT requires offering useful discussions to modify the procedure and role of multiple existing industrial systems like transport and production systems. For example, during IoT uses to construct intelligent transport systems, the transport authority tracks individual vehicles' existing location, control its movement, and prophesy its expected location and viable road traffic. Intense security research should identify who has access to which, what, and when circumstances. The Standard Models represent an organization's security plan as some set of methods, guidelines, or safety commands required now and in the eventuality by an assumed or original company in an operative environment. Presenting the right access control paradigm for IoT co-operations is an essential but severe issue. Certainly, authorization and authentication issues review by current protocols for using facts outside restrained conditions. Though, in restrained conditions, those effects are still in origin. Further and several requirements model challenges for the application of numerous protection rules. The demand rises to a fine-grained and useful Access Control device, where users guide.

Industrial IoT (IIOT) appears to describe the utilization of IoT in the industry, utilizing disruptive factors such as actuators, sensors, Machine-to-Machine (M2M)

A. Biswas
School of Computational Science, Department of IT, Maulana Abul Kalam Azad University of Technology, Simhat, Haringhata, Nadia, Kolkata, West Bengal 741249, India

D. Guha Roy (✉)
Mobile and Cloud Lab, Institute of Computer Science, University of Tartu, Ulikooli 17-324, Tartu 50090, Estonia
e-mail: roysubhraguha@gmail.com

© The Author(s), under exclusive license to Springer Nature Singapore Pte Ltd. 2021
A. Makkar and N. Kumar, *Deep Learning for Security and Privacy Preservation in IoT*,
Signals and Communication Technology,
https://doi.org/10.1007/978-981-16-6186-0_1

1

interaction interfaces, control systems, and enhanced safety devices to develop industrial operations and form the futuristic Smart Industry notion. The generation of IoT in industrial contexts and use chains permits corporations, productions, and operators to produce more efficiently. It significantly impacts numerous fields, such as industrial manufacturing, automation, logistics, trade processes, method control, and transport. Simultaneously, with the core manufacturing method's overall development, the digital conversion progressions and the continually growing node interconnectivity approve new applications to appear, often linked to process optimization, automation, optimized source expenditure, security intensification and independent system generation. It now recognizes that Industrial IoT thoroughly transforms the merchandise life circle, thus rendering a new idea of making business generally and positively influencing its overall emulations. IIoT integrates products and processes to ultimately exchange the potency industry effectiveness of peck composition to peck customization. IIoT transmutes manufacturing through immensely and innovative and flexible product services that can become somewhat autonomous, interactive, responding in real-time, and optimize the complete benefit string by presenting appropriate status data during the life circle.

While performing those goals about improved productivity, unique challenges need to address, and the most crucial difficulty is obtaining an industrial foundation and the element. Cyberattacks on critical industries and infrastructure aim attention because the casualties acquired due to those interventions are enormous. Therefore, this is required to learn from events that the industries are presently the attacker's target and an instant need to address it. IIoT assigns to the combination of Operational Technology (OT) and Information Technology (IT). Where IT includes the business network, and OT contains the factory network where production completes. The two elements have several safety demands, requiring consideration to check the understanding of Industrial IoT infrastructure. Maw et al. [1] deal with access control issues and Wireless Sensor Network (WSN) environment. Sicari et al. [2]investigate the safety, privacy, and assurance in the IoT circumstances but do not completely manage the access control problem. Atzori et al. [3] examines IoT allowing technologies and current middleware clarifications and offers privacy and security open matter, but they do not discover the connection among the mechanisms and the models. Miorandi et al. [4] chooses the foremost challenges in the IoT, including data privacy, confidentiality, and safety concerning security conditions, and reviews the prime research circumstances (i.e., projects, impact zones, and standardization exercises). Weber [5] represents the security and privacy difficulties only single of an authoritative prospect; Yan et al. [6] concentrate on first on the IoT-based trust organization. Roman et al. investigate the pros and cons of distributed and implode privacy and security structures in the IoT context, examining the primary attack threats and prototypes[7]. Gubbi et al. [8] present a representative survey of different IoT features, like applications, associated technologies, quality of service, cloud platforms, safety issues, structure, power consumption, and data drilling connections.

1.2   Existing framework

The IoT is defined by the diffusive appearance of uniquely identified things and can interact with the network's support [9]. It was introduced initially through radio-frequency identification tagging to present EPC (electronic product code). The Internet of Things includes several independent devices interconnected, applying numerous technologies and protocols to deliver the most dynamic connectivity inter-operation. Precisely, the Internet of Things defines a network of things that might assemble and share data independently without needing humans support. Examples of such things consider being various sensors that monitor and measure the environment's humidity or temperature, the expedition, or the object's location. IoT application situations consider various, varying from smart appliances to fitness devices. Although security is not immediately involved with Information Security, it is critical during IIoT development. It needs to be taken under deliberation to prevent accidents that could threaten humans and machinery's integrity and service availability. The access control model does not estimate protection under deliberation as an integrated scheme feature, so protection requirements should consider potential when performing access control guidelines.

The International Telecommunications Union (ITU) has published ITU-T Y.2060 [10], a proposal that contributes to the overview of IoT. By this proposal, IoT continues the 3rd axis in already existing "anyplace" and "anytime" conversations, which could even be presented through legacy ICT methods. This new axis is termed "anything" and describes interaction within network devices and human-thing, things, and human–human. The things signify objects which exist in the dynamic world and maybe classified and sensed. The classification can operate appropriating implicit things that may exist without the appearance of the material ones. It defines the most regularly used expressions in both associated academic literature and non-academic, although not an entire list. Industry 4.0 is an effort to secure production in optimizing outcome effectiveness and enhance product condition. The initiative's underlying theory integrates the IoT inside the legacy product area automatic data systems, forming a new idea, the IIoT. The machine improvements enable IIoT Machine communication, simplicity and network performance, integrity affected through 4G and 5G improvement and rules similar to LoRaWAN and 6LoWPAN, and meet complete IoT challenges concluding resource-constrained projects, poor connectivity, heterogeneity. During the industrial context, an essential part is a condition concerning protection also [11].

A description of the 'Industrie 4.0' a phase, which, in its English agnate, contributors explain as compatible among IIoT, is: "…we describe Industrie 4.0 as follows: Industrie 4.0 is a combined phase during concepts and technologies of value series organization. Inside every integrated smart workshop of Industrie 4.0, it creates a virtual image of the dynamic world; CPS controls physical methods and executes decentralized choices. CPS associate, support and humans in real-time over the IoT. Both cross-organizational and internal services are employed and given by partners of the value chain." via the Internet of Services (IoS) [12].

While there is various IoT information, these of significance to industrial applications make precise the sorts concerning smart elements inserted into daily purposes to incorporate IoT devices and design CPS (Cyber-Physical System).

Here are three essential descriptions are:

- A description for the IoT would be a "collection of interconnecting relevant objects, infrastructures and providing their authority, information drilling and the entrance to data they form" where relevant objects are "actuators and sensors taking out a particular purpose that can interact with different devices." [13];
- "The term 'Internet of Things' holds computing skill expansion to sensors, devices, and items broadly and network connectivity. Those things (items, objects, sensors) are not usually supposed to be the computers. These smart gadgets expect the little social interference to generate, transfer, and apply information; it should often emphasize connectivity to past data acquisition, interpretation, and administration abilities." [14];
- "The Internet of Things signifies a situation in which each gadget or 'thing' is secured by the sensor and is automatically skilled interacting its position with additional gadgets and automatic systems within the context. Various gadget implies a joint in a virtual network, incessantly broadcasting a massive amount of information about itself and adjacent of it…" [15].

1.3 Layered Architecture of IoT and IIoT Systems

Industrial IoT comprises information analytics, sensor-driven computing, and smart device utilization to accommodate performance, scalability, and interoperability, which immediately increases computerization in significant infrastructure and develops company potency [16]. Although reaching advanced control purposes, various trials are required to register, and the numerous critical difficulties securing industrial infrastructure and its components. Cyberattacks proceeding crucial infrastructure and industries propose that the losses induced due to the before-mentioned attacks would be immense. Consequently, it is expected to obtain from specific conflicts that industries are presently the attacker's main purpose, and there is a critical requirement to locate the problem. The IIoT seldom refers to the Information Technology (IT) and the Operational Technology (OT), where the OT includes a manufactory interface and IT contains the business network. Security often pretends a server-client paradigm, where interaction among the server and client occurs applying standard protocols such as UDP (user datagram protocol), TCP (transmission control protocol), IP (internet protocol), and HTTP (hyperText transfer protocol). Specific loss induced by a successful attack typically involves reputation and money and unusually includes safety intimidations. Though, the OT system plan to conduct industrial methods with safety and reliability. The operational technology elements and subsystems could not create security in cognizance and separation of the operational technology network and physical security measures. However, those security authorities are inaccurate as people have some tricks that they may use to attack.

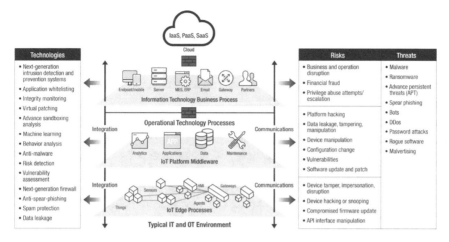

Fig. 1.1 Layered architecture of IIOT

Separating the Operational Technology networks may block an attack from a separate network but cannot confine the system's attacks. Malware can effectively deploy to negotiate the system inside an isolated network. Therefore, we require to analyze the different levels of IIoT structure. Figure 1.1 presents numerous elements at the following layers of IIoT.

1. **Layer One**: Sensor, installed devices, transmitter, actuator and motor operated on here to complete physical methods.
2. **Layer Two**: PLCs (programmable logic control), DCS (distributed control systems), and gateways communicate by the tools in layer one.
3. **Layer Three**: Data Acquisition devices, SCADA (supervisory control and data acquisition), and HMI (human–machine interface) that applies network protocol with IP-based remains in this layer.
4. **DMZ**: Demilitarized Zone applies to isolate information technology and operational technology networks. Crucial tools required to present to the surface network, such as application servers and web servers, remain in this layer. That precludes straight entrance to OT network implementing security appliances similar to a firewall.
5. **Layer Four**: Intranet service, web service, office applications and mail service expand in this layer. For site business planning, this layer is nearly reliable.
6. **Layer Five**: Data analytics, cloud computing, enterprise applications, internet and mobile device in this layer is responsible for data tunnelling and analytics, the method to conduct the erudition across the internet and also on the mobile device.

The Industry 4.0 program introduces the RAMI 4.0 (reference architectural model industry 4.0), which identifies as the DIN model (DIN SPEC 91345) and an IEC PAS 63088 (international pre-standard). RAMI 4.0 base on a 3D (three-dimensional) pattern comprising whole industrial features of the industrial authority toward the merchandise life cycle. Its 3Ds (three dimensions) are (a) Architecture, which provides a system architecture. (b) the authority represents the IIoT utilization functional areas deciding from the intelligent factory, intelligent product, and relevant world. (c) the product life period, which incorporates making, growth, and maintenance characteristics. Concentrating on these architecture dimensions, RAMI 4.0 illustrates 6 layers:

1. The **asset layer** describes the physical zone, including tools and their hardware components and the human circumstance.
2. The **integration layer** is illustrating the procurement of Asset Control Services and informational data.
3. The **communication layer** applies patterned connections combining the higher and assets layer's utilization, always observing a formality of the Integration Layer's information.
4. The **information layer** deals with a pre-processing of the generation and information of issues. In those cases of issues, the Asset Control Services might entreat.
5. The **functional layer** is getting pre-processed data from the information layer and executing precepts and decision-making inference. Moreover, the Functional layer is some exclusive access point toward the information as in those layers below, and the information protects to secure data integrity.
6. The **business layer** is the zone where the functional layer uses combines into specific business methods.

1.4   Requirements of Access Control

Access control is imperative in all methods needed to regulate and define actions or services executed through a method or user to collect system sources. An access control (AC) method estimates three concepts: AC models, methods, and mechanisms. An AC system is bound for enforcing access control methods and blocking them of destruction relied on those concepts. AC methods characterize high-level terms that define when and how a user may access the source when user or method. The Access Control methods strengthen during an access control device liable to allow either reject path. An AC model is a conceptual receptacle of a combination of access control tool applications, conserving the access control methods' logic for a structure. Thus, access control models span some considerable gaps within those methods and the access control (AC) system's mechanisms. In [17], IoT allowed ecosystem employing the idea of fog computing in intelligent transportation systems (ITSs) is exhibited. Regarding product of access control concerns given where. The subsequent conditions may extract:

*   **Context-Perception**: Contextual learning describes an entity's situation and the conditions [18]. The context may affect access control choices and support for

method work, which has analyzed parts exceeding the subject's and object's identification. Access control methods may also design, including a focus on protection
on top of data security that possesses perceptibility within the circumstances.

- **Accountability**: Audit needs to be encouraged for implementing individual stakeholders, including the capacity to control and expose every system misapplication
infractions.
- **Privacy Support**: Privacy is an imperative part required to consider deploying
all ICT solutions (separation by the scheme). It is a constitutional committee in
the European Union also established by the general data protection regulation
(GDPR) in 2018. An access monitoring device should design in a process that no
individual information should always disclose.
- **Inter-Domain Procedure**: IIoT deploys in various areas, encouraging private
sector operations following the same administrative authorization. Any access
control explication should be sufficient to support a constant procedure between
distinct regions.
- **Manageability**: There would be a centralized process to generate, confectionary,
and implement methods that would not cause additional latency and might perform
across low-bandwidth networks that might also seldom converted unavailable.
- **Resource Capability**: Maximum devices on frame designs to accomplish particular tasks and utilize less power possible. Goals accessible sources, both in
processing energy and accommodation, so several elements designed to work
should consider certain conditions.

As mentioned above, the list of conditions is not that exhaustive, but rather, that
functions while walking rocks in picking an added relevant support scheme. Here
we present further extra erudition about groups of access control paradigms and
structures towards the research in IIoT ecosystems in the comprehending.

1.4.1 Approaches of Different Access Control

While allowing attractive possibilities and new business models, IoT presents some
security and privacy issues. Focus on protecting IoT devices and resources (data,
services, applications) from unauthorized users accessed. An excellent explication
to this matter is to adopt an access control method that assures that only allowed
objects (device and user) obtain entrance to IoT resources and devices. The design
approaches of an access control system typically comprise three key components:

- The policy, which describes applause conditions consequent to which access
control improves
- The model that presents a formal description of access control procedures and the
amends
- The mechanism describes the low-level effectuation of the restriction required by
the system as established in the design

To the end, we initially perform a survey of the most current access control paradigms. We then present the demands for an access control system and that standard, whether it is performed by support structures recommended for the IoT.

AC (access control) procedures formally design consequently to an access control paradigm. Various prototypes offer inside the literature. Specific representations have different features, which may affect the suitability of a signature device for IoT. Besides, we perform a summary of the various prevalent access control paradigms. Though there is an adequacy of access control paradigms that become relevant in IIoT ecosystems, here we refine important access control family patterns. The effects in withdrawing replication of data amidst patterns have the roots in the corresponding pattern family and guidance illustrate these models' foremost characteristics. Mainly, we contribute erudition about the attribute-based, usage-based, role-based, capability-based, and limitation family patterns.

1.4.2   Capability-Based Access Control

Capability-based access control (CapBAC) emerges on the notion of abilities [19], which is identified as transmittable and unforgeable indications of authority. The capability incorporates listings for the support that a subject grants entrance also. Consequently, during a similar process to access control records, and an access control matrix considers that might comprise an object, subject, and support. In the CapBAC, authorities assign with subject and therefore support one-to-many relationships among subject and object. Subjects and objects belong to users and resources. Permissions authorize processes that a subject on an object can perform. CapBAC also supports authorization and retraction devices during capabilities. These are needed to authorize entrance (obliquely) to different subjects and withdraw entrance, respectively. The CapBAC system defined ideas and approaches by extending and addressing IoT conditions. The capability-based authorization presents the following additional characteristics that aggregate the required modification over early capability-based methods:

1. **Authorization Guide**: A subject may allow access to a different subject and allow the right to commit every or section of each ceded preference. Authorization intensity may control at each step.
2. **Data Granularity**: A capability can still specify progressive modification of the granted rights. In such a way, the service the provider can sharpen its behavior and information must provide according to what states in the capability symbol.
3. **Capability Abandonment**: Properly authorized subjects can cancel capabilities by resolving some capability proposals and results in shared circumstances.

Changeable access control, initially introduced by Lampson, was expressed through the ACM (access control matrix), where a string describes a record of sources and objects to get obtained, and wherever a series defines a file of cases, whoever requires to access the source traditionally. Two popular access control paradigms synchronize the access control list and capability-based access control. Access control list (ACL), incorporated through nature, does not recommend various granularity levels, is apt to a particular case of failure and is not scalable. The CapBAC bases on the notion of capacity that comprises rights ceded to each gadget regarding it. The ability notion also includes a tag, token, or code that allows the possessor to access an item into a computer method. The CapBAC is embraced during various largescale designs and extensively applies in the IoT domain. Implementing the capability model's original concept into the access control prototype to the IoT produces certain shortcomings. The capability configuration and cancellation hold two significant disadvantages about the conventional capability design denoted out with the Gong and to determine the classified challenges, a Secure ICAP (Identity-based Capability System), implemented.

The ICAP directs primarily to elongate the capability method approach, into which all subject or user that requires to obtain access to any particular tool or source adopts a capability. An Access grants if each subject's ability equals some capacity collected in an entity or the device that regulates the machine. The precisely that ICAP involved across the regular capability system incorporates its user or the situation in its performance. While this process, ICAP demands more effective authority in capability generation and allows more extended scalability through reducing the capabilities collected numbers, 'object server,' 'gateway,' or 'access point.' The ICAP framework and how ability, implemented objectives control, described as ICAP = (ID, AR, Rnd) where AR is the collection of access preferences for the machine with device identifier as ID, ID is the material identifier, and Rnd is the arbitrary amount to confine duplicity. It is a consequence of the way hash functions. Including connection data to obtain access control choices against an access demand of a user or subject is not granted. Its originality remains because it offers a unified appearance to access control and authentication based on the ICAP for the IoT scenario.

The introduced design is termed the identity authentication and capability-based access control (IACAC) design. In IACAC, things are connected by using an access location, and later capability-based access is permitted to another device with capability-based access control. Its capability access supports the individual establishment of the connection. Just later the capability verification, the tools can communicate with any other devices. Each device that wants to interact with the different tool can initiate the connection via transferring the appeal to a particular device. The next move is to confirm whether the requesting machine can interact with that requested device. This access license finds it verified using the ability of that machine, that connects including all devices. Its suitability to the subsequent parameters: granularity installation, scalability, and productivity time protection explained. Moreover, an analytical design to improve queuing interpretation of IACAC is performed (Fig. 1.2).

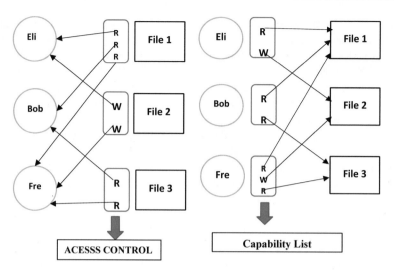

Fig. 1.2 Access control versus capability-based authorization model

1.4.3   Role-Based Access Control

In RBAC (role-based access control) [20], accessing systems' resources relied on a
user and role responsibility to roles has predefined permission. Role-Based Access
Control may carry various policies such as separation of duties, least right, and
executive functions, making it preferable for organizational circumstances. The core
RBAC design contains five static components: users, roles, also permissions; with the
end, include operations applied on objects regarding relationships between components, roles allocated to a user, and authorities, appointed on roles. Certain kinds of
associations may occur of many-to-many, such as any user may pick too multiple
roles, and numerous users may select to an only one role. The corresponding imple-
ments to grant responsibilities—negative sanctions, not recommended in role-based
access control. RBAC holds two various aspects, which are runtime and design.
While the designing form occurs, the system controller may assign individual tasks
among the computer system components. The system's responsibilities are executed
at the runtime condition by the model as defined through the design phase's security plan—runtime enforcement, instantiated over the sessions' concept. Some end
specifies RBAC of different group-based devices. Through a concourse, a subset
of users is permitted to be stimulated to functions. It implies that a user might be
selected numerous prefaces during the models' point; however, those functions do
not require to be promoted together and continuously. Applying the following mechanism, RBAC presents assistance for the policy of most insufficient opportunity.
Various restrictions get also be enforced throughout a session. Separate from the hub
prototype, role-based access control also carries authorities among roles. That mechanism presents the best flexibleness during it proceeds to the administration of the

plans. Precisely, leaders appointed through a function may quickly inherit another part without reassigning the latter's same permissions.

For instance, consider two permission sets are $PR1 = (P1, P2)$ and $PR2 = (P3, P4)$ and two roles are **R1 and R2,** which held primarily been appointed to positions **R1** and **R2**, individually. If the role **R1** obtains the role **R2**, it indicates that all of **R2**'s permits are possible with **R1**. The potential support to role **R1** is represented through the combination of consent on collections **PR1** and **PR2**. Meanwhile, authorities, expressed in charts, the direct legacy connection explains that the sign or arc's leader explains both the user and permissions association inheritance. We have **R1 → R2** in the earlier example.

User association leads to the responsibility of users in authority to roles. Users are approving to penetrates entire authorities appointed to roles either straight or by legacy contacts in such a case. Though, extra functionality implemented in hierarchical role-based access control maintains comprehensive and insufficient role authorities. Comprehensive authorities include the usual famous cases in role inheritance, and others, described as incomplete application sets. Nevertheless, the necessity for limited support authorities may occur in more restrictive environments. It involves either an individual direct descendant or ascendant role in the hierarchical formation like a tree. RBAC is further proficient in confirmative limitations by the dynamic and static detachment of accountability relationships. A static detachment of accountability relationships incorporates the implementation of the ambivalence of interest procedures. The foremost purpose of both limitations is to defend the system's protection and prevent it from occurring. Negotiated and limitations are generally applied to present industry fundamentals. For instance, considering **R1** and **R2** be two opposing roles, and **U1** is selected to **R1**. By implementing a static detachment of integrity coercion among R1 and R2, RBAC prevents user U1 with **R2** because the two roles are incompatible. This kind of limitation is established and required in RBAC while the designing phase.

The dynamic detachment of accountability relationships manages opposition of business policies in the circumstances of a session. The static detachment of integrity limitations requires the same process for all the straight inherited and assigned roles in the presence of a role hierarchy. The user holds a collection of functions initiated in this instance. The dynamic detachment of the accountability relationship is described through the design time, though it requires while runtime to limit the synchronous actuation of two or more opposing roles in the meaning of a session the same method to static severance detentions is employed, coercions are required only on a specific set of initiated roles in role hierarchies.

The authors in [21] utilize a service-based procedure to publish IoT [22, 23] where all IoT devices should extend their functionality as usual duties. The service considers the request's purpose by the service, whose permission is confirmed by access control before obtaining performances. Authors increased the RBAC prototype by adding context limitations accumulated from the mechanical object's conditions to accept contextual erudition, such as location, and time, in the conclusions. The network service technology presents exceptional interoperability among independent systems. Though the writers do not precisely define how the mechanical objective is designed on one or several numerous network services, and also necessarily, they do not recount how the contextual erudition assembles from the mechanical content conditions to incorporate during the applause method in a real-time mode. It presents their raised clarification as more suitable to design a model of context-aware access control in the network services than in an IoT ecosystem. Others have regarded only the IoT users more than tools. The purpose of intelligent gadgets in creating an access conclusion defeat. Preferably than implementation furthermore, the presented design has been just explained by case studies.

1.4.4 Usage-Based Access Control

The UCON (usage control) introduced in the [24] mod is regarded as the next generation's access control models. It proposes numerous innovations distinguished to standard access control like ABAC and RBAC. That continuously manages these authorization problems before the execution of access, throughout the execution, and afterward. Furthermore, it establishes the volatility of attributes. It implies that the access is in motion and this variation guides to dissatisfaction if the access attributes are changed, with the granted access, removed, security policy, and the method canceled. The UCONBAC model comprises eight elements: object attribute, subject attribute, authorization, object, right, obligation, and condition. The idea of objects and subjects, the connection as well as with the attributes is straightforward. Each object can interact with object attributes. A subject can be an item in a method, and its meaning and representation, presented through several features or abilities in the relevant subject's attribute. Subjects can maintain preferences on objects. A subject can permit usage or access of an object through these preferences. It deserves to mention that both object and subject attributes can obtain uncertainly. It signifies that those values can adjust through executive action only and not through its user's activity.

UCONBAC, characterized by several innovations arising essentially from the remainder of its elements. The preferences element signifies many rights and from a subject to an object that can be checked and executed. RBAC's roles, the UCONBAC theoretical structure, assists authorities with preferences in a similar way. Remark that rights, not group a priority, but it determines due to the access. From a method function, the access decision is given and considers the following factors: obligations, subject and object attributes, conditions and authorizations. In UCONBAC, authorizations are operative predicates and its evaluation uses to make decisions. Namely, access to a subject allows an object. The authorizations' evaluation is based on requested rights, object and subject attributes, and a collection of permission rules similar to the method function. Authorizations may characterize as ongoing authorizations or pre-authorizations. The prefix belongs to the time earlier on the ongoing prefix and requested right during the approach.

Moreover, UCONBAC's necessities use to obtain the conditions that need to be met of a Subject asking an Object's method. As already mentioned, those are used to evaluate access both in the usage function and authorizations. Obligations also divide into responsibilities and ongoing obligations. The previous usually uses to retrieve records data, and the end to verify whether the asked terms modified access. Eventually, requirements in the UCON uses for capturing parts that accrue to the system's context. The connotative variation among requirements and different variables, namely authorization and responsibility, holds that the past may not get uncertain considering no immediate semantic connection exists with Subjects.

1.4.5 Attribute-Based Access Control

ABAC (attribute-based access control) has reached considerable recognition during distributed networks and system's development, such as the internet, and regards it as a logical access control methodology [25]. Standardized ABAC information is yet missing invariance on RBAC, and hence differences have been raised. Though, a collection of rudders, rendered through NIST in [25]. According to the definition, ABAC may perform access choices to evaluate policy rules, attribute values, and environmental circumstances. In a system, Objects and Subjects may allow attribute states without preceding information of policy aspects. Moreover, one virtue of ABAC over different models is that its plans represent attributes without prior experience of the system's objects and subjects. It appears greatly clarify permission control.

The attribute-based access control (ABAC) paradigm forms six classes: Subjects, objects, attributes, policies, environmental requirements and operations. Attributes get to include a name-value set that is a tuple of the structure: Name, Value and both object and subject attributes may assist meta attributes. Attributes are features of the object, subject, or environmental requirements. The latter presents a separate index to refer to combinations of objects and subjects.

Authorities in ABAC support intrinsically through the meta character functionality. It provides ABAC to reveal powerful authorities with the potential connecting elements of the equivalent standard. Subjects can appoint one or more than one attribute. The subject usually explains it as a user or method to access applications for performing procedures on objects. For which the ABAC system manages access, an object may be system support. That might be programs, folders, devices, charts, records, methods, channels, or areas, including or getting knowledge. It may be the source instead demanded item and some item on which a supervisor can perform through a case, along with the information, services, applications, networks, and tools. At the appeal of a subject upon an object, service is the performance of an operation. Patterns of operations comprise the reading, writing, editing, deleting, copying, executing, and modifying commands. A system represents relationships and rules which address it probable to conclude if asked access should get approved, given the contents of the subject's characteristics, objective, and probable environmental requirements. An environment requirement is a situational and execution circumstances where access applications happen. Environment requirements are discovered environment features. Environment properties are autonomous of an object or subject, including the latest time, the weekday, current threat level and user location. The preceding descriptions consequently help while providing a recommendation form during ABAC and a precise term of it. A concise explanation of popular ABAC frames, provided in the following.

Access control structures may present applicable guidelines while regarding an access control system implementation. The NGAC (next-generation access control) and XACML (extensible access control markup language) seem to be the maximal notable structures about attribute-based access. Both current services manage, estimate choices, policies, support plans. NGAG and XACML may expedite selecting attribute-based procedures by presenting terms about balancing the elements such as policy enforcement point, policy decision point, and functional operations. We give NGAC and XACML to function as an antecedent while analyzing purposing access control systems relevant in IIoT ecosystems in the following.

1.5 Deep Learning Method

Several system designers, researchers, and software developers have shown a rising interest in applying Deep Learning proposals in modern IoT systems to address vulnerabilities and safety threats. The perspective mentioned above essentially connects with the superior achievement over classical Machine Learning methods, basically when using massive datasets. DL offers can learn data symbols with different abstraction levels applying computational designs including various non-linear processing layer. It is likewise the cause of why all get identified as the hierarchical learning techniques. Most of the latest Deep Learning techniques, relied on neural networks (NNs), during training may regulate, alternatively identified as discriminative such as convolutional and recurrent NN, unsupervised or semi-supervised conclude auto-encoders, deep Boltzmann machines, deep belief networks.

CNNs (convolutional neural networks) decrease the link connecting layers by employing parameter sharing, inadequate interactions, and analysis of invariant features.

It consists of two layers:

1. the standard layer where the data associated with different filters with the same size, and
2. the pooling layer, where several accession for the output subsampling and reducing consequent layers' size are applied.

Comparing with traditional NN, the benefits get scalability increased and training complexity decreased, while the vast selection credits to their capability to automatically learn features from raw data. Though the complexity is relatively high, producing the integration to resource-constrained things is a pretty challenging job. Successfully, CNN's have been applied for Malware detection [26] and breaking cryptographic implementations [27].

Moreover, latterly, CNN is utilized and explored for 1D sequential data analysis, including different IIoT applications. The feature learning in CNN usually accomplishes by assembling and interchanging the pooling processes and convolutional layers. These layers (convolutional layers) convolve with the provided input data in a raw manner, appropriating local procreative invariant multiple local kernel filters and features. On the opposite hand, the pooling layers liberate the implied characteristics with fixed-length sliding windowpanes of the input data's untrained form. It brings out various pooling techniques, such as average-pooling and max-pooling. The max-pooling chooses the maximum value for a specified section of the featured map being the entire valuable feature.

In contrast, the average-pooling measures the mean value of the specified section and considered it the pooling value of that section. It should note that the max-pooling is reasonably well-matched for sparse feature extraction; however, average-pooling is not optimal in all feature extraction outlines. After flourishing multi feature-learning, the fully connected layers transform the 2D feature mapping into a 1D vector and stuff it into the functional activation layer for a more suitable paradigm representation. In CNN, the most commonly used activation of the active layer is SoftMax, which generally converts the previous layer's output into the most suitable and essential output probability distribution. This layer-wise architecture is quite helpful in IIoT applications, such as identifying surface errors that transpire in the manufacturing process. CNN mainly trains by using Gradient-based backpropagation minimizes the overall CE (cross-entropy) and MMSE (minimum mean-squared-error) function for loss occurrence. CNN has various advantages over its counterparts' neural networks, including parameter distribution with several numbers and local connectivity.

The RNNs (recurrent neural networks) utilizes in purposes where information such as video, speech, sensor measures are available sequentially. Implementing the equivalent set of weights over a different graph-like structure recursively, intersect the topological structure and through this RNNs, created. Those are incredibly effective during processing data in an adaptive mode, though the primary condition is disappearing or splitting gradients [28]. Recurrent Neural Network (RNN) has an exclusive capability of hierarchical links among the neurons for modeling sequential data [29]. Figure 1.4 presents the fundamental architecture with inputs, outputs, and underlying deep hidden layers of RNN.

The input variables express as xt-1, xt&xt + 1, and defines the data of radical concealed layers, whereas o_{t-1}, o_t, and o_{t+1} give the outputs at time t. The terms U, V, and W, are the respective concealed matrices whose values change for every timestamp where the conceled states can measure as St = $f(x_{(t)} + WS_{(t-1)})$ [30]. Thus, RNNs are relevant to acquire accurate measurements from the consecutive data, allowing them to endure the hidden layers and capture the data's initial conditions. A rearranged form of RNN is used in a layer-wise architecture to efficiently calculate the variation among various time steps. The RNNs data acceptance as a persistent input in a vector where the existing hidden state, measured using an activation function. The initial portion of the data, calculated with the provided input; however, the next portion, acquired from the underlying concealed state at the earlier step time t. The objective output of then contained with these hidden layer's states' help through

SoftMax. Once the whole order of data, concocted, the hidden states describe the whole consecutive input data's learning model. Moreover, a conventional multilayer-perception is added to the uppermost layer to map the objective deputations (Fig. 1.3).

An Auto-Encoder concludes the Neural Network formed about two components, the encoder and decoder, which gets the input and provides an output code (abstraction) and vice-versa. The decoding and encoding analyses, decided by decreasing the error within the decoder's output and the encoder's input. Auto Encoders (AE)

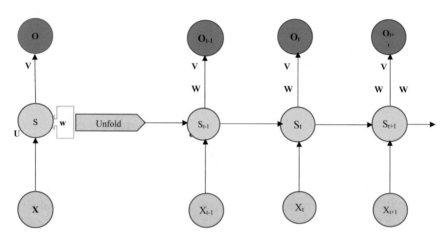

Fig. 1.3 The generic layer-wise architecture of RNN

Fig. 1.4. IIoT Market and Size Impact

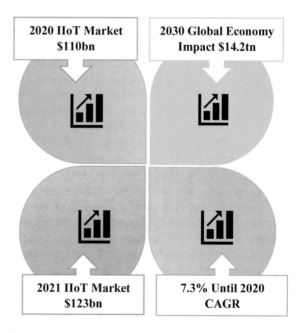

are essential for featuring dimensionality compression and ancestry without several previous erudition knowledge, though the training dataset should be descriptive of the measuring dataset for operating sufficiently, where others utilize vital computation time. Preceding researchers have applied AEs to derive characteristics explained to detect enactment attacks in WiFi environments and cyber-attacks in fog computing systems. The most crucial feature that has made the AE useful for the IIoT application is its capacity to decrease the input data dimensions and acquire non-label data features. AE can also help in the security of IIoT networks as it is capable of contributing information regarding any interference detection in the IIoT environment. Therefore, some prudent measures can take to dodge any disaster in the industrial process, such as production, safety, and warehousing.

Restricted Boltzmann Machine is essentially an Artificial Neural Network with the two-layer architecture of networking that involves a visible layer and a hidden layer. In Restricted Boltzmann Machine (RBM), only the hidden and visible layers connect; yet, there is no association among the identical layers. It is a sort of energy-based technique, where the observable era is liable for the information of input, where the unseen layer, uses for various property deductions. Besides, it considers that all the hidden nodes are tentatively self-determining and have no inter-dependency. The offsets and weights of the visible and hidden layers revolve throughout emphases to sort the visible layer and appraise input data. Conclusively, the hidden layers consider as an alternative depiction of the identical visible layer. A generalized layer-wise architecture of RBM. The hidden layers use to distinguish the input data in the realization of dimensionality compression and various data coding mechanisms. Supervised learning methods comprise naive Bayes, support vector machine, linear regression, and belief propagation for data regression and categorization. RBM usually regains the required properties from the training datasets adaptively and avoids the local least problem. RBM extensively uses as a principal learning mechanism on whose basis other variants represent.

1.5.1 Why IIoT Needs Deep Learning

The Industrial IoT (IIoT) market is expanding fast as the digital transformation in numerous industries is stimulating. Strong associations between conducting IIoT stakeholders and established some IIoT applications inspire companies worldwide to confer in the IIoT market, which expects to grow up to $123.89 billion by 2021 in Fig. 1.4. The approaching this innovative IIoT or product technology is way distinct from preceding technologies; therefore, that also terms as "Industrial Revolution." The recently IIoT technology develops people's entire working requirements and day-to-day lifestyles explicitly. Regularly, IIoT systems produce interconnected innovative industrial components for achieving high composition at a cheap cost. It is possible by real-time monitoring, explicit execution of tasks, and effective controlling of the overall industrial systems. As the quantity of internet-connected devices increases exponentially, a significant amount of data produces. In the case of IIoT, both the volume of the data and its properties needs proper deliberation because the performance of IIoT applications is undoubtedly related to the smart processing of the big data, which comes from various real-time resources. Hence, Big Data Analysis in IIoT networks requires intelligentt modeling to achieve using Deep Learning (DL) techniques.

According to the previous discussion, the most crucial factor in automation for IIoT is data analyzing, paradigm, and real-time support processing. Deep Learning (DL) used in classification, regression, and forecasting has the most potential for the IIoT systems among data analysis projects. Deep learning procedures automatically learn from the given data, identify the patterns, and make any specific decisions. With the advancements provided by DL methods, IIoT transforms into highly optimized facilities. The advantages of using DL including lower operation costs, no change with variations in consumer demands, enhancing productivity, downtime reduction, obtaining a better perspective of the market, and extracting valuables from the operations. Notably, the DL-enabled advanced analytics framework can realize the opportunistic need for smart manufacturing. It is crucial to use smart manufacturing, manufacturing, and production intelligence, which can have several advantages in IIoT. Recently, IIoT solutions are growing significantly, especially for sensor-based data consisting of various structures, formats, and semantics. Data loose from IIoT technologies is derivative from several manufacturing resources that include product line, equipment-and-processes, labor operation, and environmental conditions. Therefore, data labeling, data modeling, and data analysis play a significant role in manufacturing smarter. They are essential parts of handling high-volume data and supporting real-time data processing.

Deep Learning (DL) is a powerful machine learning (ML) that can upgrade manufacturing into highly optimized smart facilities by processing many data with its multi-layered structure. The DL assessment can give computing intelligence from unclear sensory data, resulting in smart manufacturing. DL techniques are useful for their automatic data learning behavior, identifying the underlying patterns, and making smart decisions. One of DL's advantages over traditional machine learning methods is that feature learning does automatically, and there is no need to design a separate algorithm to do this part. The comparison of DL with traditional techniques in IIoT can analyze in Fig. 1.5. Different data analysis methods can utilize to interpret IIoT data, such as descriptive analytics, prognostic analytics, prescriptive analytics and diagnostic analytics. After capturing and analyzing the operational parameters, product's condition, and the environment, we can summarize what happens; this is called descriptive analytics.

Predictive analytics utilizes statistical models and provides the prospect of making future equipment fabrication or degradation based on the provided historical data. We use diagnostic analytics to figure out the foundation cause and report failure or reducing product performance. In contrast, prescriptive analytics recommends one or more courses of action and whatever lies beyond it. Measures out of data analysis techniques are classifying to develop the production outcomes or improve the problems, depicting each assessment's probable result.

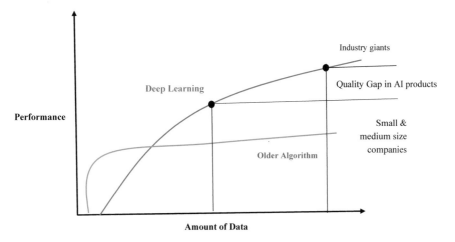

Fig. 1.5. Comparison of DL with traditional algorithms for IIoT

1.6   Detail Review on IIoT Systems

While there are various IoT descriptions, so those of significance to the industrial application form specific Smart elements inserted into familiar objects to include IoT gadgets and design components of CPS (Cyber-Physical Systems).

The three proper descriptions are:

- A description for IoT needs to be an "interconnecting connected objects, a combination of infrastructures, and enabling the supervision, data drilling and the access to information people generate" where functional objects are "sensors and actuators" bringing out a particular purpose that may interact with other devices" [30, 31].
- "IoT denotes a synopsis under which all 'thing' or object get embedded by a sensor and is expert of automatic communicating its status with another object and automated operations inside the context. Individual thing defines a link in a virtual interface, transmitting a massive volume of data continuously regarding itself and its nearby…" [32].

Based on the above definition, the initial one of IIoT might be using some IoT terms, some smart gadgets, among cyber-physical methods in a technical context to promote goals unique to the industry. The simple interpretation does present a template during a description of the IIoT, for it accurately attempts to determine IIoT through application to two fundamental characteristics: (1) the characteristic aims and purposes to which those technologies are putting and (2) the kinds of technologies that use in an IIoT setting. We require a definition with that formation, but which provides a more critical development of (1) and (2). A benefit of the simplistic concept benefit is that it clarifies the appropriate technologies applied for unique industries. It performs the essential foundation of permitting us to classify the IoT appliances from IIoT projects. As an instance, Smart kettles and Smart bike locks are not helpful in industrial applications. The simplistic opinion accurately incorporates the things as non-IIoT projects. Notwithstanding this service, the meaning persists in uninformative although. Moreover, a trap for avoiding while attempting to arrive at IIoT is representing IIoT in terms of some other conclusion, which is not distinct from the concept of IIoT itself, that would provide the uninformatively description circular.

1.6.1 Access Control in Industrial IoT

The AAA system intends for providing fine-grain and secure Access Control to the IoT systems in a regional cloud. The order of communications among the AAA system, a service consumer and producer. The AAA method consists of Authentication, Authorization and Accounting.

Authentication: The present work system uses the CoAP's DTLS (datagram transport layer security) for stable and secure connections among the IoT devices and the AAA. The CoAP protocol supports four security modes: Pre-Shared Key, No Security, Certificate, and Raw Public Key. The type of authentication obtained applying these methods explained here:

- **PSK (Pre-shared Key)**: A key that shares among the two interacting objects and they verify any other relied on that key in this method. It concludes that the key securely delivers to both parties previously. For the IoT local clouds to communicate the shared keys, the PSK is not viable for all IoT projects in a robust regional cloud.
- **No Security**: Security does not provide in this method through the protocol. Consequently, it does not apply to authenticate.
- **Certification**: X.509 certificates are generally applied and approved by a trusted source (e.g., certificate authority (CA)) in this method. The devices can authenticate with each other in a regional cloud if they manage a CA specifically to that cloud.
- **RPK (Raw Public Key)**: The IoT tools maintain an asymmetric key pair to secure the DTLS connections; however, communicating parties' authentication cannot verify in this method.

In a DTLS association, the companion starting the connection usually is the client and the other companion is the server. CoAP's DTLS is related to TLS (transport layer security); without that, it uses UDP (user datagram protocol). External of total the DTLS security procedures, the certification process is a proper model to achieve authentication in a regional cloud connection. Hence, it uses in the current work. A client (browser) validates the server's certification in a one-way and a two-way handshake is arbitrary where a server also can verify the client's authentication in TLS. Whereas both communicating objects perform a crucial role, and the AAA should confirm that a service user is an equivalent company requesting entrance into the IoT environment. The assistance customer should further guarantee that it is demanding access from the corresponding AAA policy, and they need to verify every difference by applying a two-way handshake. ECC (elliptic-curve cryptographic) keys are preferred as they present the equivalent cryptographic security to RSA keys but with smaller critical sizes in X.509 certificate generation. All these systems have a trust store, and the CA's certificate has been added to it. IoT gadgets can collect specific certifications in their limited memory and make the connection quicker during the smaller handshake information and it reduces the certificate's size. It applies to signify the AAA system's certification and all other objects in the regional cloud— if they maintain the same CA's certificate, the DTLS associations are regarded as verified. Moreover, the AAA system establishes the service user's identification using the Common Name (CN) field, which collects the service user's unique method name in a confined cloud within its record.

Authorization: Simultaneously accommodating a service customer's access demand, the Authorization assistance supports the access preferences. If access permits, the authorization policy results in an authorization privilege token to the service user. Against accepting the token, the service user submits an assistance application to a specific service generator and the token. A validity duration for those tokens can be use-case dependent. The generator decrypts that token against accepting it from the service user, confirming its validity (i.e., confirming whether that token is assigned to the corresponding user or not and verifying whether that token's authenticity has expired), and grants its services until the token's expiry. Individual tokens must be encrypted, including the service generator's public key, to maintain them secure from every unapproved access. All are self-sustaining tokens, which provide the data required for the service replacement so that every service generator does not require to validate the token by the AAA system. The assistance exchanges between a service user and a service generator while a token's validity refers to a "session" in this activity. The service user can also submit a close service application to the service generator to terminate the session before the token's expiry period if the required service is no longer needed.

Accounting: The service producer and consumer of a session needs to consider the session's relevant data of both edges into the AAA system's Accounting assistance through the regional cloud. An example set of data entered throughout a session, given here:

- Session period which can be either the time variation among the service consumer's first service request or the token expiry period set in the AAA system and the close assistance application in a session;
- Number of service exchanges in response/ request communications;
- IP address modification in a session;
- Cause for session terminus;
- The maximum and minimum packet size of the request

This data is generic to any regional cloud, and precise use-case accounting must be developed for extra secure and vital accounting requirements. The accounting data can estimate payments to service generators for measuring statistics such as security analysis, each device's representation. Erudition, such as the amount of services transfers, expedites micropayments. Data such as session time, package size, terminus, and IP address modification case can prepare every security fractures such as a (DoS) Denial of Service attack on constrained tools (assistance producer) and the service consumer's settlement in a session.

1.6.2 Deep Learning in Industrial IoT Systems

DL (deep learning) is a sub-category of ML (machine learning) that focuses on training data symbols. Based on artificial neural networks, maximum Deep learning proposals use a cascade of various layers of non-linear processing units for securing informational characteristics. Progressive layers apply the output from the preceding input layer. Deep Learning proposals may also incorporate supervised and unsupervised designs, and their main feature is their capability to acquire various devices and deep levels that communicate to various abstraction levels.

This section describes possible opportunities for DL-based IIoT, which can handle underlying smart nodes' resources and communication. One of the crucial parts of modern smart manufacturing is computational intelligence, enabling precise data insights for efficient and reliable future decision-making. As we have mentioned earlier, DL is one of the top fields in the investigation of different manufacturing lifecycle stages covering concepts, design [33], production, evaluation, sustainment, and operation. In the following, we discuss various use cases of DL in IIoT networks (Table 1.1).

1.7 An Analyzing Framework of IIoT

Ere exhibiting the IIoT Analysis Framework, analyzing the existing proclaimed material focusing on IIoT taxonomies and a scale of particular manufacturers, industrial elements, problem analyzing, and technical reports describe particular production or implementation. Classified three proclaimed IoT taxonomies in educational research address the IoT being involved and not explicitly converged on Industrial IoT.

1.7.1 Existing Taxonomy Review

The aim is to build a structure that permits us to analyze IIoT devices' aspects and the methods to be an attenuation and threat analysis process. No taxonomies describe affording adequate coverage of the attributes of devices to assist the aims. The appropriate conditions of the taxonomies summarise as follows:

Table 1.1 Deep learning models comparison in the framework of industrial IoT

Deep learning models	Application	Advantage	Limitation
Convolutional Neural Network (CNN)	Characteristic learning through accumulated pooling and convolutional layers	Minimizes scalability, shifting, and alteration	Higher hierarchical models require complex computations
Recurrent neural network (RNN)	Ephemeral framework in recurrent connections while assigned categories are in time-Series information	Temporal correlation, apprehended in progressive data with short-term info retention	Model training is challenging to keep long-term dependencies
Auto encoder (AE)	Encoding does the unsupervised learning and dimensionality reduction in data	Store only significant input information while the inappropriate data is clarified	Layer-by-layer error conception and Sparse illustration are not assured
Restricted boltzmann machine (RBM)	Hidden layer variables elaborate connectivity between input and output	Vital to input uncertainty and pretraining step do not need design training	Take much time to execute optimization of parameters

- Device-Centric Taxonomy [13]—The proposal presents useful characteristics at the device level such as communication, energy, local interface, functional properties, hardware and software sources but provides data regarding the device's performance, its mechanical, structural positions, and each division in which it applies;
- IoT-based Smart Ecosystem Taxonomy [34]—It's a bounded service as of a safety outlook as it is essential on the analysis of the web elements such as network model, communication enablers, regional area wireless patterns, technologies, features and purposes, the technology elements are comprehensive, and the aspirations (cost deduction) are challenging to allocate at the device moderately than the system level;
- IoT Design Taxonomy [35]—Connects a combination of business design or architecture and technical features such as allowing technologies, network topologies, applications, architectural demands, business objectives, and IoT stands structure types. However, given exclusively six analysis factors, it is of restricted value for analyzing devices.

Since none of the current taxonomies satisfy the conditions, as those are both too high or unfinished of a device characterization prospect, it investigates current Industrial IoT introduced and clear clarifications to improve an analytical structure for IIoT systems. Based on the published research conditions, to characterize IIoT devices, a framework has been developed. The proposals described in detail characterize devices based on four sections and some sub-sections using a (PLC) Programmable Logic Controller:

1. Devices characteristics;
2. Location;
3. Technology;
4. User

1.7.2 Devices Characteristics

The center of the aimed device's sub-sections explains as follows:

- **Function**: This section uses to represent the device's essential functions. Considering a system by analytic functions, the characteristics of the algorithm uses are suitable.
- **Criticality**: It concentrates on the device's criticality in terms of impact on the overall operational method and it is simple to correct or replace a defective device. It is more significant and challenging to repair or replace; higher security hazards arise from any analyses with any devices to conflict. Security crucial devices must be supervised and planned to advanced criteria with small results and simple to replace.
- **Management Interface**: It associates with the device configuration unless regulated or turns on/off.
- **Relationships**: The section is to understand the device association with other systems and processes, the devices, or the situation within which it operates. Such as a temperature sensor in an area links for collecting or controlling by equipment, while the purpose is for estimating that area temperature in a place where it installs, and a part of an atmosphere conditioning process, and it affects if a window or door unlocks or locks in the place inside where it locates.

The PLC can define using the category as:

Devices → Function → Control

→ Criticality → High

→ Ease of repair → Easy

→ Management interface → Remote

→ Relationships → To other devices→ Sensors → Voltage

→ Relationships → To other devices→ Actuators → Switch

→ Relationships → To other devices→ Control → RTU

1.7.3   *Location*

The proposed taxonomy that considers the IIoT device's location from several prospects is relevant in its appearance to prospects from both physical and cybersecurity aspects. Here four sub-classes propose as follows:

1. **The Purdue Model**—The Purdue model for control hierarchy [36] is a wholly recognized manufacturing industry paradigm that segments devices and apparatus into classified functions. The model uses zones for subdividing ICS and Enterprise networks toward modules that can perform similarly [37].
2. **Ecosystem**—Several models are there to offer IoT environments, but those are nonexclusive and not incorporated explicitly, including IIoT implementations. An IoT ecosystem representation is related directly to industrial purposes. The aimed classification plan adapts from the design except elongated for including some more expansive project IT for providing the operation technologies, the merging of data, and extremities, including a sub-class in Thing class "monitor" to support devices which contain broader operativity than measure (e.g., CTV cameras) [37].
3. **Physical**—This component seeks to describe the device installs' environment, allowing the physical security and vulnerability level to consider. As per example, machines located externally are expected to be enough more responsive to mechanical damage, fraud prevented, and exposure to the elements and various natural hazards [37].
4. **Mobility**—Element registers whether the device uses a set-up location or relocated everywhere about its individual or as an operation element. Mobile gadgets expect for involving a wireless communications device to conduct information and permit control and configuration, revealing the machine to the interfering or threat. Besides, it needs to geolocate or track the device to interpret the information it gives accurately [37].

The PLC can define using the category as:

Location → Ecosystem→ Concentrator → Data acquisition

→ Purdue Model → Cell/Area → 1 – Basic Control

→ Physical → External → Above Ground

→ Mobility → Fixed

1.7.4   Technology

The focus of the proposed technology of the IIoT device is on technological characteristics that need to be compelled either to alter the device's configuration or the capacity for marking attenuation. Each source of power, hardware characteristics, and uses of energy are essential. These can force the device's processing capacity, changing the security methods to defend the connection and restrict capacity to repair or modernize the tool once extended. The identification of the device producer and a novel identifier requires layout supervision plans. With the characteristics of an IIoT device and its broad application of the software, the notion of loyalty is a fundamental technological aspect. Therefore, for a component wherever the software presents the individual source of loyalty, a high level of loyalty should require and exhibit if the consequence considers notable or critical [31].

Based on the Arduino, P.L.C. can define using the category as:

Technology → Power Source → Hardware → Mains

      → Energy use → Always on

      → Operating System → Hardware & Software → Arduino

      → Software type → Open source

      → Software update → Methods → Manual

      → Hardware → CPU type → ATmega2560

      → Hardware → CPU speed

      → Hardware → Memory size

      → Hardware → Storage capacity

1.7.5   User

The proposed user properties aim to allow the classification of interacting devices. The user models are both a machine or human, like, for monitoring purposes or system control, the equipment is sensing and giving Machine-to-Machine (M2M) interface. To the user communicate with deliberations, a device needs to be:

- Direct, either active (e.g., a machine among touch-sensitive an interactive show which permits investigation regarding the material state and any direction of that) or passive (e.g., the temperature of a place thermostat showing but not permit user authority);

- Indirect, i.e., the devices can examine through another device in the IIoT system; Headless, there is no implication of device operation, measurements, or status.

The PLC can define using the category as:

User → Types of User → Machine

→User Interface →Indirect → Active

1.8   Limitations

To emerge the infrastructure of access control using deep learning in the Industrial IoT context there are some limitations in our work.

1. If some access controls correlate to the token is modified following a policy issued, measures to remove the rules which is not executed.
2. If the access control logics resides in the local devices, then it is difficult to manage and update the policies. Those need to update dynamically. Also, the access control logic may not be supported by constrained devices.
3. The trust may get approved with the decentralized than the centralized approach based on defining the network edge.

1.9   Future Scope

Security-based Datasets' availability is a significant challenge that needs to address in IIoT methods. Deep learning offers are the formation of realistic, elimination, and high-quality practice data containing several probable attacks. A necessary future analysis appearance towards the way is techniques of crowd sources to create dataset compared to the IoT attacks and [38] intimidations. This proposal might guide some formation of total potential attacks during intense practice datasets that could 'standardize new algorithms' accuracy. Nevertheless, it needs to be noted that forming a cooperative threat dataset of IoT that continuously improves, including new attacks, is a challenge practically during the enormous heterogeneity in these technological aspects of the numerous IoT gadgets. Several privacy interests also rise since crucial and sensitive erudition may be shared openly, mostly when focusing on industrial and medical IoT devices. Several editions are available to investigate and analyze privacy and security concerns associated with IIoT in common; small activity explicitly focuses on an IIoT environment. Recommend applying the classification better for learning the IIoT ecosystem and connected threat panorama to identify vulnerabilities and potential security and privacy matters.

1.10   Conclusion

This chapter presented several deep learning approaches' working principles, focusing on identifying and mitigating automated IoT vulnerabilities and safety threats. Hence, it expects to work as a practical, manual supportive researcher to develop IoT systems' defence by addressing device or end-to-end security difficulties.

Industry 4.0 is consolidating the IoT (Internet of Things) in automated applications as a conclusion. IoT technologies' performance enables effective (D2D) device-to-device interaction and produces various requirements for effective communication and security. The Analysis Access Control frame presents characteristics for approaching these conditions by the application of regional clouds. One crucial condition is protection, including (AAA) authentication, authorization, and accounting, which combines some NGAC design using a simplistic division warming use case that incorporates many investors' gadgets.

References

1. Maw, H.A., Xiao, H., Christianson, B., Malcolm, J.A.: A survey of access control models in wireless sensor networks. J. Sens. Actuator Netw. 3(2), 150–180 (2014)
2. Sicari, S., Rizzardi, A., Grieco, L.A., Coen-Porisini, A.: Security, privacy and trust in internet of things: the road ahead. Comput. Netw. 15(76), 146–164 (2015)
3. Atzori, L., Iera, A., Morabito, G.: The internet of things: a survey. Comput. Netw. 54(15), 2787–2805 (2010)
4. Miorandi, D., Sicari, S., De Pellegrini, F., Chlamtac, I.: Internet of things: vision, applications and research challenges. Ad Hoc. Netw. 10(7), 1497–1516 (2012)
5. Weber, R.H.: Internet of things-new security and privacy challenges. Comput. Law. Secur. Rev. 26(1), 23–30 (2010)
6. Yan, Z., Zhang, P., Vasilakos, A.V.: A survey on trust management for Internet of Things. J. Netw. Comput. Appl. 1(42), 120–134 (2014)
7. Roy, D.G., Mahato, B., De, D., Buyya, R.: Application-aware end-to-end delay and message loss estimation in Internet of Things (IoT)—MQTT-SN protocols. Futur. Gener. Comput. Syst. 1(89), 300–316 (2018)
8. Gubbi, J., Buyya, R., Marusic, S., Palaniswami, M.: Internet of things (IoT): a vision, architectural elements, and future directions. Futur. Gener. Comput. Syst 29(7), 1645–1660 (2013)
9. Atzori, L., Iera, A., Morabito, G.: The internet of things: a survey. Comput. Netw.
10. Molina, A.G., Escalante, R.P.: The internet of things: heteregoneous interoperable network architecture in smart cities. In; 2019 International Conference on Information Systems and Computer Science (INCISCOS) 2019 Nov 20, pp. 131–135. IEEE
11. Serpanos, D., Wolf, M.: Internet-of-Things (IoT) Systems: Architectures, Algorithms, Methodologies. Springer (2017)

12. Hermann, M., Pentek, T., Otto, B.: Design principles for industrie 4.0 scenarios: a literature review. 2015. http://www.snom.mb.tu-dortmund.de/cms/de/forschung/Arbeitsberichte/Design-Principles-for-Industrie-4_0-Scenarios.pdf. 2017 Sep.
13. Dorsemaine, B., Gaulier, J.P., Wary, J.P., Kheir, N., Urien, P.: Internet of things: a definition and taxonomy. In: 2015 9th International Conference on Next Generation Mobile Applications, Services and Technologies 2015 Sep 9, pp. 72–77. IEEE
14. Roy, D.G., Das, M., De, D.: Cohort assembly: a load balancing grouping approach for traditional WiFi infrastructure using edge cloud. In: Methodologies and Application Issues of Contemporary Computing Framework 2018, pp. 93–108. Springer, Singapore
15. Satyavolu, P.: Designing for manufacturing's 'Internet of Things'. Cognizant Report," 2014. [Online]. Available: https://www.cognizant.com/InsightsWhitepapers/Designing-for-Manufacturings-Internet-of-Things.pdf
16. Hassanzadeh, A., Modi, S., Mulchandani, S.: Towards effective security control assignment in the industrial internet of things. In: 2015 IEEE 2nd World Forum on Internet of Things (WF-IoT) 2015 Dec 14, pp. 795–800. IEEE
17. Salonikias, S., Mavridis, I., Gritzalis, D.: Access control issues in utilizing fog computing for transport infrastructure. In: International Conference on Critical Information Infrastructures Security 2015 Oct 5, pp. 15–26. Springer, Cham
18. Abowd, G.D., Dey, A.K., Brown, P.J., Davies, N., Smith, M., Steggles, P.: Towards a better understanding of context and context-awareness. In: International Symposium on Handheld and Ubiquitous Computing 1999 Sep 27, pp. 304–307. Springer, Berlin, Heidelberg
19. Wilkes, M.V., Needham, R.M.: The Cambridge CAP computer and its operating system
20. Jin, X., Krishnan, R., Sandhu, R.: A unified attribute-based access control model covering DAC, MAC and RBAC. In; IFIP Annual Conference on Data and Applications Security and Privacy 2012 Jul 11, pp. 41–55. Springer, Berlin, Heidelberg.
21. Zhang, G., Tian, J.: An extended role based access control model for the Internet of Things. In: 2010 International Conference on Information, Networking and Automation (ICINA) 2010 Oct 18, vol. 1, pp. V1–319. IEEE
22. Roy, D.G., Mahato, B., De, D.: A competitive hedonic consumption estimation for IoT service distribution. In: 2019 URSI Asia-Pacific radio science conference (AP-RASC) 2019 Mar 9, pp. 1–4. IEEE
23. Spiess, P., Karnouskos, S., Guinard, D., Savio, D., Baecker, O., De Souza, L.M., Trifa, V.: SOA-based integration of the internet of things in enterprise services. In: 2009 IEEE International Conference on Web Services 2009 Jul 6, pp. 968–975. IEEE
24. Zhang, X., Parisi-Presicce, F., Sandhu, R., Park, J.: Formal model and policy specification of usage control. ACM Trans. Inf. Syst. Secur. (TISSEC). **8**(4), 351–387 (2005)
25. Hu, V.C., Ferraiolo, D., Kuhn, R., Friedman, A.R., Lang, A.J., Cogdell, M.M., Schnitzer, A., Sandlin, K., Miller, R., Scarfone, K:. Guide to attribute based access control (abac) definition and considerations (draft). NIST Special Publication, 2013 Apr;800(162)
26. McLaughlin, N., Martinez del Rincon, J., Kang, B., Yerima, S., Miller, P., Sezer, S., Safaei, Y., Trickel, E., Zhao, Z., Doupé, A., Joon Ahn, G.: Deep android malware detection. In: Proceedings of the Seventh ACM on Conference on Data and Application Security and Privacy 2017 Mar 22, pp. 301–308
27. Maghrebi, H., Portigliatti, T., Prouff, E.: Breaking cryptographic implementations using deep learning techniques. In: International Conference on Security, Privacy, and Applied Cryptography Engineering 2016 Dec 14, pp. 3–26. Springer, Cham
28. Pascanu, R., Mikolov, T., Bengio, Y.: On the difficulty of training recurrent neural networks. In: International Conference on Machine lLearning 2013 Feb 13, pp. 1310–1318
29. Sherstinsky, A.: Fundamentals of recurrent neural network (rnn) and long short-term memory (lstm) network. Phys. D: Nonlinear Phenomena. 2020 Mar 1;404:132306
30. Khalil, R.A., Jones, E., Babar, M.I., Jan, T., Zafar, M.H., Alhussain, T.: Speech emotion recognition using deep learning techniques: a review. IEEE Access. **19**(7), 117327–117345 (2019)

31. Roy, D.G., Mahato, B., Ghosh, A., De, D.: Service aware resource management into cloudlets for data offloading towards IoT. Microsyst. Technol. **4**, 1–5 (2019)
32. Satyavolu, P.: Designing for manufacturing's 'Internet of Things', Cognizant (2014)
33. Roy, D.G., Das, P., De, D., Buyya, R.: QoS-aware secure transaction framework for internet of things using blockchain mechanism. J. Netw. Comput. Appl. **15**(144), 59–78 (2019)
34. Ahmed, E., Yaqoob, I., Gani, A., Imran, M., Guizani, M.: Internet-of-things-based smart environments: state of the art, taxonomy, and open research challenges. IEEE Wirel. Commun. **23**(5), 10–16 (2016)
35. Yaqoob, I., Ahmed, E., Hashem, I.A., Ahmed, A.I., Gani, A., Imran, M., Guizani, M.: Internet of things architecture: Recent advances, taxonomy, requirements, and open challenges. IEEE Wirel. Commun. **24**(3), 10–16 (2017)
36. Williams, T.: The Purdue Enterprise Reference Architecture, International Society of Automation. Elsevier **24**(2–3), 141–158 (1994)
37. Boyes, H., Hallaq, B., Cunningham, J., Watson, T.: The industrial internet of things (IIoT): an analysis framework. Comput. Ind. **1**(101), 1–2 (2018)
38. Lukač, D.: The fourth ICT-based industrial revolution" Industry 4.0—HMI and the case of CAE/CAD innovation with EPLAN P8. In: 2015 23rd Telecommunications Forum Telfor (TELFOR) 2015 Nov 24, pp. 835–838. IEEE

Chapter 2
Deep Learning Models and Their Architectures for Computer Vision Applications: A Review

Tanima Dutta, Randheer Bagi, and Hari Prabhat Gupta

2.1 Introduction

In recent years, deep learning techniques have executed enormous advancements in multimedia and internet of things (IoT), remarkably in the field of object detection and recognition, motion tracking, action recognition, human pose estimation, scene text spotting, and semantic segmentation [3–6, 10, 12]. Deep learning is a family of methods that uses deep neural network architectures to learn high-level feature representation. When a network has more than one hidden layer, it is of deep neural network architecture. The essence of deep learning is to compute hierarchical features, i.e., the higher-level features are derived from lower-level features. Deep learning techniques incorporate neural networks, hierarchical probabilistic models, and various unsupervised and supervised feature learning algorithms. It supports learning at multiple processing layers of the computational models. The main objective of deep learning techniques is to create a system that simulates the human brain by mimicking the procedure, how it senses and realizes the multi-modal information.

The notable factor that boosted the deep learning techniques is advancements in multimedia and IoT devices like smartphones, tablets, cameras etc. These devices generate a massive amount of visual and sensory data for the research analysis in multimedia and internet of things (IoT) tasks. Another factor is the empowerment of computing machines like parallel GPUs computing. These computationally enhanced

T. Dutta · R. Bagi (✉) · H. P. Gupta
Department of Computer Science and Engineering, IIT (BHU) Varanasi, Varanasi,
Uttar Pradesh, India
e-mail: randheerbagi.rs.cse17@iitbhu.ac.in

T. Dutta
e-mail: tanima.cse@iitbhu.ac.in

H. P. Gupta
e-mail: hariprabhat.cse@iitbhu.ac.in

© The Author(s), under exclusive license to Springer Nature Singapore Pte Ltd. 2021   31
A. Makkar and N. Kumar, *Deep Learning for Security and Privacy Preservation in IoT*,
Signals and Communication Technology,
https://doi.org/10.1007/978-981-16-6186-0_2

machines significantly accelerate the training of deep learning models. Furthermore, the evolution of powerful frameworks like TensorFlow, theano, keras, and mxnet make faster prototyping of deep learning models. In this chapter, we review the advancements in deep learning models for multimedia and internet of things (IoT) applications. It helps in selecting the deep learning models for researchers who are interested in state-of-the-art in deep learning for multimedia and internet of things (IoT) analysis.

2.1.1 Motivation for Deep Learning

The growth of machine learning in the field of computer science solves many science and engineering applications. Machine learning needs a human operator to correct the errors while training with a few hundred training data. Feature extraction in machine learning required domain expertise, which relies on humans knowledge for model learning. The first hurdle in machine learning is the scarcity of handcrafted features to develop accurate and reliable models in several practical circumstances. Unfortunately, it causes poor performance whenever tested in a new domain, even if the best algorithm for a particular application. In this scenario, deep learning plays a vital role because it works on the principle of self-learning by exploiting massive data using large-scale neural networks. Deep learning enhanced the feature generation process and graft high-level and low-level features without any human intervention. The automatic generation of features decreases human efforts and minimizes the error rate in accuracy. However, deep learning faces the challenge of additional computational cost.

The rest of the chapter is organized as follows: Sect. 2.2 describes the terminology of the deep learning models. Next, we will discuss the models of deep learning in Sect. 2.3. Applications of deep learning are described in Sect. 2.4, and in the last we will conclude the chapter in Sect. 2.5.

2.2 Preliminaries

In this section, we will discuss the terminology and the concepts that are used in deep learning models, which make different types of neural network architectures in multimedia and IoT. Some of them are described as follows:

1. **Input/Output**: A convolutional neural network usually takes images as input data and produces an output prediction score corresponding to the input image data. It considers the image as a matrix of values where each value is encoded depending on bit size.
2. **Features**: Features are grafted after convolution operation; they are distinct in nature and helpful in observing the input data patterns. Features are repeatedly emerged from the data to gain prominence.

3. **Filters (Convolution Kernels)**: Filters are also known as kernels. It is a fundamental part of the layered architecture of deep networks. Kernels are convolved with the given input volume to obtain a map called "activation maps". The value in the activation map depends on the size of the kernel.

4. **Convolution (conv)**: Convolution operation produces the feature maps after operating with a fixed kernel over the input volume [17, 29, 37].

5. **Max-pooling**: It minimizes the deep network complexity by selecting the high-level features from the input feature map. Also, it causes the loss of low-level features [17, 29, 37].

6. **Padding**: In the conv operation, we face the problem of dimension mismatch and loss of information. Therefore, padding is used to mitigate this error from the layered architecture of deep networks [17, 29, 37].

7. **Dropout**: It is used for the regularization in the layered architecture of a deep neural network to prevent the network from overfitting. It is noted that we do not use dropout in the testing phase [17, 29, 37].

8. **Gradient Descent**: It is an optimization technique that is used in deep learning models. Gradient descent is defined as a slop of a function to measure the degree of change of a variable regarding the change in another variable. There are three types of gradient descent used in a layered architecture: batch gradient descent, stochastic gradient descent, and mini-batch gradient descent.

9. **Back-propagation**: In the backpropagation, the computation begins from the last layer and stops at the first layer. It improves the accuracy by modifying the parameters like activation maps, weights, and biases between the deep network layers. Also, it reduces the cost function [17, 29, 37].

10. **Momentum**: It accelerates the training process by utilizing a stochastic gradient descent optimization. Momentum uses the moving average of the gradient, which prevents the network from getting stuck in the local minimum during training. Also, a higher momentum value overreaches its minimum and makes the network unstable.

11. **Learning Rate**: It is the step size analyzed during the training of the network that accelerates the training process. However, deciding the value of the learning rate is sensitive. A larger value of η in the network may start diverging rather than converging the loss, and if it is chosen as a small value, then the network may not converge.

12. **Activation Function**: It adds non-linearity to the deep network to solve the problem of vanishing gradient by using activation functions such as relu, tanh, elu, and sigmoid [17, 29, 37].

13. **The Fully Connected Layer**: It is fully connected with the output of the previous layer in the layered architecture of the deep neural network. It is typically used to construct the desired number of outputs from the learning models.

2.3 Models of Deep Learning

2.3.1 Categorization of Deep Neural Networks

- DEEP CONVOLUTIONAL NEURAL NETWORKS: The convolutional networks replace the matrix multiplication operation with the convolution operation in the network. Convolutional Neural Networks (CNNs) are successfully used in many complex applications of multimedia and internet-of-thing. Over the years, CNN gains considerable attention due to this; several CNN variants are developed.
- SEQUENTIAL NEURAL NETWORKS: In the sequential model, each layer has exactly one input tensor and one output tensor. It takes sequential data as an input to predict the score for the occurrence of a sequence. The input data are like text streams, audio clips, video clips, time-series data. Some of the popular sequential models are Recurrent Neural Network (RNN), Long Short Temporal Memory (LSTM), and Gated Recurrent Unit (GRU).
- DEEP GENERATIVE NETWORKS (DGNs): The generative model has gained tremendous success in the last few years because of its strength to supervise unlabeled data. It works on the zero-sum game approach, where the two networks called generator and discriminator chores against each other. The generator aims to determine the original data distribution of the training data to create new data points with some modifications as shown in Fig. 2.1.
- GRAPH NEURAL NETWORKS: The graph neural network (GNN) is a connectionist model that captures the dependence of the graphs via message passing between the nodes of graphs. GNN is challenging to train because it takes unstructured data as input. Some application areas of GNNs are social network analysis, recommender systems, visual question answering, and interaction detection (Fig. 2.2).

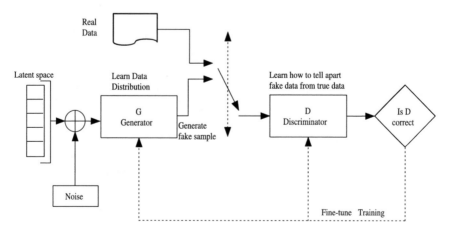

Fig. 2.1 Basic architecture of deep generative adversarial network

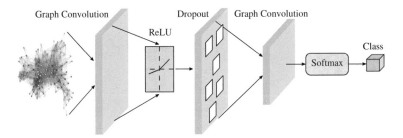

Fig. 2.2 Basic architecture of graph neural network

2.3.2   Taxonomy of Convolution Neural Network

2.3.2.1   Deep Convolutional Neural Networks

CNN [14, 29] comprises multiple layers of neural network for recognizing visual patterns in the image in a computationally efficient manner. Here, the efficiency is induced by reducing the computation requirements compared to the traditional deep neural network models. The designing mechanism of CNN compels to recognize the images' visual patterns by directly interpreting the pixels. The architecture works similar to the traditional deep learning model that produces the class score or class labels probability by taking data (images/sensory values) as input. The internal structure of CNN fabricates different operations including, convolution (abbreviated as "conv"), non-linear activation function ("Relu/Sigmoid/Tanh"), and pooling layer ("average/max pool"). At the end of the network, the fully connected ("dense") layer is added, followed by the softmax layer to generate class label probability. The basic architecture of CNN is illustrated in Fig. 2.3. The depicted architecture has gradually decreasing convolutional operations from 100×100 filters to 25×25 filters. The objective function is evaluated as:

$$J(\Theta) = \frac{1}{m} \sum_{i=1}^{m} \mathcal{L}(\hat{y}_i^{\theta}, y_i) \tag{2.1}$$

where m shows training set size, Θ model parameters, and $\mathcal{L}$ is the cost function.

Before the fully connected operation, all the layers are stacked in a one-dimensional array. To perform the stacking operation, concatenation layers are used that converts the multi-dimensional output into a single dimension. Further, the fully connected layer maps the corresponding output to the softmax operations, which results in the class label probabilities. Recent year has witnessed the CNN structure's high-level modifications to facilitate the unfolding demands of the different domains like image processing, mobile sensing IoT, etc. The varied structure is manifested by shaping the CNN architecture. It incorporates 3×3 size filter to perform the convolution in

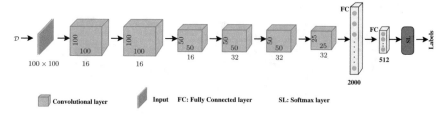

Fig. 2.3 Basic architecture of deep neural Network

the convolution layer. The maximum size of the receptive field in max-pooling is restricted to 3×3. When we increase the receptive field size, it prompts the suppression of information from data [21].

2.3.2.2 AlexNet

AlexNet [29] is one of the convolutional neural network variants and treated as one of the fundamental deep learning models. AlexNet is widely incorporated in different operations, including classification, localization, and detection using the dataset of sensors (image-based/mechanical). It comprises five convolutional layers with max-pooling layers successively. Then a fully connected layer is added at the end of the deep network. In AlexNet, Relu activation function adds non-linearity by placing it after each convolutional operation in the network. Here, data augmentation is performed to neglect incomplete input data. In the data augmentation operation like image translations, horizontal reflections, and patch extractions are conducted. It uses two GPUs in parallel for the model training, and the SGD process does the parameters tuning.

2.3.3 ZF Net

ZF Net is a classic convolutional neural network, a more refined architecture of the ALexNet. The filter size is reduced to 7×7 and the number of filters is doubled in all right convolutional layers compared to AlexNet. It has deconvolution layers alongside of the convolution layers for grafted feature maps visualization [44]. Relu added the non-linearity and cross-entropy test the error in the loss function. Accuracy is improved by tuning the parameters using the SGD process.

2.3.3.1   VGG Net

VGGNet was introduced with a reduced number of parameters in comparison to ZFnet. It uses 3×3 convolutions filters stacked on top of one another. These small filters help to increase the network's depth as well as reduced the input data dimension generating at each layer [38]. This network doubles the filter after each convolution layer and reduces the volume size using the MaxPooling operation. In the training phase, for parameter tuning, the batch gradient is used and Relu activation is enforced for non-linearity. The model is trained on 4 GPUs and used in applications like image classification and localization.

2.3.3.2   GoogleNet

The GoogleNet [40] is the extension of the previous CNN-based deep networks such as VGGNet and Resnet. The network improves the computational complexity and space complexity of previous models by utilizing multi-level feature extraction techniques. GoogleNet uses the parallel operations by introducing $1 \times 1, 3 \times 3$, and 5×5 convolutions within the same module known as the inception module. The architecture consists of convolution, maxpool, and inception modules. The inception module uses average pooling instead of max pooling and the probability was generated by a softmax layer.

2.3.3.3   ResNet

ResNet focuses on the observation that the stacking layers on the deep network architecture degrade the accuracy at some point [18, 23]. Resnet architecture introduces the "identity shortcut connections". These connections skip two or more layers and are commonly known as the residual block. These residual blocks consist of convolution, batch normalization, Relu. It provides control over the architecture because in ultra-deep networks, it is challenging to tune the parameters. It exponentially reduces the error rate due to the use of skip connections at a time of backpropagation. It uses 8 GPUs for training the model as discussed in Fig. 2.4.

2.3.3.4   Capsule Network

A capsule network [33] is generated to mimic the human visual system. It answers the actual challenge of the fundamental deep neural network i.e., CNN. The conventional approaches fail to solve the problem related to the image rotation, change in color of image, or lighting condition in an image. Capsule network preserves all the information concerning the appearance of an object and its orientation by the activity vector. It does not use pooling operations in between the deep neural network.

Fig. 2.4 Basic architecture
residual block of ResNet

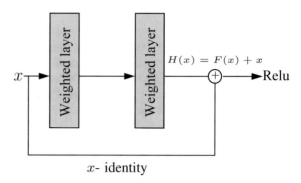

x- identity

2.3.4 Region Based CNN (RCNN)

Region-based convolutional neural networks are based on selective search algorithm [32]. The region-based convolutional network comes with a region proposal
network (RPN). RPN creates a collection of rectangular boxes, which are identified
as object proposal [13, 19]. The generated set of region proposals are fed into the
convolutional neural network for extracting the feature vector for each region. After
that, linear support vector machines (SVMs) are used for the class score prediction
of each proposal. At the same time, bounding box coordinates are obtained from the
feature vectors by utilizing the bounding box regressor.

2.3.4.1 YOLO

YOLO uses one of the fastest object detection algorithms in his deep neural network [31] which makes it suitable for real-time detection of objects in scene images.
YOLO detection algorithm develops small grids on the images; then, each grid having objects are surrounded by the bounding boxes. When the computed class score
probability of a bounding box is higher than a specific solidified threshold, it locates
the object within the image. YOLO has poor accuracy related to RCNN, yet approximately 40 frames per second quicker in test accuracy. It is also not suitable for small
object detection within the given image.

2.3.5 Mask RCNN

Mask R-CNN [19] is used for object instance segmentation. It works in two phases;
In the first phase, RPN is used to generate candidates with bounding boxes. In the
second phase, a binary segmentation mask is added to each region of interest, parallel
to softmax classification and bounding box regression.

2.3.6 Taxonomy of Sequential Neural Network

2.3.6.1 Recurrent Neural Networks (RNN)

The traditional deep network architectures proposed so far do not prove to be fascinating and efficient for sequential or time-series data. They do not capture the temporal dependency between the sequential events, which plays a crucial role in predicting the next output in the sequence. The sequential data's variable length is tedious to manage in the spatial model like a convolutional neural network. Thus, it urges a need for a network that facilitates both temporal feature sharing and handling different lengths of the input data [36, 39]. Recurrent Neural Network (RNN) deal with the sequential data and captures the temporal features to provide the faster prediction of the next input sequence. RNNs can be treated as perceptrons to store information about the input sequence by using hidden layers as shown in Fig. 2.5. It also provides the mechanism for the dynamic update of the hidden units. RNNs capture the temporal features by using only the information that is earlier used in sequence for prediction. Despite different advantages, the RNNs lag in capturing the long-term dependencies. The variables in the RNN architecture are x_t, y_t, and h_t which are input, output, and hidden state at time t. Here, h_t and y_t are formulated as:

$$h_t = \phi(U.x_t + W.h_{t-1}) \quad \text{and} \quad y_t = \psi(V.h_t) \tag{2.2}$$

where $h(t-1)$ is randomly initialized hidden state value at timestamp $(t-1)$, ψ and ϕ both are non-linear function. Also, U, V, and W are the various linear regressions parameters, preceding the nonlinear activations. The objective function is evaluated as:

$$J(\Theta) = \frac{1}{m} \sum_{i=1}^{m} \sum_{t=1}^{N_y^{(i)}} \mathcal{L}(\hat{y}_t^{(i)}, y_t^{(i)}) \tag{2.3}$$

where m is the training set size, Θ is the model parameters, N is the number of epochs, and $\mathcal{L}$ represents the cost function.

2.3.6.2 Long Short Term Memory (LSTM)

LSTM [20] is another generation of RNN that mitigates the problem associated with it. The LSTM architectures are capable of handling long-term dependency in the dataset. It introduces the memory unit in the network that captures these long-term dependencies. Thus, it can be treated as an extended version of the RNN that adds the memorizing capability and increase the computation for improving the performance using time-series data. Typically, RNNs have 'short-term memory' to capture the previous output of the model and the current input sequence for predicting the next output sequence. Thus, it helps in curtailing the extra effort needed for preserving the previous information. This stored information improves the performance on sequential data. LSTM helps to mitigate the vanishing gradient problem, where learning (or weight update) of the hidden neurons is negligible during backpropagation after certain layers in the network. The LSTM incorporates four basic units, including forget gate, input gate, output gate, and cell state. These units persist in memory blocks which are connected using multiple layers. The LSTM achieves high order performance in natural language processing, image processing, time series analysis, speech recongition [16], and image captioning etc. [20, 34].

2.3.6.3   Gated Recurrent Unit (GRU)

The gated recurrent units [9] is the sibling of the long short term memory in some aspect but has some points of difference. The GRU does not hold the output gate as in LSTM. They also compel to solve the vanish gradient problem present in the RNN in a similar fashion as LSTM perform. By eliminating the output gate, the GRU reduces the network's computation requirements and achieves performance as identical to LSTM in various cases. However, LSTM sometimes supersedes the recognition performance in the classification task of time series analysis. GRU incorporates different gated operations, including input, update, and reset. These gates control the flow of information inside the network. The update gate takes the responsibility of controlling the information into memory. The reset gate manages the flow of information from memory. These two gates are also treated as two vectors that decide which information will get passed on to the output. They train the network to ensure the persistence of the information from the past and remove irrelevant information for prediction. Thus, GRU can be treated as a fruitful mechanism for fixing the vanishing gradient problem in RNN with reduced computations.

Fig. 2.5 Basic architecture of recurrent neural network

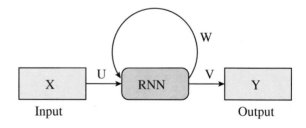

2.3.7 Taxonomy of Deep Generative Adversarial Network

2.3.7.1 Autoencoder (AE)

Autoencoder [28] takes high dimensionality data and compresses it into a small representation with neural networks without extensive data loss. It is composed of encoder and decoder networks. The encoder compresses the input data and the decoder tries to reconstruct the input data. AE estimates the reconstruction loss by computing per pixel differences between encoder input and decoder output. The reconstruction loss is calculated as :

$$\text{loss} = ||\text{input data-reconstructed data}||^2. \tag{2.4}$$

2.3.7.2 Variational Autoencoder (VAE)

Variational Autoencoder [1] is a likelihood-based generative model that includes an encoder network, a decoder network, and loss functions. The encoder embeds a data sample into discrete latent variables. The decoder network reconstructs the input sample based on the discrete latent vector without extensive input data loss.

2.3.7.3 Generative Adversarial Networks (GANs)

It is based on a zero-sum game [15] approach. It consists of two neural networks named generator (G) and discriminator (D), in which one network is acting as an adversary to another. The generator seeks to mimic the pattern of original data so that it can mislead the discriminator. The discriminator discriminates the fake data from the original data [8, 22, 25]. The cost function of the generative adversarial network is optimized after achieving the nash equilibrium between generator and discriminator. Formally, the GAN objective function can be written as a two-player minimax game with value function $V(G, D)$:

$$\min_G \max_D V(G, D) = E_{x \sim p_{data}(x)}[\log D(x)] + E_{z \sim p_z(z)}[log(1 - D(G(z)))] \tag{2.5}$$

where $D(x)$ represents probability that x came from real data and $p_z(Z)$ is the noisy input variable.

2.3.7.4 Deep Convolutional GAN (DCGAN)

It introduces to significantly stabilizes the GAN training. It also consists of two networks; the first network is CNN called a generator, whereas the second is de-CNN called s discriminator. In DCGAN [30], the layered architecture of the generator replaces all layer pooling operations with stride convolution operations. Additionally, the generator and discriminator uses ReLU and Leaky-ReLU as an activation function, respectively, with batch normalization.

2.3.7.5 Wasserstein Generative Adversarial Network (WGAN)

It is an extension of GAN, where the discriminator model is updated many more times than the generator model during the training procedure in a single iteration [2]. In this, the discriminator is known as a critic. Both models i.e., critic and generator are trained using "Wasserstein loss," which is the average product of original and predicted values from the critic. The critic learns very quickly to differentiate between fake and original data. However, the critic can not saturate and converges to a linear function that yields remarkably clean gradients everywhere.

2.3.7.6 Progressive-Growing GAN (PGGAN)

It is a multi-scale GAN network where the training of generator and discriminator started with low-resolution images and gradually increasing as the depth of the model increases. The key idea of PGGAN is to grow the generator and discriminator in synchrony. The growing training approach of PGGAN [24] facilitates stable learning for both the networks in big resolutions and reduces the training time.

2.3.7.7 BigGAN

It is one of the best GAN models that can train bigger neural networks with more parameters and generate a more detailed image without any performance degradation. BigGAN provides the exerts control over the outputs [7]. It supports interpolation phenomena, which means that it can compute the intermediate image between them and provide the best inception score if there are two images.

2.3.8 Taxonomy of Graph Neural Networks (GNNs)

2.3.8.1 Graph Attention Network

In the traditional graph convolutional network, the aggregation for each target node is contributed equally by all the neighbors. Graph attention networks [41] overwhelm this shortcoming by learning to assign different levels of importance to all the nodes in the neighborhood of a target node. Moreover, graph attention networks are generalizable for unseen nodes. It attempts to learn the propagation weight by adopting self-attention mechanism as:

$$\alpha_{i,j} = \text{softmax}(a(Wx_i, Wx_j))$$ (2.6)

$$= \frac{\exp(\text{LeakyReLU}(b^T[Wx_i||Wx_j]))}{\sum_{k \in N(i)} \exp(\text{LeakyReLU}(b^T[Wx_i||Wx_k]))}$$

where $a(.,.)$ represents a neural network, $||$ stands for concatenate operator, and $b \in \mathbb{R}^{2F}$ is the learnable vector for propagation weights.

2.3.8.2 Convolutional Graph Neural Networks (ConvGNNs)

It generalizes the convolution operation from grid data to graph data. The main concept is to create a node by aggregating neighbors' features and its own features. In this, high-level node representations are extracted by stacking multiple graph convolution layers. ConvGNNs [11, 26, 35] is useful in developing many other graph neural network models. Let a single layer ConvGNN propagates with node attributes h using a function $f(A)$ of the adjacency matrix, then the output is:

$$F(A, h) = \sigma(f(A) \cdot h \cdot W + b)$$ (2.7)

where f defines the rule of propagation, h_i is the ith node attribute, W shows weight matrix, and b represents bias.

2.3.8.3 Graph Autoencoders (GAEs)

It is an unsupervised learning framework where it encodes nodes or graphs into a latent vector space and reconstructs the graph data from the encoded information [27]. It is used to learn the generative distributions of the graph and network embeddings. It learns latent node representations through reconstructing graph structural information such as the graph adjacency matrix for network embedding. For graph generation, some methods generate nodes and edges of a graph step by step, while other methods output a graph all at once.

2.3.8.4 Recurrent Graph Neural Networks (RecGNNs)

It covers pioneer works of graph neural networks. It aims to learn node representations with the help of recurrent neural architectures. It assumes a node in a graph regularly transfers messages to its neighbor's node until a stable equilibrium is reached. RecGNN [35] is important and it inspires researchers to perform more research on convolutional graph neural networks. In particular, the idea of message passing is integrated with spatial-based convolutional graph neural networks.

2.3.8.5 Spatial-Temporal Graph Neural Networks (STGNNs)

It learns hidden patterns from spatial-temporal graphs, which play a vital role in various applications such as traffic speed forecasting, driver maneuver anticipation, and human action recognition [42, 43]. The key idea is to examine spatial and temporal dependency at the same time. Many modern research integrates graph convolutions to capture spatial dependency with RNNs or CNNs to model the temporal dependency.

2.4 Applications in Multimedia and Internet of Things

In this section, we will review some practical applications of deep learning models. Due to its ability to handle large amounts of unlabeled data, deep learning models provide powerful tools to deal with big data analysis. Deep learning techniques play·a vital role in areas of multimedia and internet of things. We have briefly summarized a general description on different applications of the deep networks: object classification, object localization, object detection, image segmentation, style transfer, image colorization, image super-resolution, and image synthesis.

1. **Object Classification**: In the object classification task, a label is assigned to the test image according to their predicted class score.
2. **Object Localization**: After the classification task, finding the location of a single object in the given classified image is known to object localization.
3. **Object Detection**: In this, multiple objects within the given test image are identified. The object within a single test image may belong to the same or another class group.
4. **Image Segmentation**: In the segmentation task, the test image pixels are grouped together according to the similarity in the properties. The segmentation algorithm depends on the kind of applications for which it is used.
5. **Style Transfer**: In style transfer, the algorithm learns style from one or more images and applies that style to another image.
6. **Image Colorization**: The task of image colorization entails transforming a grayscale image into a full-color image using deep learning models.
7. **Image Reconstruction**: The task of image reconstruction is also known as image inpainting. In this, a filling task is performed for the missing or corrupted parts of an image.
8. **Image Super-Resolution**: In the image super-resolution task, we generate a new version of the input image with a higher resolution than the original input image. Also, it can be used for image restoration and inpainting applications.

9. **Image Synthesis**: It is a broader area of research that covers various applications. In image synthesis, deep learning models generate a modified version of a given image or entirely change the given image as a new image. Using image synthesis, we can change the style of an object and add a new object to the scene image.

2.5 Conclusion

The enormous growth of deep learning techniques in multimedia and IoT is impressive and encouraging, which outperforms traditional techniques. We gain considerable progress in computational empowerment, maintaining the large dataset, and developing new ideas and algorithms to improve the architecture of deep learning models. This chapter categorizes the deep learning models according to their network architecture and the nature of problem-solving for multimedia and IoT tasks. We also explain the variants of deep learning models in each category that can help to select optimal learning architectures for the distinct multimedia and IoT tasks. Although we gain success in mimicking the human brain functionality into the deep learning models, we are still in the early phase of complete replication of the human brain into deep learning models. This is because we know very little about the human brain functionality mechanism. We do not know at what order of magnitude we need to go; to convert the complete functionality of the human brain into the different learning models. Therefore, we are expecting to have a more efficient and advanced learning model in the future.

References

1. An, J., Cho, S.: Variational autoencoder based anomaly detection using reconstruction probability. In: Special Lecture on IE (2015)
2. Arjovsky, M., Chintala, S., Bottou, L.: Wasserstein generative adversarial networks. Proc. ICML **70**, 214–223 (2017)
3. Bagi, R., Dutta, T.: Cost-effective smart text sensing spotting in blurry scene images using deep networks. IEEE Sens. J. 1–8 (2020)
4. Bagi, R., Dutta, T., Gupta, H.P.: Cluttered textSpotter: an end-to-end trainable light-weight scene text spotter for cluttered environment. IEEE Access **8**, 111433–111447 (2020)
5. Bagi, R., Dutta, T., Gupta, H.P.: Deep learning architectures for computer vision applications: a study. In: Advances in Data and Information Sciences, Springer, pp. 601–612 (2020)
6. Bagi, R., Mohanty, S., Dutta, T., Gupta, H.P.: Leveraging smart devices for scene text preserved image stylization: a deep gaming approach. IEEE MultiMedia **27**(2), 19–32 (2020)
7. Brock, A., Donahue, J., Simonyan, K.: Large scale GAN training for high fidelity natural image synthesis. In: Proceedings of ICLR (2019)
8. Choi. Y., Choi, M., Kim, M., Ha, J., Kim, S., Choo, J.: StarGAN: unified generative adversarial networks for multi-domain image-to-image translation. CoRR abs/1711.09020 (2017)
9. Chung, J., Gulcehre, C., Cho, K., Bengio, Y.: Empirical evaluation of gated recurrent neural networks on sequence modeling. In: NIPS 2014 Workshop on Deep Learning (2014)
10. Deng, S., Li, S., Xie, K., Song, W., Liao, X., Hao, A., Qin, H.: A global-local self-adaptive network for drone-view object detection. IEEE Trans. Image Proc. **30**, 1556–1569 (2021)

11. Gama, F., Marques, A.G., Leus, G., Ribeiro, A.: Convolutional Graph Neural Networks. In: Proceedings of ACSSC, pp. 452–456
12. Gao, Z., Guo, L., Guan, W., Liu, A.A., Ren, T., Chen, S.: A pairwise attentive adversarial spatiotemporal network for cross-domain few-shot action recognition-R2. IEEE Trans. Image Proc. **30**, 767–782 (2021)
13. Girshick, R.: Fast R-CNN. In: Proceedings of IEEE ICCV, pp. 1440–1448 (2015)
14. Goodfellow, I., Bengio, Y., Courville, A.: Deep Learning. MIT Press (2016)
15. Goodfellow, I.J., Pouget-Abadie, J., Mirza, M., Xu, B., Warde-Farley, D., Ozair, S., Courville, A., Bengio, Y.: Generative adversarial nets. In: Proceedings of NIPS, pp. 2672–2680 (2014)
16. Graves, A., Mohamed, A., Hinton, G.: Speech recognition with deep recurrent neural networks. In: Proceedings of IEEE ICASSP, pp. 6645–6649 (2013)
17. Guo, T., Dong, J., Li, H., Gao, Y.: Simple convolutional neural network on image classification. In: Proceeding of IEEE ICBDA, pp. 721–724 (2017)
18. He, K., Zhang, X., Ren, S., Sun, J.: Deep residual learning for image recognition. CoRR abs/1512.03385 (2015)
19. He, K., Gkioxari, G., Dollár, P., Girshick, R.: Mask R-CNN. In: Proceedings of IEEE ICCV, pp. 2980–2988 (2017)
20. Hochreiter, S., Schmidhuber, J.: Long short-term memory. Neural Comput. **9**(8), 1735–1780 (1997)
21. Hu, B., Lu, Z., Li, H., Chen, Q.: Convolutional neural network architectures for matching natural language sentences. Adv. Neural. Inf. Proc. Syst. **27**, 2042–2050 (2014)
22. Jaiswal, A., AbdAlmageed, W., Natarajan, P.: CapsuleGAN: generative adversarial Capsule Network. In: ECCV Workshops (2018)
23. Kaiming, H., Zhang, X., Ren, S., Sun, J.: Delving deep into rectifiers: surpassing human-level performance on imageNet classification. In: Proceedings of IEEE ICCV, pp. 1026–1034 (2015)
24. Karras, T., Aila, T., Laine, S., Lehtinen, J.: Progressive growing of GANs for improved quality, stability, and variation. In: Proceedings of ICLR (2018a)
25. Karras, T., Laine, S., Aila, T.: A style-based generator architecture for generative adversarial networks. CoRR abs/1812.04948 (2018b)
26. Kipf, T.N., Welling, M.: Semi-supervised classification with graph convolutional networks. In: Proceedings of ICLR (2017)
27. Kipf, T.N., Welling, M.: Variational graph auto-encoders. In: Proceedings of NeurIPS, pp. 1–11 (2019)
28. Kramer, M.A.: Nonlinear principal component analysis using autoassociative neural networks. AIChE J. **37**(2), 233–243 (1991)
29. Krizhevsky, A., Sutskever, I., Hinton, G.E.: ImageNet classification with deep convolutional neural networks. Adv. Neural Inf. Proc. Syst. **25**, 1097–1105 (2012)
30. Mehralian, M., Karasfi, B.: RDCGAN: unsupervised representation learning with regularized deep convolutional generative adversarial networks. In: Proceedings of ICAIR and ICAPIS, pp. 31–38 (2018)
31. Redmon, J., Divvala, S., Girshick, R., Farhadi, A.: You only look once: unified, real-time object detection. In: Proceeding of IEEE CVPR, pp. 779–788 (2016a)
32. Ren, S., He, K., Girshick, R., Sun, J.: Faster R-CNN: towards real-time object detection with region proposal networks. Adv. Neural Inf. Proc. Syst. **28**, 91–99 (2015)
33. Sabour, S., Frosst, N., Hinton, G.E.: Dynamic routing between capsules. CoRR abs/1710.09829, 1710.09829 (2017)
34. Sak, H., Senior, A.W., Beaufays, F.: Long short-term memory based recurrent neural network architectures for large vocabulary speech recognition. CoRR abs/1402.1128 (2014)
35. Scarselli, F., Gori, M., Tsoi, A.C., Hagenbuchner, M., Monfardini, G.: The graph neural network model. IEEE Trans. Neural Netw. **20**, 61–80 (2009)
36. Schuster, M., Paliwal, K.: Bidirectional recurrent neural networks. Trans. Sig. Proc. **45**(11), 2673–2681 (1997)
37. Shin, H., Roth, H.R., Gao, M., Lu, L., Xu, Z., Nogues, I., Yao, J., Mollura, D., Summers, R.M.: Deep convolutional neural networks for computer-aided detection: CNN architectures, dataset characteristics and transfer learning. IEEE Trans. Med. Imag. **35**(5), 1285–1298 (2016)

38. Simonyan, K., Zisserman, A.: Very deep convolutional networks for large-scale image recognition. CoRR abs/1409.1556 (2014)
39. Sutskever, I., Vinyals, O., Le, Q.V.: Sequence to sequence learning with neural networks. Adv. Neural Inf. Process. Syst. **27**, 3104–3112 (2014)
40. Szegedy, C., Liu, W., Jia, Y., Sermanet, P., Reed, S., Anguelov, D., Erhan, D., Vanhoucke, V., Rabinovich, A.: Going deeper with convolutions. In: Proceeding of IEEE CVPR, pp. 1–9 (2015)
41. Veličković, P., Cucurull G, Casanova A, Romero A, Liò P, Bengio Y (2018) Graph attention networks. In: Proceedings of ICLR
42. Wu, Z., Pan, S., Chen, F., Long, G., Zhang, C., Yu, P.S.: A comprehensive survey on graph neural networks. IEEE Trans. Neural Netw. Learn. Syst. **32**(1), 4–24 (2021)
43. Yu, B., Yin, H., Zhu, Z.: Spatio-temporal graph convolutional networks: a deep learning framework for traffic forecasting. In: Proceedings of IJCAI, pp. 3634–3640 (2018)
44. Zeiler, M.D., Fergus, R.: Visualizing and understanding convolutional networks. CoRR (2013)

Tanima Dutta Received Ph.D in Computer Science and Engineering from the Indian Institute of Technology Guwahati, India in 2014. Presently, she is an Assistant Professor in the Department of Computer Science and Engineering, Indian Institute of Technology (BHU) Varanasi, India. Her research interests include computer vision and deep networks.

Randheer Bagi Received M.Tech. degree in Computer Science from the Central University of South Bihar, India in 2015. He is currently pursuing a Ph.D. with the Department of Computer Science and Engineering, Indian Institute of Technology (BHU) Varanasi, Varanasi, India. His research interests include deep learning, computer vision, and humancomputer-interaction.

Hari Prabhat Gupta Received his M.Tech and Ph.D in Computer Science and Engineering from the Indian Institute of Technology Guwahati, India in 2010 and 2014, respectively. Presently, he is an Assistant Professor in the Department of Computer Science and Engineering, Indian Institute of Technology (BHU) Varanasi, India. His research interests include wireless networks and game theory.

Chapter 3
IoT Data Security with Machine Learning Blckchain: Risks and Countermeasures

Koustav Kumar Mondal and Deepsubhra Guha Roy

3.1 Introduction

We have seen industries change from producing only goods to developing a grid of products acknowledged as the Internet-of-Things (IoT) and finally generating a smart product grid that offers a range of irreplaceable connected services [1, 2]. As per Aksu et al. [3], every three minutes, two devices are linked to the Internet. An growing amount of network traffic has resulted from this connectivity besides the exponential development of IoT devices. Challenges such as protection and confidentiality of operator data and substantiation and confirmation of strategies have emerged due to this connectivity [4]. In 2013, for instance, hackers compromised one billion yahoo accounts [5]. One hundred and forty-six million customers of eBay were underneath outbreak in 2014[6]. In 2017, one hundred and forty-four million Equifax clienteles had their private details compromised, continuing the growing pattern of attacks. Likewise, as noted in [7], their eight hundred and twenty thousand consumer accounts were abused by a five billion dollar toy industry in 2017. Over two and half million soundtracks, of which a limited were kept for payoff, were also included. Cybersecurity disasters are full of recent cyber history, from major data breaks to safekeeping vulnerabilities in billions of computer chip and lockdowns of computer grids before a imbursement has been made [8]. IoT devices have a multitude of protection and privacy problems that are growing every day. Security and privacy are therefore major challenges in dynamic and source-inhibited IoT surroundings and essential to be addressed efficiently. As the attacks become

K. K. Mondal
School of Computational Science, Department of IT, Maulana Abul Kalam Azad University of Technology, WB, Simhat, Haringhata, Nadia, Kolkata, West Bengal 741249, India

D. Guha Roy (✉)
Mobile and Cloud Lab, Institute of Computer Science, University of Tartu, Ulikooli 17–324, 50090 Tartu, Estonia
e-mail: roysubhraguha@gmail.com

© The Author(s), under exclusive license to Springer Nature Singapore Pte Ltd. 2021   49
A. Makkar and N. Kumar, *Deep Learning for Security and Privacy Preservation in IoT*,
Signals and Communication Technology,
https://doi.org/10.1007/978-981-16-6186-0_3

sophisticated day by day, the security problems in the IoT are rising. Milosevic et al. [9] emphasized that influential computation policies, such as desktop computational devices, could be gifted to use specialised tools to detect malware. IoT systems have limited resources, however. Similarly, conventional cybersecurity frameworks and applications are not sufficiently effective to identify minor variations in attacks or zero-day outbreaks [10], meanwhile individually essential to be periodically modified. In addition, the changes are not accessible in real-time by the provider, rendering the network vulnerable. Algorithms for ML can be cast-off to progress the IoT setup (such as nifty devices and IoT entries) [11], as well as to improve the efficiency of cybersecurity systems. These procedures can analyse grid circulation, update danger information records, and retain the fundamental networks safe from novel outbreaks, based on existing knowledge of cyber threats [12]. In addition to using ML algorithms, researchers have also begun to secure the underlying structures with the groundbreaking Blockchain (BC) technique [9, 13–17]. Even though ML procedures and BC approaches have been technologically advanced to contract with IoT virtual terrorizations, compounding these deuce is somewhat new that desires to be investigated. Confidentiality drives with security hand in hand. Price et al. described confidentiality as a collection of rules based on the application [18]. The authors clarify that the instructions for in what way the data can stream be subject to on the people elaborate, procedures, regularity, and reasons for accessing the data. There are several applications that include security and privacy protection for personal information, such as wearable devices [3], Vehicular Area Network (VANET), healthcare, and smart-home [19, 20], for example. For example, the network is based on the data collected from devices in a crowdsensing application such as VANET to make smart decisions on the current traffic conditions. However, due to insufficient privacy-preserving measures and related risks, computer users may be reluctant to participate. In recent years, comprehensive studies focused on ML procedures and BC procedures [9, 12–17] have been carried out to secure system data and maintain the privacy of users.

3.2 Challenges in IoT

Internet-of-Things mentions to a huge amount of varied perception instruments, either on a LAN or over the Internet, communicating with each other [21]. Owing to the obtainable possessions of end strategies, IoT risks vary greatly from traditional networks [2]. IoT devices have limited memory and processing capacity, while powerful servers and computers with ample resources are part of the traditional Internet. Because of this, multifactor security layers and complex protocols will protect a conventional network, which is what can not be afforded by a real-time IoT device. IoT systems utilise fewer protected radiocommunication networking broadcasting, such as LoRa, ZigBee, 802.15.4, and 802.11a/b/n/g/p., as opposed toward conventional networks. Finally, IoT devices have distinct data contents and formats owing to application-precise features and absence of mutual OS, construction it difficult to establish a standard safety protocol [22]. Both of these drawbacks variety IoT vulnerable to various threats to safety and confidentiality, thereby initial places for different categories of outbreaks. In a network, the likelihood of an outbreak intensifications with the scale of the grid. The IoT grid therefore takes additional flaws than a conventional grid, such as a corporation workplace, for instance.

Furthermore, usually multi-vendor devices with various specifications and protocols are IoT devices that communicate with each other. It is a challenge to communicate between such devices that needs a trusted third party to serve as a bridge [23]. In addition, many reports have posed questions about software updates to billions of smart devices on a daily basis [15, 24]. An IoT device's computing resources are partial, thus the abilities of addressing forward-thinking terrorizations are besmirched. IoT susceptibilities could be situated secret as unique and general, to summarise. For instance, IoT devices are unique to vulnerabilities such as battery-drainage attack, standardisation, and lack of confidence, and Cyberspace-congenital exposures can be considered as communal susceptibilities. In the past [25], numerous IoT intimidations and their categorisation take be situated familiarized. We address the most common IoT threats identified in the historical period and try to categorize them hooked on categories of protection and confidentiality.

3.2.1 Security Threats

The elementary principles of protection and confidentiality orbit everywhere the CIA triumvirate of Data Concealment, Information Truthfulness, and Grid Approachability [26]. In IoT, information can be whatever, such as the identity information of a user, Wrappers submitted to a server side from a security camera, a key-fob facility provided by a operator to his vehicle, or a multimedia conversation between two individuals. Any unauthorised disclosure of information will result in either confidentiality, honesty, or availability being violated. When a threat affects confidentiality, it is a threat to privacy. Both data integrity and network stability are affected by security threats.

3.2.1.1 Denial of Service

Of all security threats, Denial of Service (DoS) has the most simple implementation in contrast. In addition, an ever rising number of malfunctioning IoT devices has made DOS an intruder favourite weapon. The main aim of a DoS outbreak is to consume invalid requests into the network refers to network capabilities, such as bandwidth ingesting, being drained. As a result, the facilities are not real Oh accessible. Users. Users. Distributed DoS (DDoS) is an enhanced DoS attack version where a single target is attacking multiple outlets, making detecting and stopping attacks even more challenging. [27, 28]. While various kinds of DDoS occurrences exist, they have all the same goal. SYN overflowing [29] (where an invader directs successive SYN applications to a target), Internet Control Message Protocol (ICMP) outbreaks [28] (a lot of ICMP packets are sent in the spoofed IP of the suspect.), conflict outbreaks [30] (using a comprehensive and dynamic botnet execution) and User Datagram Protocol (UDP) flooding are just a few variants of DDoS attacks. Botnet Attack [31] is a type of IoT network DDoS attack. The botnet is a group of Iot systems (sensors), which are conflict to strike a specific target for instance, a banking database. Malicious software intrusion can be carried out on a variety of protocols such as MQTT, DNS and Hypertext Transfer Protocol (HTTP), as specified in [31]. This is not the only solution. In the IoT setting, multiple methods are proposed for preventing DoS. Diro et al. [32] was using the auto-learning capabilities of Neural Network (DL) approaches to diagnose a threat in the fog-to-things climate. Abeshu et al. [27] recommended regulation of the DDoS outbreak by using dispersed DL on mist computation in another report. Tan et al. Intrusion Detection Method (IDS) is a series of research efforts using current ML and DL algorithms to mitigate DDoS attacks. Sharma et al. and Tselois et al. piercing obtainable, respectively, the problems of Software-Defined-Networks (SDN) flooding. The training emphasized that due to the absence of validation in the unadorned-text TCP station, the SDN's top layer was vulnerable to visceral power outbreaks.

3.2.1.2 Man-In-The-Middle Attack

MiTM was just one of a virtual world's oldest threats [33]. It is possible to categorise spoofing and impersonation as MiTM assaults. A node X intended to communicate with destination B, for example, the intruder MiTM who is trying to impersonate direction B may interact. Likewise, an intruder might use an Authenticated link, but the aim on the unsecured HTTP connection, to be able to load assaults on the database on Authentication striping. Recently, several studies have centered on enhancing MiTM defense [3, 23, 34]. Ahmad et al. [35] explored a medical situation in which a persevering gets a dose of insulin immediately. This program is vulnerable to lethal internal threats. For starters, Tang et al. effectively exposing the flow of users to Attackers in the wireless network repositories for smartphone applications; Similarly, Chatterjee et al. [36] highlighted current authentication methods in wireless mobile devices using a hidden key, in line with the impersonation attacks. This key was saved and used for digital signatures or hash-based encryption in non-volatile memory. Aside from being vulnerable, power was inefficient in this technique. Similarly, OAuth 2.0, the most recent and commonly used IoT protocol, suffers from attacks by Cross-site regeneration falsification (CSRF). The OAuth Mechanism is a time—intensive procedure which authenticates devices manually. The physical-layer security weakness in wireless authentication was stated in another study by Wang et al. They argued that, particularly in dynamic networks, the latest radio channel knowledge correlation analysis is frequently inaccessible with systems to compare the Alice channel history to detect the Eve spotter on Wi-Fi communication.

3.2.1.3   Malware

Virus is a malicious malware abbreviated form. The number of IoT devices has grown over the last few years, along with regular IoT package updates, where an intruder may use to send spam on a device and conduct fraudulent behaviors. Malicious software is widely considered to occur as a malware, spyware, worm, cheval, rootkit or malvertising [37]. A few examples that could be affected are smart home appliances, healthcare equipment, and vehicular sensors. On the Battlefield Stuff (IoBT) Internet, Azmoodeh et al. [38] studied malware. Usually, such offenders are effectively and highly qualified state-sponsored. Aonzo et al. [12], Feng et al. [39], and Wei et al. endeavored to practice various supervised ML algorithms to protect resource-constrained android devices from malware attacks. The trainings in [15, 40] as long as a thorough review of the recognition of malware and emphasized a range of safety escapes on the Android display place, in specific, on the intra application form application layer.

3.2.2   Privacy Threats

Iot nodes and their information are, in addition to safety risks, susceptible to assaults on anonymity, such as sniffing, deanonymization and assumption attacks. And if records are in motion or sleeping, the effect is on data safety. In this chapter, we deal with multiple privacy threats.

3.2.2.1   MiTM

We assume that it is possible to classify MiTM attacks into Active MiTM Attacks (AMA). MiTM Attacks (PMA) and Passive. Data transfer between two devices is passively listened to by the PMA. While privacy is violated by the PMA, they do not modify the data. An intruder who has admittance to a computer will Spot quietly for months prior to endeavoring an assault. With the rise in the number of cameras in IoT, devices such as the impact of PMA, the wake-up and the sniffing, including dolls, smartphones and wristwatches are high. The AMA however has a heavy impact on the manipulation of data. Acquired either by engaging with a consumer who pretends to be someone else, such as impersonation, For instance, authorization attack, or accessing a profile without consent.

3.2.2.2   Data Privacy

Data confidentiality attacks may be categorized as Aggressive, MiTM outbreaks, ADPA in addition Passive Data confidentiality attacks (PDPA). Data security is associated to database theft, data misuse, identity stealing and re-identification [41].

Re-identification occurrences are similarly acknowledged as inferenz outbreaks also are constructed on de-anonymisation, location recognition and aggregation of knowledge [41]. The key goal of these attacks is to gather data from different sources and to identify targets. Data from different sources. Any attackers may use the collected data to personify a particular objective. Any attack that changes information, for instance data theft, can be categorized as ADPA, while re-identification and statistics outflow are cases of PDPA.

3.3 Existing Review Papers Using ML Algorithms as a Solution

With emerging technologies, drudges are becoming advanced, making conventional attack-prevention approaches cumbersome. For a resource-constraint IoT system, protection becomes more challenging. One of the commonly used methods is ML algorithms to assist in detecting these attacks. Based on that acquired knowledge, ML could be specified as a capacity for data capability and the adjustment of ML model performance [21]. ML allows robots wise enough through learning from previous results and enhancing them to achieve more results. Many Quantitative methods have proved incredibly helpful in minimizing security and privacy risks. In the subsequent sections, we analyse these tactics in profundity.

3.3.1 Security Efforts

The programme has enhanced information exchange and interacting schemes beyond the Cyberspace. We now possess state-of-the-art, configurable software-based machines denominated Software Defined Network (SDN) that can be configured to suit a client's requirements. Cutting-edge this case, using the ML algorithms, Restuccia et al. [42] endeavored to exhibit the taxonomy of contemporary IoT preservation intimidations in addition their resolutions in SDN. They also suggested dividing the data acquisition manner into three planes, specifically IoT validation, IoT transatlantic networking, and IoT information collection & validation. An IoT system's main task is to collect data from IoT devices. The inquiry bestowed a concise summary of ML algorithms utilized to alleviate protection drives, such as distinguishing cross-layer ill-disposed strikes, using Bayesian learning, furthermore using neural networks to estimate information efficacy. The report, however, requires an in-depth knowledge of the base of the algorithms of the ML. Sharmeen et al. [43] intended to support application designers in the sustained use of Application Program Interfaces (APIs) throughout the growth of Industrial IoT mesh applications. The authors proposed that the ML example could be equipped to distinguish malware by using three varieties of latent, effective, and heterogeneous narratives.

Precise dissection of individual peculiarity type is implemented using production metrics of a dataset, wrenching peculiarity methodology, characteristic determination criteria, efficiency, and discovery process. Versatile discovery arrangements were assessed for a particular specialty set, but RF, SVM, KNN, J48, and NB are universally used. Sharmeen et al. [43] settled that variegated interpretation rendered versatility in selecting latent and changing aspects to enhance recognition process certainty. However, this article is restricted to one (android device) application and one (malware) safeguard fulmination. Between 2015 and 2018, Costa et al. [44] selected papers and affirmed that neither task contributed an in-depth appearance of the utilization of ML in every sense of apprehension of IoT transgression. The research To enhance IoT security, the state-of-the-art, as well as outmoded ML-based procedures, were checked. The most extensively utilized datasets and methodologies utilized in writing correlated to IoT protection were also discussed. However, the paper has not checked the current security or privacy risks from the IoT.

Similarly, Chaabouni et al. [10] including focused toward the apprehension systems for IoT-based channel intervention. The authors posed IoT construction and layer-wise occurrences and confidential by zones (opinion panel, chain layer, and application tier) and sketch provocations (before-mentioned as heterogeneity, versatility, reliance, and isolation, supply detentions, accessibility, and partaking of data). Some traditional IoT safety tools were obtained, including those investigating IoT regularities' Irregularity and Hybrid Network IDS (ANIDS). A thorough identification of standard NIDS was given for IoT operations treatment, apprehension methodologies, and innovative consequences. Moreover, the investigation explained whereby the IoT learning-based NIDS could determine the trials fronted through their traditional IoT commensurate systems. Finally, with an emphasis on ML algorithms, top IoT NIDS proposals were compared.

3.3.2 Privacy Efforts

Machine Learning obtains some immature data useful information, while solitude remains shielded by data concealment [45]. There are three modules in the ML method, according to Al-Rubaie et al. [41]: I information, (ii) estimate, and (iii) producing. This comparison moreover argued that solely if an indivisible personality dominated every three modules could isolation be shielded. Now, billions of IoT projects such as smartphones, wellness tracking sensors, and activity cameras, including temperature sensors, gather data worldwide, so one single-ownership situation can not be affirmed. As mentioned earlier, the problem sparked researchers' enthusiasm to propose new and improved ML algorithms that protect privacy. For instance, Zhang et al. raised the lack of privacy security mechanisms in a VANET setting. Vehicle nodes in VANET prefer to collaboratively learn, raising questions about privacy, anywhere each wicked junction may access confidential data through assuming of these data observed. They have restricted computation and memory for a single node Capabilities. Managing collaborative Characters among dispersed

ML algorithms plus addressing privacy problems, the solution was proposed by suggesting effective differential concealment principles to preserve an instruction dataset's secrecy. Transportation supervision arrangements for people, including healthcare pieces of equipment, remain pair of several standard IoT sensing technologies that necessitate perpetual development. Every robust, valuable data for the before-mentioned applications is reached immediately by Mobile Crowd-Sensing (MCS) from users. Xiao et al. checked the isolation risks associated with MCS, collecting these details of the concern and uploading the participants to the MCS server sensing reports of their climate. This exchange of information poses severe risks to the associates and the MCS server concerning sequestration. The system is vulnerable to privacy leakage, fake sensing strikes (addressing fraudulent statements to each server to limit sensing strains), including forwarding persistent fulminations (creating seclusion leakage aloft any lengthened term). This system is prone to privacy leakage. Furthermore, the survey suggested privacy protection for the DNN and CNN and counter-measurement of false sensing for the DBN, including DQN. The review was, however, limited to one application (MCS) only.

3.4   Existing Review Papers Using Blockchain as a Solution

The technology behind this notorious crypto-currency is Blockchain, frequently mistaken by some as a synonym for Bitcoin. It is a distributed ledger stored in blocks with the data. These wedges are in direction and connected to individually, creating one concatenation cryptographically into a process that performs this difficult to transform some data toward a distinct segment computationally [46]. This framework allows concerning immutation, decentralization, a threshold of faults, accountability, verification, auditability and confidence [32, 45]. There is neither a unique consensus on every BC form, although they are often unrestricted, individual, including consortium. Unrestricted rather permission-less BC is convenient to everyone to be accessed by anyone [47]. Individual/authorized blockchains, on appropriate other guidance, individual/sanctioned blockchains are performed by one or more, so not all can obtain them. The transactions here are quicker; only a few chosen can acquire a performance, thereby achieving a unison. To highlight BC techniques' importance, many reflections and critique expositions [22, 24, 31, 32, 37, 45, 48–50] have been published and may remain each valuable authorization toward these occupied in reading added wherein BC into depth. The latest research inspections approaching managing IoT protection, including isolation using BC schemes, are reviewed in this section.

3.4.1 Security Efforts

For all cases of IoT use, protection has been the prime subject of concern. Lots of things to address security problems in the IoT domain, work focused on BC techniques has emerged. Banerjee et al. [51] presented a report on IoT protection, characterized by safety procedures such as trespass apprehension and restraint regularity (IDPS), cooperative protection, including the ominous token. In addition, IDPS is defined by techniques, chain construction, including utilization. Collaborative safety furthermore auspicious protection exist addressed in-depth after that. Collaborative protection methods are categorized in the same study by network architectures and applications.

Security concerns associated with key superintendence, path administration, and corporation superintendence in IoT continue to be addressed in another study by Khan et al. [52, 52] classified those preservation intimidations toward IoT panels, including their explications based on BC. Low-level intermediate-level, and high-level security problems were categorised as IoT security issues. Khan et al. [52] assume that the low-level safety problems are squeezing foes, precarious initialization, parodying, fragile environmental interface, including slumber divestment initiatives. Micro intermediate-level preservation concerns are reiteration, RPL routing strikes, sinkhole, Sybil assault approaching amid layers, transport-level end-to-end sanctuary, assembly substantiation, including authentication. Insecure interfaces, CoAP Internet protection, insecure applications, and middleware security are high-level security concerns. The analysis then produced a thorough mapping of the preceding issues among those IoT architecture zones that affected various of them amidst suggested clarifications. Toward every point, the writers explored whereby some of the most important IoT security issues could be resolved and solved using BC techniques. This study highlighted the preservation uncertainties associated with an individual panel of IoT nevertheless failed to address the provision of BC-based explications to certain preservation fulminations.

Furthermore, Reyna et al. studied in [17] whence BC methods in the IoT could theoretically boost protection (data reliability). Since the whole concerning the summonses for BC procedures, each study listed security threats. Most attacks, double-spend attacks, and DoS attacks were the security threats identified in the report. The research also highlights the integration of BC methods, BC utilization, and BC principles with IoT. However, this research created not embrace many distinct IoT-related safeguard assaults, which was a drawback of this survey.

On the other hand, during extension to preservation issues, fresh advances within IoT, including BC integration, Panarello et al. [53] comprehensively analysed BC consensus protocols. The past literature was classified based on domain measures, accompanied by a comprehensive outline regarding specific contemporary BC-based solutions.

Kumar et al. [54] provided a concise summary regarding IoT security problems, including difficulties, before-mentioned as False authentication including Spoofing. Tamper-proof data, conferred, dynamic information, robustness, and assigned and authorized information distribution are some of BC's benefits for large-scale IoT systems. They were following that the review presented the request wise BC founded IoT provocations. The authors of [55] emphasized IoT preservation problems furthermore presented their solutions based on BC. That thought preeminent highlighted specific criteria for IoT safeguard and its hurdles under six separate operation fields, such as intelligent cities, healthcare, intelligent networks, transportation, intelligent houses, furthermore development. The writers addressed the taxonomy of IoT preservation explications before-mentioned, as confidentiality was also prepared comprehensively. Specific study of procedures that obtained sufficient for various IoT was also investigated Requesting.

3.4.2   Privacy Efforts

Strong cryptographic steps have been used in previous studies, such as [56], to defend upon spiteful third multitudes, including to provide culpable IoT path. Nevertheless, as one of their tools, they didn't use either ML or BC. Kshetri et al. [7] demonstrated how compared to a conventional network for cloud-based services, BC techniques can provide better privacy-preserving solutions.

It also stressed BC's dominance in the management of identity and the establishment of admittance control. The research showed how using BC techniques, an invasion toward the IoT system could remain delimited. In this literature, though, a detailed privacy-preserving IoT fulmination pattern utilizing BC procedures was obtained needing. A short summary of IoT privacy concerns and problems, such as data sharing, was posed by Kumar et al. [54]. The work subsequently proposed BC-based explications over specific problems furthermore explored many sectors of application toward the implementation of BC. In contrast, the paper addressed BC's problems within every IoT utilization, which requires one detailed examination of IoT security and seclusion fulminations. These writers concerning [55] highlighted IoT solitude concerns furthermore presented their solutions based on BC. Attaining one "trio" regarding anonymity, unlinkability, moreover obstinacy was the prime purpose of privacy-preserving techniques. Based on conventional cryptographic techniques, the key security services, such as confidentiality, privacy and availability, have been discussed. The research harangued those impressions regarding IoT information distribution, information protection, moreover user behaviour and explored their solutions, such as data tagging, zero-knowledge evidence, pseudonyms, and the model of k-anonymity. In a conventional Identity Management (IdM) scheme, Zhu et al. highlighted privacy vulnerabilities, in particular because of their centralised architecture and reliability for so-called trusted third parties. Scarce seclusion interventions, before-mentioned being phishing also information leakage, can result in these vulnerabilities. The authors argued that due to certain fundamental IoT features such as scalability, versatility, and usability, standard IdM arrangements could no transpire explicitly emigrated until IoT ecosystems. The study further illustrated the privacy issues in conventional IdM systems and explored their BC-based solutions.

A comprehensive sketch regarding sequestration culmination in BC-based IoT policies was presented by Hassan et al. [57]. BC-based IoT network-related privacy attacks before-mentioned while Label reuse, Deanonymization, Charges by Sybil, Communications Spoofing, moreover Associating obtained highlighted. This trade further examined these implementations within BC-based implementations of the five diverse, widespread secrecy protection routines (Encryption, Smart Contract, Anonymization, Mixing, including Differential Privacy). The IoT privacy problems and their new BC-based solutions were analysed by Ali et al. [58]. Inside any centralised IoT paradigm before-mentioned records protection furthermore information confidentiality, they raised questions regarding privacy. Current centralised privacy solutions, such as the use of a privacy broker, the use of community signatures, the use of k-anonymity, and aliases, entirely rely profoundly covering third parties concerning their co-operations. The study provided a thorough analysis of the BC-based IoT privacy solutions to counter these problems.

3.5 Solutions to IoT Threats

Security experts have mitigated zero-day security, or privacy risks considering those commencements regarding one initial virus (Creeper) during 1970 before that Whatsapp scribbler proceeding 15 May 2019 and succeeding. Several solutions to mitigate protection and privacy problems have been suggested in this regard. However, within the aforementioned part, we concentrate upon particular latest paper recommending safe moreover privacy-preserving methods toward specific IoT specialties. We address significant explications given through primary utilizing ML algorithms essentially a guide, when over practicing BC methods, furthermore conclusively over merging both.

3.5.1 Existing Solutions Using Machine Learning (ML) Algorithms

ML implies we utilized in every application since each information processing pipeline. Notwithstanding instance, an ML prototype can dissect statistics traffic inserting a chain to kind an well-versed verdict. Figure 3.1 displays the key apparatuses of the ML hazard model for IoT. Additionally, for an attacker, the figure provides a survey concerning goal circumstances, before-mentioned since facts also output. Exploratory or poisoning attacks may occur on the information data of authorization upon IoT junctions and IoT junctions upon the ML design. Attacks of honesty and inversion are possible at performance [59]. Therefore, it must be protected as well as privacy-preserved for an entire system to be fully resistant to attacks.

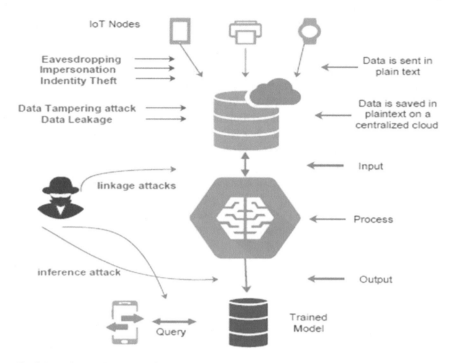

Fig. 3.1 An illustration of ML threat model for IoT

3.5.2 Existing Solutions Using Blockchain (BC) Technology

The BC network is protected, tolerant to errors, transparent, verifiable and auditable [60, 61]. Decentralized, P2P, open, trust-less, eternal, are the commonly used keywords to explain BC benefits. Such Features made a BC secure rather than a trusting fundamental client–server system. The smart convention is a BC programming protocol that ensures that a scheduled event is carried out [46]. The blockchain guarantees data integrity and authenticity, according to Restuccia et al. [42], making it an effective solution for defence against data tampering in IoT devices.

Several BC strategies for supply chain, identification, access and IoT management were suggested However, the current methods don't take into account time, and aren't applicable to resource-con IoT devices. And in comparison, other experiments examined time reaction of IoT devices, not just machado et al. [62] provided a three-layered architecture for Cyber-Physical Systems (CPS): an IoT (internal) architecture, a fog (external) design, and a cloud (external) design. First, IoT devices in the same network entity use the Proof-of-of-Trust (PoT) protocol (PoT). In IoT, Formal: Proof-of-of-Luck (PoL) was castoff to generate fault-tolerant cryptographic data, which provides an audit trail the first level's data was run via SHA-256 and temporarily stored. The consensus was achieved, and the data was saved at the third stage of the cloud which is a distributed ledger. Aside from data integrity, there were also included the methods of key management and the node's position. The multi-lateration method was used to locate the node, and time synchronization was given by TSTP. It suggested the usage of various consents, like PoT and PoL, but ignored some privacy issues. Publication demonstrated a method of ensuring data privacy by utilizing public BC DroneChain introduced had four elements; the drones, the control system, the cloud, and the BC network. Drones were being operated by the controller, the data was processed and encrypted in the cloud using the decentralized BC. The resulting machine had accurate and up-to-date data with a fault-tolerant backend. The research however did not use Proof of Work (PoW), a real-time IoT application including drones notwithstanding. Additionally, the service did not have sidecoin data and encryption has not been seen to function. A DoS assault is one of the attacks that are widely used due to its simple implementation and the ever-increasing number of vulnerable computers. With the low cost of IoT technology, it is easy to get several machines under control to initiate an assault. The SDN is vulnerable to brute-force assaults. SDN is susceptible to attacks such as DoS/DDoS, because it is under the influence of machines. In a lightweight multi-standard IoT setting, earlier means of prevention may not be efficient. In addition to that, SDN is vulnerable to floods, saturation, MiTM assaults, and Man-in-the-the-middle.

attacks attributable to unauthenticated data in the unencrypted TCP channel Their formal argument has it that BC offers a stronger protection against the threats of network attacks and maintains confidence between multi-vendor devices; moreover, they asserted that BC is fault-tolerant and, tamper-proof. It is vulnerable to data tampering and flooding attacks because of these important attributes. However, all of the theories listed above were just theory; they've never been tried in practice. In a previous article, Sharma et al. enhanced protection in distributed SDN IoT proposed DistNet. This BC was used to ensure the current forwarding devices had the correct flow rule table checked, validated, and downloaded. DistNet's technologies were contrasted with those already in use, and the findings were higher in terms of real-time vulnerability monitoring and overhead. The researchers discovered a major protection loophole in the MiTM attack; a malicious attacker might alter user data that was transmitted across the internet with little difficulty. Furthermore, consumers were unable to scrutinize their expensive power bills since the grid was not equipped on early-with-early-warning functions. To prevent the above problems, this study suggested utilizing public and private keys and cryptographic data transfer on BC. The use of this methodology provided an eternal, stable, and transparent method. However, Proof of Work is not always cheap or resource-intensive.

It is claimed that the current logistics networks are neither simple nor dependable in [transparent and trustworthy]. Established networks were decentralized, leveraged several TTPs, and placed all their energy on a single point of energy transfer. Hasan et al. [57] introduced the BC distribution method. Nodes may be regarded as buyer, seller, courier services, as well as Smart Contract Verifier (SCAA). The contract was successfully put on Inter-Planetary File System (IPFS) and implemented after both the parties had come to an understanding. As per specifications of the object was moved between multiple transporters (maximum three times in this paper). When the object has been delivered and paid for, the customer releases the funds to the vendor. If the deal is rejected, the arbitrator steps in, resolves the disagreement and redistributes the sum. The planned physical distribution method defends against Man-in-the-the-the-Middle and DOS threats. However, little regard has been given to manipulator ID administration or data privacy. In the paper by Gupta et al. [63], the writers appear to have dealt with phyical or programmatic Sybil attacks as well as the reiteration occurrences in an IoT network. The problem is not just because of the two additional layers in the current IoT design, but because they didn't have this latest one from the start. They clarified their algorithm, concept, and work in terms of transaction, block, and space use (Mmempool). IDS (now also known as Netflow) is one of the main ways to track unusual and malicious traffic patterns. The writers claimed in a report by Golomb et al. [64] that the new anomaly IDSs aren't effective because only innocuous traffic was used in the training process [64] Using this loophole, an adversary may introduce malicious data that is considered safe. Second, the qualified models could be lacking such event-driven IoT traffic, for example, including a fire alarm. Both of these questions is addressed using a CIoTA (Collaborative Internet of Things Anomaly) Detection approach, where all BC IoT devices of a since too many IoT devices were trained on their own traffic, there was a lower risk of an adversary assault. Any machine will form a locally trained model which would be collaboratively combined with other machines to form a globally trained model The CIo experiment proved to be an effective method for countering adversary assaults. However, the stand-alone model IoT node will, however, increase the volume of info. Complementing the study on widely studied risks such as Data privacy, as well as DoS mitm-based assaults, several remedies have been investigated. Sharma et al. introduced an inexpensive, always-on, and continuously-available methodology for cloud architecture. The introduction of SDN to the network along with BC was responsible for securing the fog nodes. To help maintain protection and also reduce end-to-to-end latency, the research study took the resource near to the IoT network. According to the developers, the model was flexible because of the observed risks and assaults, as well as streamlining the administrative procedures, it reduced their workload. The key goal of this paper was to create a BC-cloud architecture that was scalable, stable, and robust. It was measured in terms of production, reaction time, and false alarm. Nevertheless, there was no care given to either of data protection, user ID management, or key management was addressed. With regards to the unified infrastructure, Sharma et al. have maintained that the current Mobile Device Management (MDM) lacks robustness to security threats. They reported that their proposed system had increased latency, delay, and energy usage, while also keeping the original network architecture intact. Unfortunately, the thesis used Proof of Work (PoW) consensus, which is energy-hung and offers little consumer protection.

3.5.3 Existing Solutions Using Machine Learning (ML) and Blockchain (BC)

With the combination, Agrawal et al. reported to delete spoofing attacks ML algorithms and BC methods [65]. The user in a legitimate IoT-zone is constantly monitored by securing the user-device contact, and the BC is preserved in correspondence logs. Records are ongoing and repetitive events may be tracked. Current user authentication methods involve single-password (OTP) or safekeeping problems that are restricted to solo validation. Through using Distributed ledgers as that of the BC network, the researchers fixed the situation that use the IoT-zone recognition, IoT-token creation and the credential authentication. Nevertheless, the study found the Blockchain to be a communication core that reversed the notion of decentralization. No consumer or database protection was concerned and indeed the data collection for a Dnn models would be too small. Android's open nature raises new threats and attacks in terms of security. Gu et al. [66] illustrated that when examined overtime, the ransomware, Trojan horses, and extortion have targeted Android-based networks aggressively. Real programs, which may also be classified as non-linear analyses, get some drawbacks, including large computational time costs and styles of obfuscation of text, such as adjustable indoctrination and encrypting [67]. Gu et al. implemented a novel Multi Feature Based Paradigm (MFM), in which a malicious code index will be used by the BC Conglomerate for Malware Detection and Evidence Retrieval, on android platforms (CB-MDEE). In relation to past simulations, CD-MDEE obtained greater accuracy with decreased working time. The proposed architecture uses the Exonum BC platform and DNN ML algorithms to exploit BC's information sending and selling assets as and when needed to have management and future control of their health data [68]. The storage breach would not lead to data leakage, since the encrypted data in the store. In order to guarantee the acceptance and authenticity of the user records, the system utilizes hash features and public signature.

To maximise their target audience, many businesses rely on large datasets. However these information covers confidential private details, including political opinions that could be influenced and their profits raised by interested persons. Therefore, to protect and, if possible, protect the confidentiality of these customers, reimbursing them used for their donations is important. Moreover, a lot of evidence could be beneficial for design and technology in some dimensions, however the information can indeed be distributed with private entities. Moreover, this very same information collected can be modified and questions regarding their credibility can be raised. The above model has been improved by many reports. The proposal is [69, 70]. Mendis et al. [15] proposed that completely independent individual contributors cooperate de-centrally without interfering with their latter improved overall production efficiency and functionality [16]. In every case, over than 94% of the CNN sample size was compared with domain adaptation for the CNN model. The peer-to-peer transactions were conducted through smart contracts incentivizing the machine contributors. That being said, in their analysis [16], encoding time was increased by 100%. Furthermore, the construction was centered on the cryptocurrency BC having a teaching effectiveness wedge time which might not be practicable, for examples for video transmission in a legitimate IoT program.

DeepChain proposed a value-driven, BC-based reward system for solving security problems. For the model training process, DeepChain guarantees data protection and auditability. Confidentiality is used for the Threshold Paillier algorithm, which gives a homomorphic additive property. Therefore more parties engaged in joint training, the greater the precision of training was shown by DeepChain, utilizing CNN protocols and MNIST datasets.

ML classification methods requires datasets in order to train. Because of multiple concerns surrounding confidentiality, including data theft, data confidentiality and custody, these databases are extracted from separate individuals, who usually do not want their communication to occur. Users are not sure of why and how their information will be used. In order to secure these confidentiality matters, Shen et al. [37] planned merging machine learning into cryptocurrency. A privacy-conserving SVM constructed classification had been cast-off to prepare the authenticated information obtained from Remote devices, although the BC system provided shared data between multiple service providers.

3.6 Deep Learning Approaches-Based IoT Data Privacy and Security

Throughout this section, detection equipment based on deep learning strategies are clarified. As seen in Fig. 3.2 There are ten supervised neural approaches used for detecting intrusion from information technology, namely (1) DNN; (2) FFDNN; (3) RNN; (4) CNN; (5) RBM; (6) DBN; (7) DA (Fig. 3.2);

Fig. 3.2 Deep learning techniques used for intrusion detection in computer defense. FFDNN: Deep neuronal network feed forward; CNN: Convolutionary nerve-network; DNN: deep neural network; RNN: Recurrent neural network; DBN: Deep conviction network; STL: Self-tapping; ReNN: Neural network replicator. DBN: deep neural network

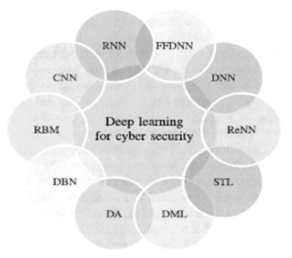

3.6.1 Deep Neural Network

Tang et al. [10] suggested a network monitoring approach that uses a deep learning approach for a software-defined framework. In the SDN controller which can monitor all openflux transitions the proposed Method framework is introduced. The study used the NSL-KDD 2-class (i.e. regular and phenomenon class) dataset, which involved of four classes, including four groups. (1) Attacking DoS, (2) attacking R2L, (3) attacking U2R, and (4) attacking sample. Exploratory findings found that the 0.001-learning threshold is more effective than others because of the receiver's largest operational curve (AUC). Potluri et al. [71] used this deep neural technique as a complex classifier for the management of enormous grid statistics. They just cast-off the NSL-KDD statistical model, which contains 39 detection techniques clustered in four inflammatory factors. Their analysis reveals that 2 classes had a good detection accuracy (i.e. normal and attack). Kang et al. [48] recommended an intrusion recognition process for vehicular networks founded on DNN. The scenario attack was carried out on malicious data packets which are inserted into the network bus of the in-vehicle controller region. To differentiate shipments into two categories (i.e., a regular packet in addition an outbreak packet), the proposed sys-temp inputs the function vector to the input nodes. Outputs are computed (e.g., ReLU) based on the activation function. Then, with these outputs, the next hidden layers are connected. The proposed system reaches a detection ratio of 99% if the untruthful optimistic fault is fewer than 1–2%. Zhou et al. [72] recommended an intrusion finding process founded on the DNN to help identify cyber-outbreaks. Specifically, three stages are used by the system, namely (1) DAQ, (2) data pre-processing, besides (3) deep classification of the neural network. For SVM model with a learning rate of 0.01, training epochs 10 and input elements 86, the stratagem accomplishes an accuracy of 0.963. The findings show this technique to marginally outperform the three methods to machine learning: (1) linear regression (LR), (2) random forest (RF), besides (3) k-nearest neighbourhood (KNN). Feng et al. [26] explains a plug-and-play framework using a network packet tool and mitigation paradigm that is used to track access denial (DoS) and ad hoc network incidents. The model suggested uses two types of in-depth processing, namely fully convolutional neural (CNN) as well as good memory for XSS and SQL challenges (LSTM). A deep neural network is used for the developed framework to detect DoS tacks. The survey was using the KDD CUP 99 database, which is split by 30% in evaluation and 70% in preparation. In comparison, the study reported an efficiency of 0.57 and 0.78% for the identification of XSS attacks by deep neural netting and convolutionary neural network.

A clear example of profound adversarial learning and predictive learning methods to detect net-work intrusions is the research by Zhang et al. [25]. By using data augmentation and advanced classification techniques, the analysis will classify a number of network intrusions. There are two elements used in the proposed method, the differential amplifier and the operator, in particular. The neural network is used as a predictor to reject enhanced infiltration information since actual illustrations while the compressor is used to produce expanded intrusion data. Kim et al. [73] worked on data set from KDD in 1999 to run a deep neural network with ever-changing networks. In the suggested intrusion prevention scheme, design variables are used: four hidden layers and one hundred hidden units. ReLU is used as the initialization function as well as the simulated annealing mechanism for deep neural network testing. The classification results approximately 99% precision. Zhang et al. [46] have introduced a two-stage exploitation deletion method, known as CAN IDS, for detecting autonomous driving malicious attacks. In the first stage, a robust rule-based method is used, while for anomaly detection, the second stage uses deep learning net-work. Three datasets, including the Honda agreement, the Asian brand and the US brand car, are used in the assessment of results. Training database provides only regular traffic from all three sets, while testing set contain normal traffic and malicious activity, including falling strikes, direct attacks, zero-identification attacks, vulnerability scanning and spoof attacks.

3.6.2   Feedforward Deep Neural Network

For intrusion detection by Kasongo et al. [34], Feed forward deep neural network (FFDNN) was used. To create optimal subsets of features with minimal redundancy for wireless networks, Using FFDNN for a function selection technique dependent on target. The main training dataset was divided into 2 major sets i.e. data set for preparation and data set for evaluation) by the proposed intrusion detection system. Then a two-way process of normalisation and a process of feature transformation are involved. Finally, the pro-posed method utilises the FFDNN for model curriculum and research. The database NSL-KDD was castoff in addition the KDDTrain + and KD-DTest + were chosen. The estimation of results indicates that 99.69% including its proposed system with an operating rate of 0.05 and 30 neurons blowout over three hidden layers is correct.

3.6.3   Recurrent Neural Network

Kim et al.'s framework uses the KDD Cup database for the 1999 execution of a long, selective memory framework for a recurring neural remote monitoring model [74]. The effects were used as a feature vectors by the output vector (41 functions) (4 attacks and 1 non-attack). We also used step-by-step extent 100, load extent 50 also epoch 500. The intrusion optimal location is stated to be 98.8% across total attack occurrences. Loukas et al. [75] pro-posed a cyber-physical intrusion detection device to detect cyber attacks against vehicles. The method uses both the recurrent architecture of the NN and the DMP, highly efficient than conventional machine learning methods for high precision (e.g., k-means clustering and SVM). The computer is assessed against such a vehicle model using different categories of injection controls:

guidance attack, access denial intervention and perhaps a Network adapter vulnerability attack. Taylor et al. [1] suggested an anomaly detector to detect car algorithms rely on a recurrent neural network architecture. As a RNN, LSTM is used, which would be training to anticipate and its failures are used for detecting abnormalities new frame relay values. In an IDS method for supervised classification learning, Yin et al. [76] attempted to incorporate recurrent neural networking. The study used three performance metrics for the NSL-KDD dataset, this requires specificity, high false rates, and real positive rates. The consequence of outlier detection with a back propagation of = 0.1 and hidden neurons of = 80 is indicated as higher precision. The article also highlights the benefits of a repeating neural network for infiltration de-section schemes. Tang et al. [19] have suggested the use of a probabilistic neural unit, recurring mathematical computation for endpoint protection in software-defined networking. The paper reveals an 89% identification rate exploitation a minimal quantity of functions. The NSL-KDD dataset is being cast-off in network quality with four measurement parameters, i.e. recovery, F-Mail, precision and accuracy. Jiang et al. [20] has developed a cross intrusion detection method utilizing re-current neural networks for long-term memory. The NSL- KDD dataset is being cast-off for evaluating the effectiveness of the new outbreak recognition classification. The reliability of the reminiscence recall recurring neural networks is calculated at a speed of 99.23%, with a number of iterations of 9.86% and a precision of 98.94%.

3.6.4 Convolution Neural Network

Basumallik et al. [49] used convolutionary neural networks for packet-data anomaly detection in the state estimator based on phasor measurement units. To derive case fingerprints (features) from calculating units of phasor, they use a convolutionary neural network based data philtre. The IEEE-30 bus and IEEE-118 bus structures are being cast-off by means of phasor extent device buses. The analysis indicates a likelihood of 0.5 with a completely connected layer of 512 neurons and a precision of 98.67%. The authors say that, The neuronal philter is superior in its recital concluded all additional machine learning methods, namely RNN, LSTM, SVM, bagged then enhanced. The design constructed by Fu et al. [77] practices a convolutive neural network to monitor the inherent outlines of cheating events, in fact for the detection of credit card fraud. Zhang et al. [69] has used B2C banking institutions online transaction information for education and analysis, using the convolutionary network of neurons. One month's data was split into training sets and test sets. A 91% accuracy rate and a 94% recall rate are indicated in the report. These findings, relative to the work proposed by Fu et al. [77], are increased by 26% and 2% respectively. Nasr et al. [13] provided an invasion exposure classification, called DeepCorr, Centered on a convolutionary computer program to learn the role of differentiation. DeepCorr focuses mainly on two turnout layers and network layer of a fully linked neural network. Experimentation found that the unsurpassed recital is with a 0.0 0 01 learning rate, and with a false positives of 10–3, the DeepCorr reaches a true positive rate similar to 0.8. Zhang et al. [78] introduced the model of a 2 layers neural network detection algorithm in which the primary layer is an improved neural network convolutionary LetNet-5 feature. Zhang et al. The upper method enables a long-term memory.

3.6.5 Restricted Boltzmann Machine

For intrusion detection, the constrained Boltzmann mechanism was castoff by Fiore et al. Towards syndicate the communicative ability of generative models with good classification, they use a discriminative restricted Boltzmann machine [79]. With a set of 41 traits and 97,278 examples, the KDD Cup 1999 dataset was used. Salama et al. [80] combine the Boltzmann restricted machine and the intrusion detection sup-port vector machine. The NSL-KDD dataset containing a total of 22 types of training attacks was used through an supplementary 17 kinds cutting-edge the difficult package. The training notes that a developed proportion of sorting is seen in this combination than by using the help vector machine. Alrawashdeh and Purdy [24] used the deep belief network of the restricted Boltzmann machine and hand-me-down the KDD 1999 information set comprising 494,022 training archives in addition 311,028 research records. C++ and Mi-crosoft Visual Studio 2013 are used to implement the detection algorithm. The research shows that 92% of attacks were categorised by the restricted Boltzmann machine. The paper combined the findings with Salama et al. [48work,]'s which shows both greater precision and speed of detection. Aldwairi et al. proposed a simulated study of Boltzmann limited hacker remote monitoring machines [81]. The analysis in specific demonstrates the efficiency of Boltzman restricted machines to discern among NetFlow traffic normal and anomalous. The research suggested was extended to the ISCX [82] database which had the maximum precision of 78.7 ± 1.9% so when study rates were set at 0.004. In comparison, the highest accuracy rates at the 0.004 learning scale are high, 74.9 ño 4.6% and 82.4 ± 1.8%. Gao and others are inclined and extended in the field of intrusion identification to the inclusion of multilayer unregulated training programs [83].The research is conducted using a limited Boltzmann machine with two levels of profound neural networking: (1) instruction of the Boltzmann machine on a small n-layer basis, and (2) fine tuning the whole Boltzmann machine parameter. The study reveals that the quality of the fully connected web on KDD CUP 1999 is greater than the quality of a vector supporting computer and a genetic algorithms built on the limited Boltzmann method. Alom et al. [64] identified an intrusion detection device that uses a stack-restricted Boltzmann computer. The main purpose of this strategy is to identify events that are Abnormal or malignant. The paper includes the NSL-KDD repository and is divided into five forms of attacks. The results reveal that the suggested solution achieves approximately 97.5% experiment precision at only 40% of the evidence used in testing. Yang et al. [84] therefore New approach suggested using the vector help machine, called SVM-RBM, based on restricted

Boltzmann machines, to provide enhanced traffic detection. For training functionality, the restricted Boltzmann computer is used. The authors continued to adjust the number of units in the hidden layers during the process of feature extraction. Then once the good features were obtained, the authors suggested that the trained prototype of a support vector process that uses the gradient downward algorithm with the trainable parameters. The SVM-RBMS algorithm suggested shows that perhaps the maximum precision approaches 80%.

3.6.6   Deep Belief Network

Thamilarasu et al. [40] used the deep-seated conviction framework for vulnerability scanning. They choose a deep belief network to develop a feed-forward-profile computer program for the IoT devices. The developers specifically introduced a binary interentropy prediction error in command to keep the overall cost of the IDS model to a minimum. The Keras archive, the Cooja Network Emulator and Texas Instruments CC2650 Sor markings are also used for process improvement. The Keras library is being castoff for the development of a procedural deep learning model. The theoretical prototypical was verified for 5 assaults (1) sinkhole, (2) wormhole, (3) blackhole assaults, (4) opportunistic service attack, and (5) DDoS attacks. The findings demonstration a 96% sophisticated meticulousness and a 98.7% reminiscence proportion for sleuthing DDoS outbreaks. Zhao et al. [85] in some other study, a based Protocols method utilizing the deep belief network and the cognitive deterministic network. The study contrasts the 10% learning database with the 10% reference data collection remote management model with the KDD CUP 1999 dataset. The findings show that it is stronger than three versions, namely (1) classical probability—based neural network, (2) the key component study of a generic probabilistic neural network, and (3) the non-optimized deep-faith network of the algorithm. Zhang et al. [63] analyzes are a prime example of how to incorporate enhanced genetic algorithms with a strong network of beliefs to predict computer security infringements. The study uses many restricted machines from Boltzmann which mainly lead to unsuited data learning. The profound beliefs framework is split into two phases in the performance evaluation: (1) each Boltzmann restricted computer is trained independently and (2) the whole last layer of that same deep beliefs network is formed as a network of neural proliferation. The NSL KDD database performance measurement suggests a detection rate of 99%.

3.6.7   Deep Auto-Encoder

The deep self-encoder has been cast-off by Shone et al. to identify interference in cyber protection [86]. In contrast with deep belief networks, to facilitate improved classification performance, they are using an auto encoder with—anti different classifiers. The research uses five metrics per format datasets of the KDD Cup'99 and NSL-KDD, including precision, accuracy, false warning, F-score and recall. The test results for KDD Cup'99 suggest that an average of 97.85% of the developed framework can be higher than the work in [24]. In addition, the findings of the NSL-KDD data set assessment indicate that the counter model has reached a cumulative precision rate of 85%, an increase of 5% on the deep-believe training algorithm. The two-phase deeper learning model has been used by Khan et al. [53] to propose a method of Intrusion Detection (TSDL). The TSDL framework contains a softmax auto module stacked with three primary layers (1), (2) the input layer, and (3) the output layer. A feed-forward neural network analogous to an inter sensor is employed by these three layers. Two public datasets, like KDD99 and UNSW-NB15, are being used in the analysis. High recognition rates, up to 99.996%, are reached by the KDD99 data set performance. Furthermore, up to 89.134% of the results on the UNSW-NB15 dataset reach high recognition rates. The use of auto-encoder techniques is proposed by Papamartzivanos et al. [67] Develop a detection system for peer and automatic violation assault. The proposed framework is explicitly based on four stages, including (1) tracking, (2) observing, (3) preparation, (4) exercise, and (5) information. The surveillance method decides any modification activity requiring an improvement to a sensor network. In order to convert raw traffic to real networks, the review program utilizes network auditing instruments (such as Argus and CICFlowMeter).

3.6.8   Deep Migration Learning

For cyber security intrusion detection, Li et al. are used for profound mobility learning [87]. The analysis explicitly integrates the deep learning model with the method of intrusion detection. Profound migration can be learned as per this article, four categories are divided, including the technical variable migration process, the simulation sample methodology, and the corresponding information migration methodology. The study utilises collection of KDD CUP 99 with 10% of the training examples as investigational information. Mostly throughout test, the study chooses the pooled haphazardly 10.0 0 0 data sets as classification model and the sampled 10.0 0 0 knowledge sets as the prototype test sets. The results show a 91.05% average precision and a untruthful positive rate of 0.56%.

3.6.9   Self-taught Learning

Javed et al. is using personality learning in order to detect information security attack. The suggested approach uses classification phases for the supervised learning except the overview of learning attributes and the obtained representation [88]. For validation of findings the study uses the NSL-KDD dataset. The pro-position scheme contains three different forms of classification: (1) 2-class (i.e. ordinary and abnormal), (2) five-class (i.e. regular and four separate attack groups), and (3) 23-class (i.e. standard and 22 diverse outbreaks). The study used tenfold inter on formation data to determine the self-classification learning's consistency for those three modes of learning.

3.6.9.1   Replicator Neural Network

Cordero et al. [89] was using the cognitive replicator models to detect interference in cybersecurity. To locate anomalies, the analysis uses the dropout method. The extraction of entropy is composed of three steps. The aggregation of packets is the first level. The process consists of splitting the fluxes into service times. The final move is to collect those flows' fascinating features. The database is used to introduce inserting engineered attacks (e.g. SYN DDoS) into the information source for performance evaluation. The original data has been used.

3.7   Discussion of Taxonomy of Machine Learning Algorithms

Determining the role that each data set of data set serves in expanding an algorithm. You would still want to search for relevant or weird points of data to build up an algorithm features, as well as investigate value categories or hypotheses.

An unstructured dataset is typically best interpreted using clustering algorithms, which will aid in identification of form. Because K-means is the most commonly used and deals with a large volumes of data with a wide variety of data forms, it is able to provide significant performance when dealing with large volumes of data. Many [26] References (K and F together) have established a way to use the K-means algorithm for smart city and smart home data management (both long term and day-to-day data collection). Web databases, including the CitizensWire and The paraphrase: Oracle has also works for cluster database-scanning citizen web sources, which groups data found unlabeled these two databases by employing an Oracle-specific index, [5].

Using two techniques, odd and clever data points and anomaly-detection algorithms, it is possible to locate irregularities and strange facts in intelligent data of particular importance, these are one-instance and multilabel support vector machine learning (SVM) and spectral principal component analysis (PCA) techniques, which can both identify irregularities and poor or noisy data with excellent accuracy. Refs. [40, 85] used a single-class SVM to detect human behavior was considered to be effective in this task.

Two well accepted algorithms to make good predictions on and sequence data classified by the linear regression and the machine learning techniques were used. Data is usually consists of enormous quantities that need to be processed and trained at a high speed to perform accurately. By example, in [83, 80] a simple regression algorithm was used for real-time prediction. An alternative that has proven useful for other rapid categorization and trend detection methods is the classification and regression tree, which has also been used to address problems with citizen behaviors.

To guess at the purposes, neural networks are an effective in helping to determine how various functions will be, they are well-suited learning models. Another reason for multi-class neural networks to have a good alternative is that it would take time to learn well and gather information to be of great accuracy. A good examples of FFNN use in use cases such as reducing potential energy demand include forecasting the data that will be produced and at future dates and how that data will be superseded, in each individual instances [use, as in which we see future redundancy in each specific instance is present on the list of items being removed] Another classification method, which is capable of managing enormous volumes of data and correctly classifying each of its categories, is the SVM Because of the capability of SVM to manage a large data sets and diverse kinds of features, it is widely used in various kinds of machine learning applications. Also, for example, the SVM was used to identify the results.

PCA and CA (both by the way of using a PC with an additional component and adding components to improve functionality) are two methods for enhancing the overall data features. Moreover, CCA is able to demonstrate a connection between two different types of data. Anomalies in a non-expanded PCA and CCA and non-PCA systems are often discovered using PCA and CCA techniques. For Reference [66], the PCA and CCA algorithms were applied to public areas and social venues to identify, capture, and record noteworthy data was developed.

The algorithm must be applied and designed correctly such that it arrives at a proper conclusion.

3.8 Research Challenges

3.8.1 Challenge to Machine Learning Algorithms in IoT

After practicing on several datasets, they may reasonably expected to the required performance, ML algorithms are used for analysis. For example, these models can be used in the navigation of a machine or language comprehension either that does not and could be used for individual know-how. To analyse threats against several cybersecurity domains, ML algorithms have also been used very efficiently. Although in many areas, they still have drawbacks on the Iot system: ML techniques rely well:

- **Scalability and Complexity**: In recent research some ML algorithms minimized cyber assaults successfully. That being said, Ai systems are not an optimal alternative for IoT implementations due to various their shortcomings. Diro et al. demanded that scalability, feature extraction, and accuracy of the traditional ML algorithms were restricted [34]. Whereas Moustafa et al. [31] argued that many problems could not be solved by ML algorithms, Emotional and practical in a resource-restricted complex Distributed device. Another work of Abeshu et al. [27] shows that conventional ML algorithms are less efficient in addition less precise in a large distributed ledger including certain IoT. Various studies recently learned, after contrasting contemporary ML algorithms and DL methodologies, that most Modulus of elasticity use pretraining for dimensionality reduction. DL not just to avoided the problem, but also decreased the dimensionality of the function [54, 88, 90] by reducing repetition.

- **Latency**: Some authors, such as Xiao et al., have suggested using ensemble ML algorithms as a solution to the above problems. The aggregate theoretical framework superior than each Neural network independently, but computation was expensive. Most studies have pointed out as an alternative to classical ML, that DL is a better IoT choice.
- **Vulnerability**: Securing oneself from any security or privacy attacks is one of the main ML/DL strategies problems for IoT. Adversarial attacks may degrade system performance against machine learning models, as such attacks significantly decrease the accuracy of output [91]. The strength of the intrusion determines the amount of data given to the opponent of the method [71], which is very difficult to counter.

3.8.2 Challenges to Blockchain in IoT

- **Latency and speed**: While BC engineering was launched a era ago, its actual reimbursements have only been understood freshly. Numerous previous findings attempt to implement BC have included transportation, nutrition, electricity cities, VANET, 5G, wellbeing and operating expenditure in several applications. However, the current solutions do not meet latency concerns with BC and are not applicable to commodity IoT devices [19, 62]. PoW is the most common BC assumption, as seen in Table 10. PoW is sluggish and needs substantial resources (limited to 7 cycles per second, compared to the national average of 2000 network visa data per second).
- **Computation, processing, and data storage**: The maintenance of a BC across a vast network of peers [72] involves a substantial cost of computation, power, and memory. The size of the bitcoin ledger exceeded 196 GB in May 2018, according to Song et al. For an IoT device, these boundaries recommend underprivileged scaling in addition contract rapidity. Whilst it was an option to uploading the computing activities to a remote computer—cloud or quasi server—fog, there are still latencies throughout the network.
- **Compatibility and standardisation**: One of the BC challenges, like any emerging technology, is its standardisation, for which legislation needs to be renewed [90]. It would have been naive to expect that we all will see a degree of protection and privacy which will remove the chance of security breaches on IoT devices in the immediate future. Nevertheless a "reasonable" protection and privacy standards

can be ensured by a protocol specification. There are a range of essential protection and privacy features in every IoT system.

- **Vulnerability**: A decentralized framework is only as reliable as the platform's entry point even though the BC is non-repudiable, trustless, decentralised, and tamperproof. Anyone can access and view the content of data in a public BC-based scheme. While one of the solutions to the above problem is the private blockchain, other concerns are raised, such as trustworthy third parties, centralized management and user access regulation. In general, IoT solutions allowed to blockchain have to comply with either the security requirements like that of the data that I have to store for safe and confidential transmission; (ii) secure transmission of data; (iii) stable and responsible exchange of data; (iv) protection of identity and non-reputed properties; (iii) sharing of personal information; and Increasing the sharing of IoT solutions.

3.8.3 Challenges to Machine Learning (ML) and Blockchain (BC) in IoT

It is our view that a single device or tool, including such BC or ML, is not enough to provide maximum security and privacy for the IoT networks. The merger of BC and ML thus takes a long time for the scientific community to investigate the stability and anonymity of IoT.

Subsequent challenges:

- **Storage**: ML algorithms perform better with larger datasets, as discussed in Sect. 3.4 [27, 28]. That being said, the rise in BC's data will hinder its performance [70]. A simple research concern is the selection of a combination that will be suitable for IoT systems.
- **Latency challenges**: An IoT network can generate a significant amount of information depending on the scenario, more preparation and computation time is needed, which could theoretically boost the overall efficiency of typical Different classifiers (i.e. latency) [19, 62].
- **Scalability**: ML as well as BC have computation complexity both with respect to production and connectivity costs. Multiple ML algorithms place higher computing costs and connectivity costs as traffic increases, which is unavoidable for many of these IoT networks. Also, the BC is poorly managed with growing numbers of users and networking knots [76]. An Ethereum BC executes an increase of 11 transactions a second in standard IoT implementations, with bitcoin transactions taking place per second [62].
- **Selection of right algorithm**: The selection of correct algorithm is not limited to dozens, but a number of publicly accessible options are. There are basic rules that apply to all algorithm design projects: Algorithms should be used in all kinds of design scenarios, although there are exceptions to which one will be more appropriate. Expensively incorrect algorithm selection will result in useless

results or drag down the project over months of work, meaning that the efforts end result will be useless or will be delayed indefinitely.

- **The collection of data you are using for machine learning**: garbage in garbage out one must pay careful attention to the consistency, quantity, planning, and collection of the data used in machine learning projects to ensure their effectiveness. The data may be biased because of the following factors: The data must be carefully selected to prevent prejudice from influencing its results, and it is especially necessary to choose those who reflect all the events.
- **Data preparation**: The data has quality issues ranging from lost values to worthless values, which makes the results hard to trust and unreliable data is essential for data-normalization processes. Converting, truncation, refactoring, and cleaning of this data may be very time-consuming. Feature properties and feature requirements have to features should be studied and strategies including feature scaling has to be added to help avoid them dominating the blueprint.
- **Data Labelling**: are the ones used in supervised machine learning algorithms, which make the classification and recommendation processes both more straightforward and correct For a newly-implemented algorithm, unsupervised algorithm, this can be a very long and difficult operation, always involving many futile cycles of expanding and re-expanding. Only supervised machine learning algorithms need to be trained on labeled results. It's a job that requires plenty of effort, but outsourcing can't be trusted, so data marking must be done as part of the process. For example, health care services are a classic test of well-being because of the precariousness of their finances. Expanded vocabulary: In order for the predictive diagnosis to be effective, relevant medical evidence needs to be labelled. The marking relies on regular feedback from medical professionals and physicians but these people see the activity of labelling certain things like a trained doctors find it a waste of time.

In addition to these obstacles, there are plenty of others. Working with the developers, developing and maintaining product variants, creating and handling a separate copy of the results, and so on this is something that everybody employed on challenging projects knows about and understands: It's difficult to find good ML engineers, and if they constantly switching teams creates challenges for them, the job becomes overwhelming. It's an ongoing operation, and as time goes on. As time goes on, the system's specifications change, the algorithm should be given daily updates so it can have them as part of its environment.

Vulnerability: While ML and BC can significantly improve safety and confidentiality, there are also many challenges. On real time IoT platforms the difficulty of finding, working to prevent threats, namely malware and harmful programs, is growing. The ML training phase takes longer, and while malicious traffic can be detected, only a qualified model can do that [50]. Ledger will, but at the other hand, guarantee data non-repudiation and can understand their transformations. The dilemma, however, has been the compromised data before accessing the blockchain. Furthermore, the malfunction of sensing devices cannot be detected from the beginning before such a malfunction is established. The instrument [17] was tested. Besides

the aforementioned concerns, because the collected data are relevant to all stakeholders and is freely available, public BC is open to privacy infringement. One of
the solutions to these challenges is the use of private BC, This will therefore restrict
access to a considerable amount of information needed to successfully achieve ML
[62].

3.9   Conclusion and Future Work

Throughout this segment, we discussed and categorized the latest risks to IoT as
security and privacy. They briefly mentioned their consequences, type of actions,
the interaction layer as well as the responses. We instead discussed and outlined the
deficiencies in the new IoT regarding health and safety survey using both ML and BC
architectures. This article provides the new IoT security and privacy strategies using
Neural networks, BC methods and the implementation of both strategies. In order to
better explain security and privacy issues in an IoT ML we have indeed attempted
to present a regression analysis previous researcher. In conclusion, we have a range
of study concerns on IoT Different classifiers, IoT BC approaches and IoT ML and
BC mixture problems. The Digital gateway has essential for data collection, storage,
study and correspondence. There is a performed a comprehensive, through initiatives
such as adherence to best practises and continuous testing, where a vulnerability-free
framework needs to be developed. As malicious activities are dynamic, the apparatus
should be able to respond to the new hazard innovations (zero-day attacks). In this
respect, in the study of traffic, ML/DL can be extremely helpful. At the same time, in
an IoT environment, a log and correspondence directory will be maintained by the BC.
As this information is unalterable, it can be used in the courts with trust as testimony.
Majority of them should have concentrated on ensuring defense or anonymity in the
fields of IoT defense and safety. We agree that both protection and privacy are equally
necessary for a system to be secure. Moreover, the most important aspect is data
protection, which can only be true when considered end-to-end. Present frameworks
ignore the credibility of databases used only to create a network. These datasets can
be tampered with by any opponent to achieve their desired performance. Currently,
ML algorithms are being combined with BC techniques to achieve IoT protection
and Privacy, which needs more exploration, is a relatively new field. Any concerns
concerning analysis, however are: By mixing it, I could use BC with ML algorithms
to eradicate DDoS attacks on an IoT network? (ii) Can the resource-constrained
IoT system exploit the inherited encryption of BC for real-time performance? (iii)
Can BC create trust in conventional IoT Intrusion Prevention Mechanisms based
on collaborative ML? In addition, many organisations depend on the data generated
by IoT devices, both public and private. Whether in motion or at rest, how can we
trust the data? In a centralised IoT architecture based on the cloud, this question
becomes more difficult to address. We significant data can be derived ML algorithms
that secure privacy, while BC should maintain protection and trust. We plan to build

and create a privacy-preserving IoT platform in the future, which will provide data sharing and privacy-preserving data analysis to preserve privacy.

References

1. Taylor, A., Leblanc, S., Japkowicz, N.: Anomaly detection in automobile control network data with long short-term memory networks. In: 2016 IEEE International Conference on Data Science and Advanced Analytics (DSAA). IEEE; 2016. pp. 130–9
2. Cicds2017 Dataset. https://www.unb.ca/cic/datasets/ids-2017.html. Last Accessed 30 May 2019
3. Hidayet Aksu, A., Uluagac, S., Bentley, E.: Identification of wearable devices with bluetooth. IEEE Trans. Sustain. Comput. **2018**, 1–1 (2018)
4. Song, H., Fink, G.A., Jeschke, S.: Security and Privacy in Cyber-Physical Systems: Foundations, Principles, and Applications, pp. 1–472. Wiley
5. Goel, V., Perlroth, N.: Yahoo Says 1 Billion User Accounts Were Hacked. (2016). https://www.nytimes.com/2016/12/14/technology/yahoo-hack.html
6. Peterson, A.: eBay asks 145 million users to change passwords after data breach (2014). https://www.washingtonpost.com/news/the-switch/wp/2014/05/21/ebay-asks-145-million-users-to-change-passwords-after-data-breach/
7. Kshetri, N.: Blockchain's roles in strengthening cybersecurity and protecting privacy. Telecommun. Policy **41**(10), 1027–1038 (2017). https://doi.org/10.1016/j.telpol.2017.09.003
8. Giles, M.: Five emerging cyber-threats to worry about in 2019. (2019). https://www.technologyreview.com/s/612713/five-emerging-cyber-threats-2019/
9. Milosevic, J., Malek, M. and Ferrante, A.: A friend or a foe? Detecting malware using memory and CPU features. In: Proceedings of the 13th International Joint Conference on e-Business and Telecommunications (ICETE 2016), vol. 4. pp. 73–84
10. Chaabouni, N., Mosbah, M., Zemmari, A., Sauvignac, C., Faruki, P.: Network intrusion detection for IoT security based on learning techniques. IEEE Commun. Surv. Tutor. **21**(3), 2671–2701 (2019)
11. Dartmann, G., Song, H., Schmeink, A.: Big Data Analytics for Cyber-Physical Systems: Machine Learning for the Internet of Things. Elsevier, pp. 1–360 (2019)
12. Aonzo, S., Merlo, A., Migliardi, M., Oneto, L., Palmieri, F.: Low-resource footprint, data-driven malware detection on android. IEEE Trans. Sustain. Comput. **3782**, c, 1–1 (2017). http://ieeexplore.ieee.org/document/8113505/
13. Nasr, M., Bahramali, A., Houmansadr, A.: Deepcorr: strong flow correlation attacks on TOR using deep learning. In: Proceedings of the 2018 ACM SIGSAC Conference on Computer and Communications Security. ACM, 2018. pp. 1962–76
14. Ferdous, M.S., Chowdhury, M.J.M., Biswas, K., Chowdhury, N., Muthukkumarasamy, V.: Immutable autobiography of smart cars leveraging blockchain technology. Knowl. Eng. Rev. **22**, e3 (2020)
15. Song, J., Takakura, H., Okabe, Y.: Description of Kyoto University Benchmark Data; 2006. Available at link: http://www.takakura.com/Kyoto_data/ BenchmarkData-Description-v5.pdf. Accessed on 15 March 2016
16. Mawi Dataset. http://www.fukuda-lab.org/mawilab/data.html. Last Accessed 30 May 2019
17. Reyna, A., Martín, C., Chen, J., Soler, E., Díaz, M.: On blockchain and its integration with IoT. Challenges and opportunities. Fut. Gener. Comput. Syst. **88**, 173–190 (2018)
18. Price, W.N., Cohen, I.G.: Privacy in the age of medical big data. Nat. Med. **25**(1), 37–43 (2019). https://doi.org/10.1038/s41591-018-0272-7
19. Tang, T.A., Mhamdi, L., McLernon, D., Zaidi, S.A.R., Ghogho, M.: Deep recurrent neural network for intrusion detection in SDN-based networks. In: 2018 4th IEEE Conference on Network Softwarization and Workshops (NetSoft). IEEE, 2018. pp. 202–6

20. Jiang, F., Fu, Y., Gupta, B.B., Lou, F., Rho, S., Meng, F., et al.: Deep learning based multichannel intelligent attack detection for data security. IEEE Trans. Sustain. Comput. (2018)
21. Hussain, F., Hassan, S.A., Hussain, R., Hossain, E.: Machine learning for resource management in cellular and IoT networks: potentials, current solutions, and open challenges. IEEE Commun. Surv. Tutor. C **2020**, 1–1 (2020)
22. Makhdoom, I., Abolhasan, M., Lipman, J., Liu, R.P., Ni, W.: Anatomy of threats to the Internet of Things. IEEE Commun. Surv. Tutor. **21** (2), 1636–1675 (2019)
23. Brass, I., Tanczer, L., Carr, M., Elsden, M., Blackstock, J.: Standardising a moving target: the development and evolution of IoT security standards. In: Living in the Internet of Things: Cybersecurity of the IoT, pp. 1–9
24. Alrawashdeh, K., Purdy, C.: Toward an online anomaly intrusion detection system based on deep learning. In: 2016 15th IEEE International Conference on Machine Learning and Applications (ICMLA). IEEE; 2016. pp. 195–200
25. Zhang, H., Yu, X., Ren, P., Luo, C., Min, G.: Deep adversarial learning in intrusion detection: a data augmentation enhanced framework (2019). arXiv preprint, arXiv: 1901.07949
26. Feng, F., Liu, X., Yong, B., Zhou, R., Zhou, Q.: Anomaly detection in ad-hoc net- works based on deep learning model: a plug and play device. Ad Hoc Netw. **84**, 82–89 (2019)
27. Abeshu, A., Chilamkurti, N.: Deep learning: the frontier for distributed attack detection in fog-to-things computing. IEEE Commun Mag 56(2):169–175 (2018)
28. Elejla, O.E., Belaton, B., Anbar, M., Alabsi, B., Al-Ani, A.K.: Comparison of classification algorithms on ICMPv6-based DDoS attacks detection. Lect. Notes Electr. Eng. **481**(2019), 347–357 (2019)
29. Otoum, S., Kantarci, B., Mouftah, H.: Adaptively supervised and intrusion-aware data aggregation for wireless sensor clusters in critical infrastructures. In: 2018 IEEE International Conference on Communications (ICC). IEEE; 2018, pp. 1–6
30. Rezazad, M., Brust, M.R., Akbari, M., Bouvry, P., Cheung, N.M.: Detecting target-area link-flooding DDoS attacks using traffic analysis and supervised learning. Adv. Inf. Commun. Netw. 180âĂŞ202 (2018). https://doi.org/10.1007/978-3-030-03405-4_12
31. Moustafa, N., Turnbull, B., Choo, K.K.R.: An ensemble intrusion detection technique based on proposed statistical flow features for protecting network traffic of Internet of Things. IEEE IoT J. **6**(3), 4815–4830 (2019)
32. Diro, A., Chilamkurti, N.: Leveraging LSTM networks for attack detection in fog-to-things communications. IEEE Commun. Mag. **56**(9), 124–130 (2018)
33. Roy, D.G., Das, P., De, D., Buyya, R.: QoS-aware secure transaction framework for internet of things using blockchain mechanism. J. Netw. Comput. Appl. **15**(144), 59–78 (2019)
34. Kasongo, S.M., Sun, Y.: A deep learning method with filter based feature engineering for wireless intrusion detection system. IEEE Access **7**, 38597–38607 (2019)
35. Ahmad, U., Song, H., Bilal, A., Saleem, S., Ullah, A.: Securing insulin pump system using deep learning and gesture recognition. In: Proceedings—17th IEEE international conference on trust, security and privacy in computing and communications and 12th IEEE international conference on big data science and engineering, Trustcom/BigDataSE 2018:1716–1719 (2018)
36. D., Maity, S., Sen, S.: 2018. RF-PUF: IoT security enhancement through authentication of wireless nodes using in-situ machine learning. In: Proceedings of the 2018 IEEE International Symposium on Hardware Oriented Security and Trust, HOST 2018, c (2018), pp. 205–208
37. Shen, M., Tang, X., Zhu, L., Du, X., Guizani, M.: Privacy-preserving support vector machine training over blockchain-based encrypted IoT data in smart cities. IEEE Internet Things J. **2019**, 1–1 (2019)
38. Azmoodeh, A., Dehghantanha, A., Choo, K.K.R.: Robust malware detection for internet of (Battlefield) things devices using deep Eigen space learning. IEEE Trans. Sustain. Comput. **3782**, c, 1–1 (2018). http://ieeexplore.ieee.org/document/8302863/
39. Fu, K., Cheng, D., Tu, Y., Zhang, L.: Credit card fraud detection using convolutional neural networks. In: International Conference on Neural Information Processing, 2016. pp. 483–90. Springer

40. Thamilarasu, G., Chawla, S.: Towards deep-learning-driven intrusion detection for the internet of things. Sensors **19**(9), 1977 (2019)
41. Al-Rubaie, M., Chang, J.M.: Privacy preserving machine learning: threats and solutions. IEEE Security and Privacy Magazine (2018)
42. Restuccia, F., D'Oro, S., Melodia, T.: Securing the Internet of Things in the age of machine learning and software-defined networking. IEEE IoT J. **1**(1), 1–14 (2018)
43. Sharmeen, S., Huda, S., Abawajy, J.H., Ismail, W.N., Hassan, M.M.: Malware threats and detection for industrial mobile-IoT networks. IEEE Access **6**(2018), 15941–15957 (2018)
44. da Costa, K.A., Papa, J.P., Lisboa, C.O., Munoz, R., de Albuquerque, V.H.C.: Internet of Things: a survey on machine learning-based intrusion detection approaches. Comput. Netw. **151**, 147–157 (2019). https://doi.org/10.1016/j.comnet.2019.01.023
45. Ji, Z., Lipton, Z.C., Elkan, C.: Differential privacy and machine learning: a survey and review. CoRR abs/1412.7584 (2014). http://arxiv.org/abs/1412.7584
46. Zhang, L., Shi, L., Kaja, N., Ma, D.: A two-stage deep learning approach for can intrusion detection. In: Proceedings Ground Vehicle systems Engineering and Technology Symposium (GVSETS), pp. 1–11 (2018)
47. Fernández-Caramés, T.M., Fraga-Lamas, P.: A review on the use of blockchain for the Internet of Things. IEEE Access **6**(2018), 32979–33001 (2018)
48. Kang, M-J., Kang, J-W.: Intrusion detection system using deep neural network for in-vehicle network security. PLoS ONE, **11**(6), e0155781 (2016)
49. Ferrag, M.A., Maglaras, L.: Deepcoin: a novel deep learning and blockchain-based energy exchange framework for smart grids. IEEE Trans. Eng. Manage. (2019)
50. Center for Applied Internet Data Analysis. https://www.caida.org/data/overview/. Last Accessed 30 May 2019
51. Banerjee, M., Lee, J., Choo, K.K.R.: A blockchain future for internet of things security: a position paper. Digit. Commun. Netw. 4(3):149–160 (2018). https://doi.org/10.1016/j.dcan.2017.10.00
52. Khan, M.A., Salah, K.: IoT security: review, blockchain solutions, and open challenges. Fut. Gener. Comput. Syst. **82**, 395–411 (2018). https://doi.org/10.1016/j.future.2017.11.022
53. Khan, F.A., Gumaei, A., Derhab, A., Hussain, A.: Tsdl: a two stage deep learning model for efficient network intrusion detection. IEEE Access (2019)
54. Kumar, N.M., Mallick, P.K.: Blockchain technology for security issues and challenges in IoT. Procedia Comput. Sci. **132**, 1815–1823 (2018). https://doi.org/10.1016/j.procs.2018.05.140
55. Kouicem, D.E., Bouabdallah, A., Lakhlef, H.: Internet of things security: a top-down survey. Comput. Netw. **141**, 199–221 (2018). https://doi.org/10.1016/j.comnet.2018.03.012
56. Ferretti, L., Longo, F., Colajanni, M., Merlino, G., Tapas, N.: Authorization transparency for accountable access to IoT services. In: Proceedings—2019 IEEE International Congress on Internet of Things, ICIOT 2019—Part of the 2019 IEEE World Congress on Services (2019), pp. 91–99
57. Hassan, M.U., Rehmani, M.H., Chen, J.:. Privacy preservation in blockchain based IoT systems: integration issues, prospects, challenges, and future research directions. Fut. Gener. Comput. Syst. **97**, 512–529 (2019). https://doi.org/10.1016/j.future.2019.02.060
58. Ali, M.S., Vecchio, M., Pincheira, M., Dolui, K., Antonelli, F., Rehmani, M.H.: Applications of blockchains in the Internet of Things: a comprehensive survey. IEEE Commun. Surv. Tutor. **21**(2):1676–1717 (2019)
59. Lbnl Dataset. https://powerdata.lbl.gov/download.html. Last Accessed 23 Juin 2019
60. Baxter, R., Hastings, N., Law, A., Glass, E.J.: Future Uses of Blockchain. vol. 39, pp. 561–563. https://www.thestreet.com/technology/cybersecurity/five-future-uses-for-blockchain-14589274
61. Christidis, K., Devetsikiotis, M.: Blockchains and smart contracts for the Internet of Things. IEEE Access **4**, 2292–2303 (2016). http://ieeexplore.ieee.org/document/7467408/
62. Salah, K., Rehman, M.H.U., Nizamuddin, N., Al-Fuqaha, A.: Blockchain for AI: review and open research challenges. IEEE Access **7**, 10127–10149 (2019)

63. Zhang, Y., Li, P., Wang, X.: Intrusion detection for IoT based on improved genetic algorithm and deep belief network. IEEE Access **7**, 31711–31722 (2019)
64. Alom, M.Z., Bontupalli, V., Taha, T.M.: Intrusion detection using deep belief networks. In: 2015 National Aerospace and Electronics Conference (NAECON). IEEE, 2015. pp. 339–44
65. Agrawal, R., Verma, P., Sonanis, R., Goel, U., De, A., Kondaveeti, S.A., Shekhar, S.: Continuous security in Iot Using Blockchain 6423–6427 (2018)
66. Gu, J., Sun, B., Du, X., and Senior Member.: Consortium blockchain-based malware detection in mobile devices. IEEE Access **6** (2018)
67. Ikram, M., Beaume, P., Kâafar, M.A.: DaDiDroid: an obfuscation resilient tool for detecting android malware via weighted directed call graph modelling. In: Proceedings of the 16th International Joint Conference on e-Business and Telecommunications, ICETE 2019 - Volume 2: SECRYPT, Prague, Czech Republic, July 26–28, 2019. SciTePress, pp. 211–219. https://doi.org/10.5220/0007834602110219
68. Homoliak, I., Barabas, M., Chmelar, P., Drozd, M., Hanacek, P.: ASNM: advanced security network metrics for attack vector description. In: Proceedings of the International Conference on Security and Management (SAM). The Steering Committee of The World Congress in Computer Science, Computer âQ; 2013. p. 1
69. Feng, P., Ma, J., Sun, C., Xu, X., Ma, Y.: A novel dynamic android malware detection system with ensemble learning. IEEE Access **6**(2018), 30996–31011 (2018)
70. Song, J.C., Demir, M.A., Prevost, J.J., Rad, P.: Blockchain design for trusted decentralized IoT networks. In 2018 13th System of Systems Engineering Conference, SoSE 2018
71. Potluri, S., Diedrich, C.: Accelerated deep neural networks for enhanced intrusion detection system. In: 2016 IEEE 21st International Conference on Emerging Technologies and Factory Automation (ETFA). IEEE; 2016. pp. 1–8
72. Zhou, L., Ouyang, X., Ying, H., Han, L., Cheng, Y., Zhang, T.: Cyber-attack classification in smart grid via deep neural network. In: Proceedings of the 2nd Inter- national Conference on Computer Science and Application Engineering. ACM; 2018. p. 90
73. Kim, J., Shin, N., Jo, S.Y., Kim, S.H.: Method of intrusion detection using deep neural network. In: 2017 IEEE International Conference on Big Data and Smart Computing (BigComp). IEEE, 2017. pp. 313–16
74. Roy, D.G., Das, M., De, D.: Cohort assembly: a load balancing grouping approach for traditional WiFi infrastructure using edge cloud. In: Methodologies and Application Issues of Contemporary Computing Framework 2018 (pp. 93–108). Springer, Singapore
75. Loukas, G., Vuong, T., Heartfield, R., Sakellari, G., Yoon, Y., Gan, D.: Cloud-based cy- ber-physical intrusion detection for vehicles using deep learning. IEEE Access **6**, 3491–3508 (2017)
76. Yin, C., Zhu, Y., Fei, J., He, X.: A deep learning approach for intrusion detection using recurrent neural networks. IEEE Access **5**, 21954–21961 (2017)
77. Basumallik, S., Ma, R., Eftekharnejad, S.: Packet-data anomaly detection in PMU-based state estimator using convolutional neural network. Int. J. Electric. Power Energy Syst. **107**, 690–702 (2019)
78. Zhang, Y., Chen, X., Jin, L., Wang, X., Guo, D.: Network intrusion detection: based on deep hierarchical network and original flow data. IEEE Access **7**, 37004–37016 (2019)
79. Roy, D.G., Mahato, B., De, D., Buyya, R.: Application-aware end-to-end delay and message loss estimation in Internet of Things (IoT)—MQTT-SN protocols. Futur. Gener. Comput. Syst. **1**(89), 300–316 (2018)
80. Salama, M.A., Eid, H.F., Ramadan, R.A., Darwish, A., Hassanien, A.E.: Hybrid intelligent intrusion detection scheme. In: Soft Computing in Industrial Applications, 2011. pp. 293–303, Springer
81. Aldwairi, T., Perera, D., Novotny, M.A.: An evaluation of the performance of restricted Boltzmann machines as a model for anomaly network intrusion detection. Comput. Netw. **144**, 111–119 (2018)
82. Jing, X., Yan, Z., Jiang, X., Pedrycz, W.: Network traffic fusion and analysis against DDoS flooding attacks with a novel reversible sketch. Inf. Fusion **51**, 100–113 (2019). https://doi.org/10.1016/j.inffus.2018.10.013

83. Gao, N., Gao, L., Gao, Q., Wang, H.: An intrusion detection model based on deep belief networks. In: 2014 Second International Conference on Advanced Cloud and Big Data. IEEE; 2014. pp. 247–52
84. Yang, J., Deng, J., Li, S., Hao, Y.: Improved traffic detection with support vector machine based on restricted Boltzmann machine. Soft Comput. **21**(11), 3101–3112 (2017)
85. Zhao, G., Zhang, C., Zheng, L.: Intrusion detection using deep belief network and probabilistic neural network. In: 2017 IEEE International Conference on Computational Science and Engineering (CSE) and IEEE International Conference on Embedded and Ubiquitous Computing (EUC), vol. 1. IEEE; 2017. pp. 639–642
86. Shone, N., Ngoc, T.N., Phai, V.D., Shi, Q.: A deep learning approach to network intrusion detection. IEEE Trans. Emerg. Top. Comput. Intell. **2**(1), 41–50 (2018)
87. Javaid, A., Niyaz, Q., Sun, W., Alam, M.: A deep learning approach for network intrusion detection system. In: Proceedings of the 9th EAI International Conference on Bio-inspired Information and Communications Technologies; 2016, pp. 21–6
88. Roy, D.G., Mahato, B., De, D.: A competitive hedonic consumption estimation for IoT service distribution. In: 2019 URSI Asia-Pacific Radio Science Conference (AP-RASC) 2019 Mar 9, pp. 1–4. IEEE
89. Iscx Dataset. https://www.unb.ca/cic/datasets/ids.html. Last Accessed 23 Juin 2019
90. Niwa, H.: Why Blockchain is the future of IoT? (2007). https://www.networkworld.com/art icle/3200029/internet-of-things/why-blockchain-is-the-future-of-iot.html
91. Roy, D.G., Mahato, B., Ghosh, A., De, D.: Service aware resource management into cloudlets for data offloading towards IoT. Microsyst. Technol. **4**, 1–5 (2019)

Chapter 4
A Review on Cyber Crimes on the Internet of Things

Mohan Krishna Kagita, Navod Thilakarathne, Thippa Reddy Gadekallu, Praveen Kumar Reddy Maddikunta, and Saurabh Singh

4.1 Introduction

IoT (Internet of things) is developing very rapidly and it offers various types of services that made it the fastest-growing technology with a big influence on society and business infrastructures. IoT has become an integral part of human's modern life like in education, every type of business, healthcare, stores the sensitive data about companies and individuals, information about financial transactions, development of the product, and its marketing [1, 2]. In IoT, Transmission from connected devices has generated huge demand to concentrate on security as millions and billions of users perform sensitive transactions on the internet. Cyber threats and attacks are rising daily in both complexity and numbers. Potential attackers are increasing with the growth in networks and also the tools or methods they are using are becoming more effective, efficient, and sophisticated [3]. Hence, to get the full potential of IoT, it is needed to be protected from threats and attacks [4] (Fig. 4.1).

M. K. Kagita (✉)
School of Computing and Mathematics, Charles Sturt University, Melbourne, Australia
e-mail: mohankrishna4k@gmail.com

N. Thilakarathne
Department of ICT, University of Colombo, Colombo, Sri Lanka
e-mail: navod.neranjan@ict.cmb.ac.lk

T. R. Gadekallu · P. K. R. Maddikunta
School of Information Technology and Engineering, Vellore Institute of Technology, Vellore, India
e-mail: thippareddy.g@vit.ac.in

P. K. R. Maddikunta
e-mail: praveenkumarreddy@vit.ac.in

S. Singh
Department of Industrial and System Engineering, Dongguk University, Seoul, South Korea
e-mail: saurabh89@dongguk.edu

© The Author(s), under exclusive license to Springer Nature Singapore Pte Ltd. 2021
A. Makkar and N. Kumar, *Deep Learning for Security and Privacy Preservation in IoT*,
Signals and Communication Technology,
https://doi.org/10.1007/978-981-16-6186-0_4

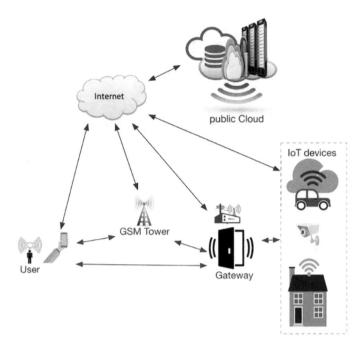

Fig. 4.1 A high level of system model of IoT

These smart technologies indeed have many advantages to offer but still, it has many loopholes that result in the possibility of cyber-attacks that will cause huge damage to life and property. In today's scenario, it becomes essential that technologies with proper security systems should be adopted in the whole ecosystem to finish the possibilities of hacking or fraud. 98% of all the IoT devices traffic is un-encrypted, exposing personal and confidential data on the network [5]. The most used IoT device in the bossiness and every day in the office space is IP-Phones which has 44% of enterprise IoT Devices but has only 5% of security issues when compared to other IoT devices. Most security issues are faced by cameras that have 33% of risk but only 5% of usage in the business world [6, 7] (Fig. 4.2).

As per the reports of Australia cyber security center, there has been one reported incident for every 10 min, which costs Australian economies $328 million annual losses. The Top five Cybercrime types targeting Australians are Identity theft, Online fraud, and Shopping scams, Bulk extortion, Online romance scams, Wire-fraud, and Business email compromise [8]. The period of December 2019 to June 2020 Agari data finds 68% of the identity-deception based attacks aimed at impersonating a trusted individual or a brand. As per the reports from Kaspersky estimate of 105 Million attacks on IoT devices are coming from 276,000 unique IP addresses. Cyber-criminals uses network to infect smart devices to conduct DDOS attacks as a proxy services. Further, 51% of health care devices attacked, mostly involving medical

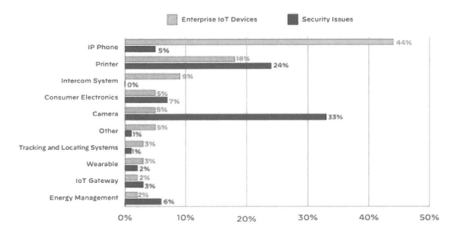

Fig. 4.2 Industrial usage of IoT devices

imaging devices [9]. New techniques, such like peer-to-peer command and worm-like features for self-propagation, are used to infect vulnerable IoT devices on same network [10] (Fig. 4.3).

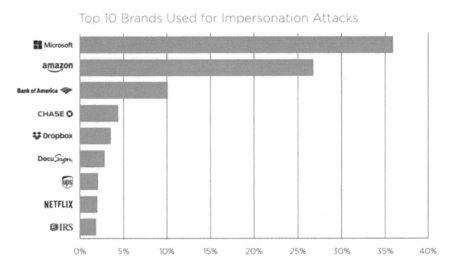

Fig. 4.3 Email fraud and identity deception trends by Agari

4.2 Literature Review

Lu and Xu [11] explore that IoT, modernized the network globally including smart equipment, Humans, intelligent objects, and information. IoT provides an opportunity to increase integrity, confidentiality, accessibility, and availability. It is evident that IoT are still on the developing stage and contain many issues that are necessary to be solved [11]. System security is a base for expansion in IoT. In this study, cyber security is studied thoroughly. The main focus is on the protection and integration of various smart devices and technologies in information communication. This study helps other researchers and experts who want to do researches in IoT in the future can get useful information [12]. The study shows the research of cyber security on IoT, taxonomy, and architecture of IoT cyber security, strategies, and other trends in research and challenges.

Hilt et al. [13] deliberate that IoT is influencing every field of today's society. The ongoing progress of IoT becomes the temptation for cybercriminals [13]. Various studies are done on how criminals can attack IoT and what impact will it laid on. In this research IoT cybercrime underground is selected to collect ideas about the current fears from different minds that consider them. Five underground groups are analyzed which are categorized based on the language used in discussions among community i.e. English, Spanish, Portuguese, Russian and Spanish. Many research and tutorials are gathered on the method of hacking, exploitation of vulnerability but no symbol of any intensive determination from the criminal's clusters to enormous damage of IoT Structures are found. Cybercriminals are usually inspired by financial profit and until now there are few ways of making money from the attack on IoT. New devices are invented by cybercriminals with which they find new ways to infect and make a lot of money with these infections.

Venckauskas et al. [14], found that IoT can be described as a physical system of world wide web that unites all types of physical things on the internet. The big size, scope, and vast physical distribution of IoT make it difficult to protect it from threats and attacks of cybercrimes [15]. Limitations of the IoT like low power add a contribution to the problems by prohibited the usage of high security but techniques of resource greedy cryptography [16]. IoT provides a stage for cybercrimes. Hackers or attackers take benefit of a low level of understanding among users of IoT technologies and safety measures to cheat them. New methods for digital forensics in IoT should be increased as the number of threats and attacks of existing and futuristic will increase day by day. New technologies and new strategies are continuously developing that create new challenges for digital forensics. IoT has a large amount of information. Huge scope, a large number of data, diverse nature of the Internet of things, methods in which information is shared, combines and handled need the inventions of new strategies by the digital forensic examinations. It is found that traditional forensic methods used in investigating cybercrimes that are not effective at all, as new tools and devices are developed by cybercriminals to defraud the user on IoT [17].

Abomhara and Koien [18] found that in the field of IoT security, still lots of work to be done by merchants and end-users. It is necessary to find out the limitations of

IoT security as the internet on things is growing so fast. Threats and attacks of IoT infrastructure should be thoroughly studied along with the consequences of these threats and attacks against IoT [18]. It is advised that effective security devices for controlling access, authentication, manage identity, flexible faith management structure should be taken care of at the starting of the development of the product. This research is useful for the researchers who study the field of security by helping in finding the mains problems insecurity of IoT and provide a clear understanding of threats and attacks and the factors instigating from various organizations or intelligence agencies. This research helps in better clarity on various threats and their factors inventing from various burglars such as intelligence and organizations [19]. The procedure of finding threats and vulnerabilities is important to make healthy and completely secured IoT and make sure that the security solution is secure enough to protect from malicious attacks.

Iqbal and Beigh [20], explore that as the use of the internet is increasing in the world, cybercrime is also increasing at the same pace, particularly in India. IoT covers vast areas all over the world in the same way Cybercrime is not bound to a specific geographical area. So, these crimes can't be controlled by local laws. Cyber laws in the context of India are still in the early developing stage. India has done many bilateral agreements related to Cybercrime such as the agreement with Russia, a basic agreement with the US, and a framework cyber agreement with Israel to modernize it cyber space. But scope of these bilateral agreements is limited, ineffective and insufficient to deal cybercrime. This research found that India should make multilateral treaty that blends its laws on common criminal policy and deal to reduce cyber-crimes at global level with international co-operation. This treaty will help in framing active regulations and strong analytical methods, which result in increasing internationally co-operation to control cyber-crime [21]. Budapest convention council of Europe on cybercrime is one of the multilateral international treaties that deal with international co-operation for fighting cyber-crimes globally. India should also join this Budapest Convention as US and Israel also whom India has bilateral agreement are already part of this cyber- crime convention.

Sarmah et al. [22] found that with the development of new technologies are increasing; it also led to increase in crimes related to IoT. Cyber-crime is actually a threat to people, so it is necessary to take steps to protect IoT from cyber-crimes for welfare of society, cultural and countries security aspect. Indian government has passed an IT act, 2000 to control cybercrimes issues. Cyber-crime is not bounded to any particular geo-graphical area. It passes national boundaries on internet and creates legal and technical difficulties in investigation and accusing the crimes. Hence it is necessary that proper action should be taken to control cybercrimes internationally. Proper cooperation and coordination among various countries are necessary to fight against cybercrimes. The main objective of this study is to create awareness among common people about Cyber-crime. It is important that users who become the victim of cyber-crime should come forward and report s file against cyber criminals so that strict actions can be taken against them and an example can be set for future cyber criminals.

Anisha [23] argue that main reasons of cybercrime is technology and dangerous infrastructure of IoT. As the ratio of users on IoT is increasing, it leads to increase risks of different types of cyber-crimes. Crimes are unpredictable due to development of new technologies. Crimes based on technologies are increasing day by day and it is necessary that these are solved on the priority basis [23]. Cybercrimes are not limited to computers only, electronic devices such as telecommunication tools, financial transaction machines etc. IoT is diversified in nature that makes it difficult to find out the problems of cyber security that results in unawareness on issues of security. It is suggested that free advertisements and workshops can be organized to generate awareness among users with the help of NGO'S and government. Cybercrime issues and threats should be acknowledged from the grassroots level i.e. institutes, schools, colleges, computer centers etc. Indian government has taken many effective steps to control cybercrimes like Information technology act, 2000 has been passed. But a fixed cyber law is not effective in cybercrime context as IoT has a vast and diversified nature and new type of crimes keeps on inventing. So, it is necessary that cyber law keep close eyes on cybercrime and updated its law and regulations accordingly.

Husamuddin and Qayyum [24], explore that IoT are developing as an important technology. Information's transferred with RFID tags or sensors include sensitive data which should be secure from unauthorized access. There is no security in between 2 nodes of IoT communication and security of IoT should not be negotiated [24]. To get more secure communication it is necessary that IoT should have services like end to end environments, real time access control, protection of critical infrastructure and encryption. It is difficult to think or stay ahead of the cyber-criminal. It can be expected in future that smart equipment's will include privacy security which will help users to perform more tasks conveniently by using IOT. With improved privacy, information protected methods and ethical practices, IoT will gain the trust and faith of users in this connected world.

Marion [25] argues that the Council of Europe's (CoE) Agreement on Cybercrime is studied as representative mechanisms. This research shows that the Agreement includes the features of figurative policy like comforting the users that proper action taken to control cybercrime, educate the users about cybercrime, and act as a warning for those who commit cybercrimes. It leads to the serious consequences in IoT [25]. Crimes related to computers are not bound to any particular nation while it is an international matter. Countries should co-operate and make synchronized laws to have control on cybercrimes. The CEO Treaty is such an important step towards cybercrime control globally. As Cybercrimes scope is very wide hence it is difficult to have proper control on it.

In development of this treaty, representatives from different countries discuss and argue on the acts committed on internet and define the actions that can be taken to fight against cybercrimes [26]. A reliable international method is used to control cybercrimes that include co-operation in law execution agencies and investigating offence. The finding shows that the effectiveness of CEO Treaty is questionable as resolutions made in this treaty are actually figurative like issues related to privacy, powers of investigators and it's kind of difficult to enforce co- operation among countries. There are many loopholes in this treaty that result in criminals to continue commit crimes. To have more effective and efficient treaty it is required that more and more countries sign this treaty and make national laws and keep on updating the laws as per new types of crimes.

Moitra [27], explore in this research that there are various concerns that are very important for the development of policies related to cybercrimes. Various concerns or issues are categorized in 5 questions that are 1. Criminals, 2. Crimes, 3. Occurrence of cybercrime, 4. Effect on victim's and 5. Response of society. It is also discussed in this research that why each concern is important in making policies. Europe Council enrolled its Agreement on Cybercrime in 2001, and various initiatives are launched by European Union to control cybercrime. Standardization and coordination that is necessary for common classification of cybercrime is also discuss in this study. Hacker behavior, victim response, legal activity and criminal justice policies are some of the features that are to be studied thoroughly before making rules and regulations in cyber law. It is necessary to study cybercrime further as new problems may occur in future and new types of cybercrimes may appear, although policies still exist in various countries like in US, Agreement on Cybercrime (EU), Information technology act 2000 but up gradation is needed on timely basis. Finding shows that reliable information is to be collected and evaluated before developing new policies. Suggestions given in this research can help those countries as well which are still on development stage of making policies. This research has some limitations like it is limited to only some salient features and lots of other factors are still left.

Oriwoh et al. [28] introduce some guideline principles for vendors, consumers, governments and law makers who use or work on IoT (Internet of Things). Usually new technologies and new applications of prevailing technologies show future prospects and appropriate uses where it can be used. Security concern importance in development of any technologies in IoT at early stage is acknowledged by various researchers. Laws are already in existence and new laws also provide guidance to the users of IoT and ensure that there should be no fraud or breach in usage of technologies; if it is detected then proper action should be taken to scold the offender [29]. Hence it is important that appropriate principles for guidance should be done to introduce the laws to the interesting users.

Maung and Thwin [30], found that new challenges in forensic of cybercrimes develop with new and latest operating systems. On one side these new versions of Windows make the things easy for users and on the other possibilities of new crimes arise. Cybercrime forensics investigations are not a new arena and, but it is necessary that it keep updated its methods to catch cyber criminals. Computer forensics experts make cybercrime investigations based on Quality, effectiveness, legal obligations and flexibility. Objective of investigation must be customized, expertise, systematic and comprehensive enough that the process of investigation complete in less time and relevant information can be gathered and investigated accordingly[31]. Digital evidence in cybercrime means the digital data that shows crime has committed and there is a relation between victim and crime or criminal and crime.

IT Security is very difficult in this digital world as these exposed to various threats and malware's like viruses, spies, worms and Trojans affect IoT almost on daily basis [32]. This research shows various solutions that can be used systematically to get sound evidence forensically. These solutions help and support in collecting evident information in various forensic areas like cloud, static, and social network [33]. The main objective of this study is to find an appropriate solution for the country, Myanmar.

4.3 Types of Cyber Attacks on IoT Devices

4.3.1 Physical Attacks

Physical attacks can happen when an IoT device is accessed physically. This kind of attack can be performed by the same company employee who has access to the IoT device.

4.3.2 Encryption Attacks

Encryption attack can be done when the IoT device is unencrypted, attacker can sniff the data with the help of an intruder. Encryption attacks strike at the heart of your algorithmic system. Hackers analyze and deduce your encryption keys, to figure out how you create those algorithms. Once the encryption keys are unlocked, cyberassailants can install their own algorithms and take control of your system.

4.3.3 DoS (Denial of Service) Attack

This kind of attack may not steal the data from services like websites [34]. Attackers target service with a large number of botnets sending thousands of requests to the service and making them crash, which makes services unavailable.

4.3.4 Firmware Hijacking

Firmware kind of attacks can be done when an IoT device is not updated up today. Attackers can hijack the device and download malicious software. Computers contain a lot of firmware, all of which is potentially vulnerable to hacking.

4.3.5   Botnet Attack

A Botnet attack is which can be done when an IoT device is turned into remotely controlled bots, which can be used as a part of the botnet. Botnets can connect to the network and transfer the private and sensitive data. Two types of Botnet attacks (a) The Mirai botnet (b) The PBot malware.

4.3.6   Man-In-The-Middle Attack

A man-in-the-middle attack can be done when a hacker breach the communication between two systems. By spying on communication between two parties [35]. There are 7 types of Man-in-the-middle attack (a) IP spoofing (b) DNS spoofing (c) HTTPS spoofing (d) SSL hijacking (e) Email hijacking (f) Wi-Fi eavesdropping (g) Stealing browser cookies.

4.3.7   Ransomware Attack

Ransomware is a type of attacks when a hacker encrypts the data and lock down the access. Then the hacker sells the decryption for his price. This kind of attack will disrupt daily business [36]. Types of Ransomware attack (a) Scareware (b) Screen lockers (c) Encrypting ransomware.

4.3.8   Eavesdropping Attack

Eavesdropping is a kind of attack when a hacker intercepts network traffic to get access to sensitive and private data via a weekend connection between an IoT device and a server [37]. Eavesdropping attack can prevent by using personal firewall, keeping antivirus software updated, and using a virtual private network.

4.3.8.1   Privilege Escalation Attack

In this particular kind of attack the hacker looks for an IoT device bugs to gain access. In this attack, the use their newly gained privileges to deploy malware. Hacker exploits a bug, design flow, or configuration error in an application or operating system to gain elevated access to the resources that should normally be unavailable to the third person.

4.3.8.2 Brute Force Password Attack

In the attack, the hacker uses password hashing or password cracker software's to hit the server with the possible tries. Until the hacker gets the correct credentials. Hacker uses trail-and error method to guess Login credentials, encryption keys, or finding hidden web pages. Types of Brute force attacks: (a) Simple brute force attacks. (b) Dictionary attacks (c) Hybrid brute force attacks (d) Reverse brute force attacks (e) Credential stuffing.

4.4 Smart Home and It's Subsystems

Smart homes are equipped with advanced automated internet connected devices which makes your life much easier like Multimedia kits, Automatic door and window operators, smart home appliances etc., but on the side of the coin, If one of the device of your smart home is vulnerable and unencrypted your data will be on Network like Google dorks, Shodan which the hackers first place to search [38]. The smart home appliances are mostly with three important entities: Physical Components, communication system and intelligent information processing. Which makes the most sophisticated smart home devices.

Adopting IoT Technology into our house will raise more security concerns and challengers, because the IoT based smart home devices are highly vulnerable to attack as compared to other devices [39]. If the Smart home device is attacked and compromised the potential to invade the user's privacy and steal the personal information and can be monitored as well [40] (Fig. 4.4).

4.5 Challenges for the Current Approaches

4.5.1 Testing Drawbacks

Due to insufficient testing and updating of current IoT devices i.e., Approx. 30 billion devices present connected to the internet, which makes the IoT devices vulnerable to cyber-attacks. Some IoT manufacturers offers firmware updates but unfortunately due to lack of automatic updates according to the zeroth day hacks, These Devices exposed to internet and prone by the hackers[41].

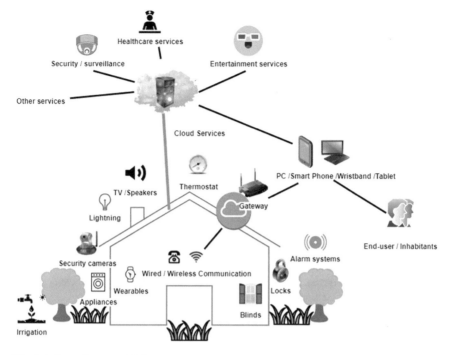

Fig. 4.4 Smart Home and Subsystems

4.5.2 Default Passwords

According to some the government reports that advised to the manufactures against selling the IoT devices with default credentials (admin/password) [42]. Weak passwords and default passwords of IoT devices are identified as the most vulnerable devices with password hacking and brute-forcing.

4.5.3 IoT Ransomware

The ransomware depends on encryption to lock out completely different users with different devices and platforms [43]. The ransomware could potentially protect the device from attack but eventually hacker can seal some personal data with the malware.

4.5.4   IoT AI and Automation:

The amount of data gathered by the sensors and IoT is becoming enormous day by day. AI tools and Automation are already been used in shifting massive information form network to network. However, using this AI tools for make autonomous decisions can affect Millions of functions across infrastructure such as like healthcare, transport etc., [44, 45].

4.5.5   Botnet Attacks

When a hacker creates a collection of malware infected botnet and sends thou- sands of requests per second and brings down the target is called as botnet attack [46]. A single IoT device infected with malicious code or malware may not possess any real threat [47]. When the hacker uses DDOS attacks using thousands of IP cameras, home routers, Smart devices were infected and directed with bringing down the DSN provider platforms like Netflix, GitHub etc., [48].

4.6   Future Directions

Based on our review we have noted that the cybercrimes that targets the IoT ecosystem are increasing day by posing a huge question for security experts, IoT devices manu-factures and academia. With the exponential growth of cybercrimes approaches to mitigate this cyber-attacks are also increasing. Thereby the main intention of this section is to provide readers with a brief understanding of future directions of cyber-crime resolution. Integrating with other enabling technologies will strengthen the ability to fight against cybercrimes. Artificial Intelligence (AI), Machine Learning, Big Data analysis, Blockchain are just a few of the technologies which will further fuel this cybercrime mitigation approaches. Such examples includes predictive threat analysis using AI so before the attack is onset they authorizes have the power to miti-gate it. On the other hand security would be an integral part of IoT manufacturing as device manufactures are highly concern about the security of devices like never before. Due to this robust security schemas we could expect that the damage that brings IoT ecosystem by cybercrimes will be lessen.

4.7   Recommendations for Cyber Hygiene of IoT Devices

Installing updated firmware as soon as possible, where the manufacture released all the patches for the vulnerability's found in previous version of the device [49]. By updating the firmware one can be protected from the attacks by bugs from older versions of the software. It is recommended to change the pre-installed password or manufacture default passwords which makes your device default password attacks. Always reboot the device when you think the device acting strange or when noticed suspicious activity [50]. It might help in getting rid of existing malware. Keeping access to IoT device restricted by a local VPN can be protects from attacks.

4.8   Conclusion

IoT becomes the most important for every human being in this connected world. IoT (internet of things) make the world so small. Every human being is connected with each other by using internet. Lots of transactions are done over IoT and chances of crimes have increases. Crimes in cyber space are not bound to a particular location or country, its scope is very wide [51]. Risks related to Cyber- attacks can't be ignored so while adopting IoT on regular basis it is important to take adequate measures. Simple steps that can be done by users to get safe can be by installing software protection firewall, antiviruses, antimalware etc. Awareness should be spread regarding the types of cybercrimes in IoT and how it can be avoided. Various international treaties are executed to control cybercrimes. Current Multilateral and local legal devices and national laws include different concept and content, and their coverage of criminalizing, investigation powers and methods, digital evidence, risk and regulations, and control and cooperation internationally [39]. These treaties are different in different geographic scope like multilateral or regional and its applicability. These differences cause obstacles in identification, examination and taking action against cybercriminals and taking preventive measures in cybercrime. So, it is concluded that a common, cooperative, and flexible international treaties should be formed between the countries so that the same laws are followed everywhere on IoT and there is no confusion. Strict punishments should be imposed on cyber criminals so that potential criminals left the idea to do any crime. It should ensure that laws formed must be followed properly and restrictions if any applied on internet access and content should not be neglected [52]. These laws should be according to the law and rights of humans [53]. Challenge is generated due to the scope and effect of cyber laws in different countries like the content on the internet is acceptable in one country while the same content is illegal in other countries than it is difficult to make common global laws [54].

References

1. Bhattacharya, S., Kaluri, R., Singh, S., Alazab, M., Tariq, U.: A novel PCA-firefly based XGBoost classification model for Intrusion Detection in Networks using GPU. Electronics **9**(2), 219 (2020)

2. Hathaliya, J.J., Tanwar, S., Tyagi, S., Kumar, N.: Securing electronics healthcare records in healthcare 4.0: a biometric-based approach. Comput. Electr. Eng. **76**, 398–410 (2019)

3. Carruthers, K.: Internet of Things and beyond: cyber-physical systems-IEEE Internet of Things. IEEE IoT. Newslett. **2014** (2016)

4. Tong, J., Sun, W., Wang, L.: An information flow security model forhome area network of smart grid. In: Cyber Technology in Automation, Control and Intelligent Systems (CYBER), 2013 IEEE 3rd Annual International Conference on, pp. 456–461. IEEE, (2013)

5. Maddikunta, P.K.R., Srivastava, G., Gadekallu, T.R., Deepa, N., Boopathy, P.: Predictive model for battery life in IoT networks. IET Intell. Trans. Syst. (2020)

6. Padyab, A.M., Paivarinta, T., Harnesk, D.: Genre-based assessment of information and knowledge security risks. In: System Sciences (HICSS), 2014 47th Hawaii International Conference on, pp. 3442–3451. IEEE (2014)

7. McCune, J.M., Perrig, A., Reiter, M.K.: Seeing-is-believing: using camera phones for human-verifiable authentication. In: Security and Privacy, 2005 IEEE Symposium on, pp. 110–124. IEEE (2005)

8. Ch, R., Gadekallu, T.R., Abidi, M.H., Al-Ahmari, A.: Computational system to classify cybercrime offenses using machine learning. Sustainability **12**(10), 4087 (2020)

9. Krishna Kagita, M., Varalakshmi, M.: A detailed study of security and privacy of Internet of Things (IoT). Int. J. Comput. Sci. Netw. **9**(3), 109–113 (2020)

10. Krishnasamy, L., Dhanaraj, R.K., Ganesh Gopal, D., Reddy Gadekallu, T., Aboudaif, M.K., Abouel Nasr, E.: A heuristic angular clustering framework for secured statistical data aggregation in sensor networks. Sensors **20**(17), 4937 (2020)

11. Yang Lu and Li Da Xu: Internet of Things (IoT) cybersecurity research: a review of current research topics. IEEE IoT. J. **6**(2), 2103–2115 (2019)

12. Alazab, M., Layton, R., Broadhurst, R., Bouhours, B.: Malicious spam emails developments and authorship attribution. In: 2013 4th Cybercrime and Trustworthy Computing Workshop, pp. 58–68. IEEE (2013)

13. Hilt, S.; Kropotov, V.; Merces, F.; Rosario, M., Sancho, D.: The Internet of Things in the cybercrime underground. Trend Micro Res. 1–46 (2017)

14. Venckauskas, A., Damasevicius, R., Jusas, V., Toldinas, J., Rudzika, D., Dregvaite, G.: A review of cybercrime in Internet Of Things: technologies, investigation methods and digital forensics. Int. J. Eng. Sci. Res. Technol. Venckauskas **4**(10):460–477 (2015)

15. Azab, A., Layton, R., Alazab, M., Oliver, J.: Mining malware to detect variants. In: 2014 5th Cybercrime and Trustworthy Computing Conference, pp. 44–53. IEEE, (2014)

16. Madakam, S., Ramaswamy, R., Tripathi, S.: Internet of Things (IoT): a literature review. J. Comput. Commun. **3**(05), 164 (2015)

17. Iwendi, C., Jalil, Z., Javed, A.R., Reddy, T., Kaluri, R., Srivastava, G., Jo, O.: KeySplitWatermark: zero watermarking algorithm for software protection against cyber-attacks. IEEE Access **8**, 72650–72660 (2020)

18. Abomhara, M., Koien, G.M.: Cyber security and the internet of things: vulnerabilities threats, intruders and attacks. Journal of Cyber Security **4**, 65–88 (2015)

19. RM, S.P., Maddikunta, P.K.R., Parimala, M., Koppu, S., Reddy, T., Chowdhary, C.L., Alazab, M.: An effective feature engineering for DNN using hybrid PCA-GWO for intrusion detection in IoMT architecture. Comput. Commun. (2020)

20. Iqbal, J., Beigh, B.M.: Cybercrime in India: trends and challenges. Int. J. Innov. Adv. Comput. Sci. **6**(12), 187–196 (2017)

21. Bali, R.S., Kumar, N.: Secure clustering for efficient data dissemination in vehicular cyber–physical systems. Futur. Gener. Comput. Syst. **56**, 476–492 (2016)

22. Sarmah, A., Sarmah, R., Baruah, A.J.: A brief study on cyber crime and cyber law's of India. Int. Res. J. Eng. Technol. **04**(06), 1633–1641 (2017)

23. Anisha, M.S.: Awareness and strategy to prevent cybercrimes: an Indian perspective. Indian J. Appl. Res. **7**(4), 114–116 (2017)

24. Husamuddin, M., Qayyum, M.: Internet of Things: a study on security and privacy threats. In: The 2nd International Conference on Anti-Cyber Crimes (ICACC) Organized by IEEE (2017)

25. Marion, N.E.: The council of Europe's cyber crime treaty: an exercise in symbolic legislation. Int. J. Cyber Criminol. **4**(12), 699–712 (2010)
26. Numan, M., Subhan, F., Khan, W. Z., Hakak, S., Haider, S., Reddy, G. T., ... Alazab, M.: A systematic review on clone node detection in static wireless sensor networks. IEEE Access, **8**, 65450–65461 (2020)
27. Moitra, S.: Developing policies for cybercrime. Euro. J. Crime Crim. Law Crim. Justice **13**(3), 435–464 (2005)
28. Oriwoh, E., Sant, P., Epiphaniou, G.: Guidelines for Internet of Things deployment approaches—the thing commandments. In: The 4th International Conference on Emerging Ubiquitous Systems and Pervasive Networks, pp. 122–131 (2013)
29. Singh, A., Maheshwari, M., Kumar, N.: Security and trust management in MANET. In: International Conference on Advances in Information Technology and Mobile Communication, pp. 384–387. Springer, Berlin, Heidelberg (2011)
30. Maung, T.M., Thwin, M.M.S.: Proposed effective solution for cybercrime investigation in Myanmar. Int. J. Eng. Sci. **6**(1), 01–07 (2017)
31. Garg, S., Singh, A., Batra, S., Kumar, N., Yang, L.T.: UAV-empowered edge computing environment for cyber-threat detection in smart vehicles. IEEE Netw. **32**(3), 42–51 (2018)
32. Alazab, M., Venkatraman, S., Watters, P., Alazab, M.: Information security governance: the art of detecting hidden malware. In: IT Security Governance Innovations: Theory and Research, pp. 293–315. IGI Global (2013)
33. Holmberg, D.G., BACnet wide area network security threat assessment, Technical report, National Institute of Standards and Technology, 2003
34. Wood, D., Stankovic, J.A.: Denial of service in sensor networks. IEEE Comput. **35**(10), 54–62 (2002)
35. Savage, K.: IoT devices are hacking your data amp; stealing your privacy-infographic (2017)
36. Vijay, M.: An updated new security architecture for IoT network based on software-defined networking (SDN). Int. Res. J. Comput. Sci. IRJCS **5**, 77–81 (2018)
37. Reddy, T., RM, S.P., Parimala, M., Chowdhary, C.L., Hakak, S., Khan, W.Z.: A deep neural networks based model for uninterrupted marine environment monitoring. Comput. Commun. (2020)
38. Anthi, E., Williams, L., Slowi nska, M., Theodorakopoulos, G., Burnap, P.: A supervised intrusion detection system for smart home IoT devices. IEEE IoT. J. (2019)
39. Iwendi, C., Maddikunta, P. K. R., Gadekallu, T. R., Lakshmanna, K., Bashir, A. K., Piran, M. J.: A metaheuristic optimization approach for energy efficiency in the IoT networks. Softw. Pract. Exp. (2020)
40. Radanliev, P., De Roure, D.C., Nurse, J.R., Burnap, P., Anthi, E., Ani, U., Maddox, L., Santos, O., Montalvo, R.M.: Cyber risk from IoT technologies in the supply chain—discussion on supply chains decision support system for the digital economy. Oxford, 2019
41. Alazab, M., Huda, S., Abawajy, J., Islam, R., Yearwood, J., Venkatraman, S., Broadhurst, R.: A hybrid wrapper-filter approach for malware detection. J. Netw. **9**(11), 2878–2891 (2014)
42. Chaudhary, R., Kumar, N., Zeadally, S.: Network service chaining in fog and cloud computing for the 5G environment: Data management and security challenges. IEEE Commun. Mag. **55**(11), 114–122 (2017)
43. Patel, H., Singh Rajput, D., Thippa Reddy, G., Iwendi, C., Kashif Bashir, A., Jo, O.: A review on classification of imbalanced data for wireless sensor networks. Int. J. Distrib. Sens. Netw. **16**(4), 1550147720916404 (2020)
44. Deepa, N., Prabadevi, B., Maddikunta, P.K., Gadekallu, T.R., Baker, T., Khan, M.A., Tariq, U.: An AI based intelligent system for healthcare analysis using Ridge Adaline Stochastic gradient descent classifier. J. Supercomput. (2020)
45. Vora, J., Italiya, P., Tanwar, S., Tyagi, S., Kumar, N., Obaidat, M. S., Hsiao, K. F.: Ensuring privacy and security in E-health records. In: 2018 International Conference on Computer, Information and Telecommunication Systems (CITS) (pp. 1–5). IEEE, (2018)
46. Paul, L.: New reaper IoT Botnet Leaves 378 Million IoT devices potentially vulnerable to hacking (2017)

47. Schiefer, M.: Smart home definition and security threats. In: IT Security incident Management IT Forensics (IMF), 2015 Ninth International Conference on, pp. 114–118. IEEE (2015)

48. Azab, A., Alazab, M., Aiash, M.: Machine learning based botnet identification traffic. In: 2016 IEEE Trustcom/BigDataSE/ISPA, pp. 1788–1794. IEEE (2016)

49. Krishna Kagita, M.: Security and privacy issues for business intelligence in a IoT. In: Proceedings of 12th International Conference on Global Security, Safety and Sustainability, ICGS3 2019 [8688023] (2019)

50. Gubbi, J., Buyya, R., Marusic, S., Palaniswami, M.: Internet of things (IoT): a vision, architectural elements, and future directions. Futur. Gener. Comput. Syst. **29**(7), 1645–1660 (2013)

51. Maddikunta, P.K.R., Gadekallu, T.R., Kaluri, R., Srivastava, G., Parizi, R.M., Khan, M.S.: Green communication in IoT networks using a hybrid optimization algorithm. Comput. Commun. (2020)

52. RM, S.P., Bhattacharya, S., Maddikunta, P.K.R., Somayaji, S.R.K., Lakshmanna, K., Kaluri, R., ... Gadekallu, T.R.: Load balancing of energy cloud using wind driven and firefly algorithms in internet of everything. J. Parallel Distrib. Comput. (2020)

53. Farivar, F., Haghighi, M.S., Jolfaei, A., Alazab, M.: Artificial intelligence for detection, estimation, and compensation of malicious attacks in nonlinear cyber-physical systems and industrial IoT. IEEE Trans. Industr. Inf. **16**(4), 2716–2725 (2019)

54. Thilakarathne, N.N., Kagita, M.K., Gadekallu, T.R.: The Role of the Internet of Things in health care: a systematic and comprehensive study. Int. J. Eng. Manage. Res. **10**(4), 145–159 (2020)

Chapter 5
Deep Learning Framework for Anomaly Detection in Iot Enabled Systems

B. Selvakumar, S. Sridhar Raj, S. Vijay Gokul, and B. Lakshmanan

5.1 Introduction

Internet of Things (IoT) is rapidly gaining popularity and emerges as a novel paradigm that prevalent across various application areas. The IoT enables us to connect with other devices that intelligently monitor and exchange the data in modern wireless communication [1]. The IoT systems are widely used in various daily life applications like health care [2–6], intelligent transportation systems [7–9], smart cities, and home [10–14]. With the advancement in data processing power, people are being familiar to work with IoT sensor data to extract useful patterns for prediction tasks. Now, machine learning algorithms are used along with IoT for various applications like disease prediction using Radiation images, interpreting ECG and EEG signals, pattern analysis in genomics data in bioinformatics, and all complex operations which require machine learning techniques [15]. In IoT based system, where they monitor the physical events and communicate the acquired data with remote users through a network-based router or base stations. With rapid growth and demand in the IoT based network system, the IoT enabled devices gets vulnerable and complicated nowadays.

In IoT-based devices, a security breach is a major problem due to the growing complexity of the IoT infrastructure and results in undesirable weakness to IoT

B. Selvakumar (✉) · B. Lakshmanan
Department of Computer Science and Engineering, Mepco Schlenk Engineering College, Sivakasi, Tamilnadu 626005, India
e-mail: selvakumar.b@mepcoeng.ac.in

B. Lakshmanan
e-mail: lakshmanan@mepcoeng.ac.in

S. Sridhar Raj · S. Vijay Gokul
Department of Electronics and Communication Engineering, Mepco Schlenk Engineering College, Sivakasi, Tamilnadu 626005, India

A. Makkar and N. Kumar, *Deep Learning for Security and Privacy Preservation in IoT*,
Signals and Communication Technology,
https://doi.org/10.1007/978-981-16-6186-0_5

99

devices. The transmission of data through the wireless medium is the easiest target for an attack [16] and attacks in IoT-based systems result in devastating effects on IoT sites since IoT systems increases over a larger area.

Therefore, an efficient deep learning model has been studied and the proposed model can categorize anomaly from normal behaviors based on the various types of attacks in the IoT systems.

The key contribution of the deep learning framework is based on.

(a)   To design a deep learning framework for detecting anomalies in IoT based network systems.
(b)   To analyze the various factors that influence the performance of cyber attacks
(c)   To classify different categories of attacks

The book chapter is organized as follows: Section 2 presents recent literature on detecting anomalies in IoT based systems. Section 3 describes the methodologies of our work; Section 4 discusses the dataset description, experimental setup, results, and comparisons with the existing state-of-the-art methods, while Section 5 presents the conclusion and future directions of the method.

5.2   Related Works

Many automatic anomaly detection methods are already developed for preventing attacks in a network system. Nowadays, security in IoT-based network-based systems gets much focus and there is a need for developing efficient and affordable anomaly detection applications for such an environment. From the extensive literature study, there are few studies on deep learning approaches for IoT based network system is presented in this section.

Aloqaily et al. [17] proposed a method named deep belief combined decision tree-based hybrid intrusion detection system for connected vehicles in smart cities environment. The algorithm has been designed in two-step processes: (a) deep belief network for dimensionality reduction (b) decision tree algorithm for classifying the type of intrusion such as Denial of Service (DoS) attacks, User to Root (U2R) attacks, Probing attacks, Remote to Local (R2L) attacks and normal. The authors tested their algorithm on NS3 collected traffic dataset with the NSL-KDD dataset. This algorithm achieved an accuracy of 99%, a detection rate of 99.92%, and reported false-positive rate of 0.96% and 1.53% false-negative rate. Anthi et al. [18] have used a three-layer supervised approach for intrusion detection systems to detect attacks on the IoT network system. The system has three major functionalities (a) categorize the type and profile the normal behavior of the IoT system (b) detects the malicious packets (c) classify the attack types. Their approach was successfully evaluated within a smart home testbed. The supremacy of the approach is evaluated by detecting and classifying 4 network-based attack categories. The achieved F-score of 0.962 for first functionality, 0.90, and 0.98 for second and third functionality respectively. Rahman et al. [19], proposed the use of a combined method called semi-distributed and distributed methods which performs feature extraction and selection and is followed by fog-based analytics. The authors designed the algorithm for monitoring malicious traffic in an IoT based network. In this work, the novel network-based IDS framework will detect various types of attacks in an IoT environment. They used the AWID dataset. This approach achieves a detection accuracy of 97.80% with the lowest CPU time to build the model (73.52 s).

Alhakami et al. [20], a nonparametric Bayesian model for detection of known and unknown intrusions has been discussed. They addressed the classification of intrusion anomaly by designing a mathematical Bayesian model that groups the network traffic behaviors into multi-classes. The model was tested on KDD Cup'99,Kyoto 2006+, and the ISCX dataset. Selvakumar et al. [40] proposed an NIDS based on the mutual information based firefly algorithm to select appropriate features for detecting attacks on network and evaluated the effectieveness using Decision Tree and Bayesian Networks. Elsaeidy et al. [21] used Restricted Boltzmann machines for intrusion detection in a smart city environment. They used a dataset related to the Smart water distribution system and achieved an F-score value of 0.9. In Li et al. [22], the authors reviewed the deep migration learning model for the intrusion detection system. The algorithm learns with a deep migration model for an intelligently-based model, which merges intrusion detection technology with a deep learning model. The algorithm was tested on KDD CUP 99 dataset. The authors concluded that their method has a higher detection rate with a shorter detection time.

Tekouabou et al. [23] used an integrated system composed of IoT and an ensemble predictive model for checking parking space availability in smart parking. They tested on Birmingham parking data set and achieved improved performance over 6.6% compared to other state-of-the-art techniques and also reduce the system complexity. In the method proposed by Shafiq et al. [24], IoT network for attacks identification was done by the bijective soft set approach used for selection of effective machine learning (ML) algorithm from a set of ML algorithm. They used the BoT-IoT dataset and 44 effective features selected from the entire dataset. They concluded that their approach is effective compared to other methods. Mishra et al. [25] introduced a cloud-based intelligent system for improving human life quality in smart cities. The system will alert and send a warning to remember and recall day-to-day activities in daily life. The authors suggested that new approaches need to be designed for the security of the IoT based system. Li et al. [26], presented a method to describe the activity pattern of private vehicles and also describe the framework for location-based urban vehicle network (LUV) for collecting local IoT information. The model also reduces the data collection costs in the IoT environment.

Alrashdi et al. [27] used a random forest algorithm for anomaly detection for IoT systems. The model shows the effective detection of anomalies in a distributed fog environment. Their approach tested on a modern dataset and shows a classification accuracy of 99.34%. Hasan et al. [28] reviewed various machine learning models and compare their performance on prediction of attacks and abnormal behavior on IoT based network systems. The authors used machine learning models such as Support Vector Machine (SVM), Decision Tree learning algorithm (DT), Random Forest method (RF), Logistic Regression algorithm (LR), and Artificial Neural Network

(ANN) for experimental purpose. Their approach achieved 99.4% accuracy for DT, ANN, and RF methods. The authors suggested that RF performs comparatively better than other machine learning algorithms.

In Pajouh et al. [29], a two-layer dimension reduction and a two-tier classification framework for intrusion detection have been discussed. The framework was designed to detect malicious activities in the network environment. The authors used naive Bayes for the classification module and k-Nearest Neighbor to identify abnormal behaviours. They used the NSL-KDD dataset for their model evaluation. The authors concluded that their approach outperforms other methods in detecting U2R (User to Root) and R2L (Remote to Local) attacks. Deng et al. [30], proposed an intrusion detection method combined with principal component analysis (PCA) and Fuzzy C-means (FCM) clustering algorithm. The authors discussed the various security issues of IoT, security features, security architecture, and followed by key management. They used the KDD-CUP99dataset and the method shows improved detection accuracy with less false positive rate. In Liu et al. [31], presented the model which constitute three major functionalities (a) Trust estimation, (b) Trust aware routing, and (c) Light probe routing. Their approach identifies the malicious nodes accurately and reduces the error rate. The authors concluded that their model works effectively compared to other methods.

5.3 Materials and Methods

5.3.1 Data Set Description

The experiment is carried out on Bot-IoT, which consists of various types of attacks like DoS, DDoS, OS and Service scan, Keylogging, and Data exfiltration attacks and also incorporates simulated and legitimate IoT network traffic data. The dataset consists of normal/ benign network traffic data for smart home configuration. In this configuration setup, they considered five IoT devices namely Smart Refrigerator, Weather Monitoring System,Smart Garage door, Smart Lights, and Smart thermostat. BoT-IoT (UNSW-NB15) dataset [32] consists of total records of 73,360,900 (includes all types of attacks such as Service scanning, OS Fingerprinting, DDoS, DoS, Keylogging, Data theft) in which 5 percent data taken with 10 important features selected using Correlation Coefficientand Joint Entropy and selected features are srate, drate, rate, max, state number, mean, min, stddev, gs number, seq. For experimental purposes, they provideda training dataset with 1,048,575 records and a testing dataset with 733705 records.

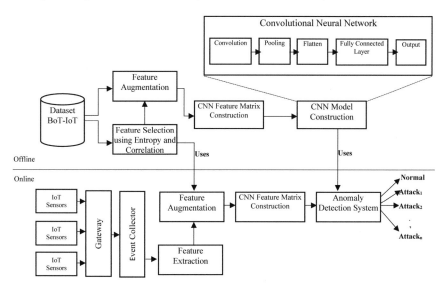

Fig. 5.1 Block diagram for a proposed deep learning-based anomaly detection system

5.3.2 Deep Learning Framework for Securing IoT Based Network System

Machine learning techniques are generally used for various applications to good accurate results. The learning is broadly classified into supervised learning and unsupervised learning. Here, in supervised learning, the algorithm process the input data with a class label. Whereas, in unsupervised learning, it processes data without class labels. In this work, we used a deep neural network which gains popularity recently for its good performance and is trained in end-to-end fashion in a supervised manner. The most popular deep learning architectures are convolutional neural networks (CNN) and it's variant LeNet-5.

The block diagram for proposed deep learning-based anomaly detection in the IoT environment is shown in Fig. 5.1. In the proposed system, the anomaly detection model is constructed using CNN. Input to the CNN is a feature matrix which is constructed from the augmented features of BoT-IoT data.

The following section discusses the deep learning framework used for detecting anomalies in IoT network systems.

5.3.2.1 Feature Augmentation and Feature Matrix Construction:

LeNet-5 CNN architecture requires an input matrix size of 32×32. In order to increase the size of the existing feature set, we perform augmentation by replicating original features. The augmented features are converted into feature matrix and it is fed as input to CNN model construction.

5.3.2.2 Convolutional Neural Network (CNNs)

The deep learning approaches are widely applied in intrusion detection system to detect the anomalies in IoT enabled systems [33–37].

CNN is a multi-layer feed-forward neural network that mimics the functionality of the human nervous system and it is introduced by LeCun et al. [38]. CNN network is widely used in various applications like image classification, object detection, face recognition. Deep neural networks integrate all levels of features such as low/medium and high-level features [39] and network training is performed in an end-to-end multilayer stacked fashion. The objective of CNN is to extract high-level features such as edges and corners from the given input image. The level of features gets enriched when we go deeper and the network is trained to identify the complex features such as shapes, faces, and digits, etc., In CNN, it processes the input image as tensors, where tensors are matrices of numbers with additional dimensions.

CNN is consists of two main components: (a) Feature learning and (b) Classification.

In general, CNN perform four main operations:

1. Convolution operation layer
2. Pooling layer
3. Activation function
4. Fully connected layer

Convolution Operation Layer

The main function of convolution is to extract the features from the input data. The layer applies a set of kernel filters on the input data to produce a "feature map" or "convolved feature". Final output of the layer can be obtained by stacking all the resultant convolved feature together.

Let deep convolutional network is denoted by 'g' and that has stacked order of 'l' layers ie., $(g_1, g_2, g_3 ..... g_l)$ that feed to the input data vector 'v' to an output vector 'o'.

Mathematically we can represented by Eq. 5.1:

$$o = g(v; h_1, h_2, \ldots h_l)$$
$$= g_1(.; v_1) \circ g_2(.; v_2) \ldots g_l(.; v_l) \qquad (5.1)$$

where 'h_l'represents network bias and weights vector for the layer 'l'. For a given training set 'N' which has input and output pairs, we can obtain parameters $h_1 \ldots h_l$ by solving numerical optimization problem and it can be performed by methods like backpropagation and stochastic gradient descent technique.

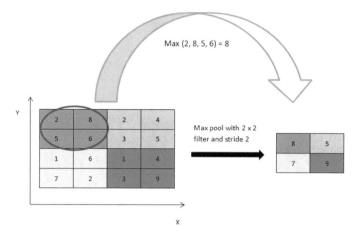

Fig. 5.2 Max pooling operation

Pooling Layer

This layer is sometimes called as subsampling layer, where dimensionality of the feature maps gets reduced. The most common methods used in pooling is (1) Average pooling and (2) Max pooling. Figure 5.2 shows max pooling operation by considering 2 × 2 filter size. The operation is performed by taking the largest element from the feature map within that window size.

Activation Function:

Activation function is helps to determine the output of the neural network ie., True or false. The resulting output value is mapped between the range of 0 to 1, −1 to 1 and so on.

In general, activation function is divided into two types:
(1) Linear activation function and (2) Non-linear activation function.

In our work, we used non-linear activation function called ReLU (Rectified Linear Unit).ReLU performs non-linear opearation and it is mathematically represented by Eq. 5.2:

$$f(x) = \max(zero, x) \tag{5.2}$$

Fully Connected Layer

It takes the output of the previous layers in the network, and this layer produces a single vector that can be an input for the next layer. Fully connected layer uses

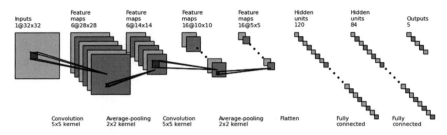

Fig. 5.3 Architecture of LeNet-5 CNN model

Table 5.1 Parameters used in LeNet-5 CNN model

Layer	Feature map	Size	Kernel size	Stride	Activation
Input image	1	32×32	–	–	–
Convolution-1	6	28×28	5	1	tanh
Average Pooling-1	6	14×14	2	2	tanh
Convolution-2	16	10×10	5	1	tanh
Average Pooling-2	16	5×5	2	2	tanh
FC–1	–	120	–	–	tanh
FC–2	–	84	–	–	tanh
FC–3	–	5	–	–	Softmax

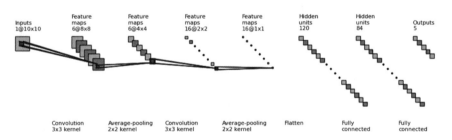

Fig. 5.4 Architecture of CNN-10 model

softmax function in the output layer. It also uses other classifier such as support vector machine, random forest, linear discriminant analysis etc.

Model construction using LeNet-5 CNN architecture:

LeNet-5 model is considered as one of the best performing frameworks for classification in various applications. The architecture of LeNet-5 is shown in Fig. 5.3. The architecture details are elaborately discussed in [38]. The model parameters are tabulated in Table 5.1.

Model construction using CNN-10 architecture:

In this model, the Input size of 10 X 10 feature matrix is constructed and fed into the CNN model for anomaly detection in IoT enabled system and it is depicted as

Table 5.2 Parameters used in CNN-10 model

Layer	Feature map	Size	Kernel size	Stride	Activation
Input image	1	10×10	–	–	–
Convolution-1	6	8×8	3	1	tanh
Max Pooling-1	6	4×4	2	2	tanh
Convolution-2	16	2×2	3	1	tanh
Max Pooling-2	16	1×1	2	2	tanh
FC–1	–	120	–	–	tanh
FC–2	–	84	–	–	tanh
FC–3	–	5	–	–	Softmax

shown in Fig. 5.4. The model parameters for CNN-10 architecture are given in Table 5.2.

5.4   Results and Discussions

To study the effectiveness of the proposed model for anomaly detection, we used evaluation criteria like precision (P), detection rate (DR), and F1 measure (F1). Both deep neural networks are performing well for DDoS, DoS, and Reconnaissance attacks. But still,there is scope to improve detecting information theft attack, since data instances for that category is very low which results in poor detection. Table 5.3 shows the performance of CNN-10 and Lenet-5 on the BoT-IoT dataset. A comparison of the deep learning framework is shown in Fig. 5.5.

The overall accuracy of the deep learning models for BoT-IoT is depicted in Fig. 5.6. It shows that LeNet-5 performs comparatively better than CNN-10.

5.5   Conclusion

This proposed work presented the problems associated with the security attacks in IoT enabled network systems. We made use of the deep learning models using CNN-10 and LeNet-5 and compared them for effectiveness. The performance metrics like accuracy, detection rate, precision, and F1-measure are considered, and the experiments were conducted on the BoT-IoT data set. The adaptation of deep learning methods for classifying the anomalies in the IoT environment is explored and shows-better results. In the future, various optimization techniques can be used for feature selection and class weight enabled CNN models can be designed to improve the detection rate of attacks with very smaller attack records.

Table 5.3 Performance of deep learning models on BoT-IoT dataset

Techniques / Attacks	DDoS			DoS			Normal			Reconnaissance			Theft		
	DR	P	F1	DR	P	F1	DR	P	F1	DR	P	F1	DR	P	F1
CNN10*	0.95	0.98	0.96	0.98	0.94	0.96	0.22	0.63	0.33	0.91	0.82	0.87	0.0	0.0	0.0
LeNet-5	0.95	0.98	0.97	0.98	0.95	0.96	0.04	0.40	0.07	0.96	0.82	0.88	0.0	0.0	0.0

* CNN10 – custom-designed CNN network with 10 * 10 feature matrix

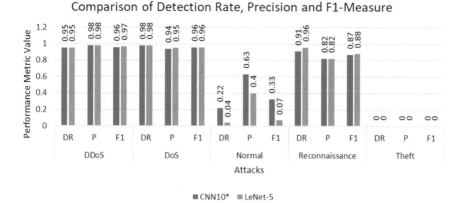

Fig. 5.5 Comparison of evaluation metrics for CNN-10 and LeNet-5 on BoT-IoT dataset

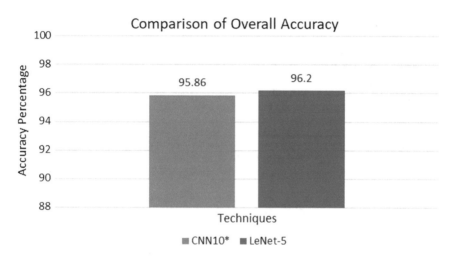

Fig. 5.6 Comparison of the overall accuracy of CNN-10 and LeNet-5

References

1. Atzori, L., Iera, A., Morabito, G.: The Internet of Things: a survey. Comput. Netw. (2010). https://doi.org/10.1016/j.comnet.2010.05.010
2. Rohokale, V.M., Prasad, N.R., Prasad, R.: A cooperativeinternet of things (IoT) for rural health-care monitoring andcontrol. In: Proceedings of the 2011 2nd International ConferenceonWireless Communication, Vehicular Technology, InformationTheory, and Aerospace& Electronic Systems Technology (WirelessVITAE), pp. 1–6, IEEE (2011)
3. Fan, Y.J., Yin, Y.H., Xu, L.D., Zeng, Y., Wu, F.: IoT-basedsmart rehabilitation system. IEEE Trans. Industrial Informatics **10**(2), 1568–1577 (2014)
4. Farahani, B., Firouzi, F., Chang, V., Badaroglu, M., Constant, N., Mankodiya, K.: Towards fog-driven IoT eHealth: promises and challenges of IoT in medicine and healthcare. Future Generation Comput. Syst. (2017)

5. Catarinucci, L., de Donno, D., Mainetti, L., et al.: An IoT-awarearchitecture for smart healthcare systems. IEEE Internet Things J. **2**(6), 515–526 (2015)
6. Riazul Islam, S.M., Kwak, D., Humaun Kabir, M., Hossain, M., Kwak, K.-S.: The internet of things for health care: acomprehensive survey. IEEE Access **3**, 678–708 (2015)
7. Yang, Z., Wang, X., Sun, H.: Study on urban its architecture based on the internet of things. In: LTLGB 2012, pp. 139–143, Springer (2013)
8. Ibá̄nez, J.A.G., Zeadally, S., Contreras-Castillo, J.: Integrationchallenges of intelligent transportation systems withthe connected vehicle, cloud computing, and Internet of Thingstechnologies. IEEEWireless Commun. Mag. **22**(6), 122–128 (2015)
9. Siegel, J.E., Erb, D.C., Sarma, S.E.: A survey of the connectedvehicle landscape–architectures, enabling technologies,applications, and development areas. IEEE Trans. Intelligent Transp. Syst. (2017)
10. Li, B., Yu, J.: Research and application on the smart homebased on component technologies and internet of things. Proc. Eng. **15**, 2087–2092 (2011)
11. Kelly, S.D.T., Suryadevara, N.K., Mukhopadhyay, S.C.: Towards the implementation of IoT for environmental conditionmonitoring in homes. IEEE Sens. J. **13**(10), 3846–3853 (2013)
12. Zanella, N., Bui, A.P., Castellani, L., Vangelista, Zorzi, M.: Internet of things for smart cities. IEEE Internet Things J **1**(1), 22–32 (2014)
13. Tsai, K.-L., Leu, F.-Y., You, I.: Residence energy control systembased on wireless smart socket and IoT. IEEE Access **4**, 2885–2894 (2016)
14. Sotres, P., Santana, J.R., Sanchez, L., Lanza, J., Munoz, L.: Practical lessons from the deployment and management ofa smart city internet-of-things infrastructure: the smartsantandertestbed case. IEEE Access **5**, 14309–14322 (2017)
15. Deo, R.C.: Machine learning in medicine. Circulation **132**(20), 1920–1930 (2015)
16. Liu, X., Liu, Y., Liu, A., Yang, L.T.: Defending on–offattacks using light probing messages in smart sensors for industrial communication systems. IEEE Trans. Ind. Inf. **14**(9), 3801–3811 (2018)
17. Aloqaily, M., Otoum, S., Al Ridhawi, I., Jararweh, Y.: An intrusion detection system for connected vehicles in smart cities. Ad Hoc Netw. **90**, 101842 (2019)
18. Anthi, E.,Williams, L., Slowinska, M., Theodorakopoulos, G., Burnap, P.: A supervised intrusion detection system for smart home IoT devices. IEEE Internet Things J. 9042–9053 (2019)
19. Rahman, M.A., Asyhari, A.T., Leong, L.S., Satrya, G.B., Hai Tao, M., Zolkipli, M.F.: Scalable machine learning-based intrusion detection system for IoT-enabled smart cities. Sustain. Cities Soc. **61**, 102324 (2020)
20. Alhakami, W., ALharbi, A., Bourouis, S., Alroobaea, R., Bouguila, N.: Network anomaly intrusion detection using a nonparametric Bayesian approach and feature selection. IEEE Access. **7**, 52181–52190 (2019)
21. Elsaeidy, A., Munasinghe, K.S., Sharma, D., Jamalipour, A.: Intrusion detection in smart cities using Restricted Boltzmann Machines. J. Netw. Comput. Appl. **135**, 76–83 (2019)
22. Li, D., Deng, L., Lee, M.,Wang, H.: IoT data feature extraction and intrusion detection systemfor smart cities based on deep migration learning. Int. J. Inf. Manage. **49**, 533–545 (2019)
23. Koumetio Tekouabou, S.C., AbdellaouiAlaoui, E.A., Cherif, W., Silkan, H.: Improving parking availability prediction in smart cities with IoT and ensemble-based model. J. King Saud. Univ. Comput. Inf. Sci. (2020). https://doi.org/10.1016/j.jksuci.2020.01.008
24. Shafiq, M., Tian, Z., Sun, Y., Du, X., Guizani, M.: Selection of effective machine learning algorithm and Bot-IoT attacks traffic identification for internet of things in smart city. Future Gener. Comput. Syst. **107**, 433–442 (2020)
25. Mishra, K.N., Chakraborty, C.: A novel approach toward enhancing the quality of life in smart cities using clouds and IoT-based technologies, pp. 19–35 (2020)
26. Li, H., Liu, Y., Qin, Z., Rong, H., Liu, Q.: A large-scale urban vehicular network framework for IoT in smart cities. IEEE Access **7**, 74437–74449 (2019)
27. Alrashdi, I., Alqazzaz, A., Aloufi, E., Alharthi, R., Zohdy, M., Ming, H.: AD-IoT: anomaly detection of IoT cyberattacks in smart city using machine learning. Paper presented at: 2019

IEEE 9th Annual Computing and Communication Workshop and Conference (CCWC), 0305–0310 (2019)

28. Hasan, M., Islam, M.M., Zarif, M.I.I., Hashem, M.M.A.: Attack and anomaly detection in IoT sensors in IoT sites using machine learning approaches. Internet of Things **7**, 100059 (2019)

29. Pajouh, H.H., Javidan, R., Khayami, R., Dehghantanha, A., Choo, K.-K.R.: A two-layer dimension reduction and two-tier classification model for anomaly-based intrusion detection in IoT backbone networks. IEEE Trans. Emerg. Top Comput. **7**(2), 314–323 (2019)

30. Deng, L., Li, D., Yao, X., Cox, D., Wang, H.: Mobile network intrusion detection for IoT system based on transfer learning algorithm. Cluster Comput. **22**(S4), 9889–9904 (2019)

31. Liu, X., Liu, Y., Liu, A., Yang, L.T.: Defending ON-OFF attacks using light probing messages in smart sensors for industrial communication systems. IEEE Trans. Ind. Informatics **14**(9), 3801–3811 (2018)

32. Koroniotis, N., Moustafa, N., Sitnikova, E., Turnbull, B.: Towards the development of realistic botnet dataset in the Internet of Things for network forensic analytics: Bot-IoT dataset. Futur. Gener. Comput. Syst. (2019). https://doi.org/10.1016/j.future.2019.05.041

33. Vinayakumar, R., Alazab, M., Soman, K.P., Poornachandran, P., Al-Nemrat, A., Venkatraman, S.: Deep learning approach for intelligent intrusion detection system. IEEE Access (2019). https://doi.org/10.1109/ACCESS.2019.2895334

34. Gamage, S., Samarabandu, J.: Deep learning methods in network intrusion detection: a survey and an objective comparison. J. Netw. Comput. Appl. (2020). https://doi.org/10.1016/j.jnca.2020.102767

35. Bu, S.J., Cho, S.B.: A convolutional neural-based learning classifier system for detecting database intrusion via insider attack. Inf. Sci. (Ny) (2020). https://doi.org/10.1016/j.ins.2019.09.055

36. Nguyen, M.T., Kim, K.: Genetic convolutional neural network for intrusion detection systems. Futur. Gener. Comput. Syst. (2020). https://doi.org/10.1016/j.future.2020.07.042

37. Bhuvaneswari Amma, N.G., Selvakumar, S.: Anomaly detection framework for Internet of things traffic using vector convolutional deep learning approach in fog environment. Futur. Gener. Comput. Syst. (2020). https://doi.org/10.1016/j.future.2020.07.020

38. LeCun, Y., Bottou, L., Bengio, Y., Haffner, P.: Gradient-based learning applied to document recognition. Proc. IEEE (1998). https://doi.org/10.1109/5.726791

39. Zeiler, M.D., Fergus, R.: Visualizing and understanding convolutional neural networks. In: ECCV (2014)

40. Selvakumar, B., Muneeswaran, K.: Firefly algorithm based feature selection for network intrusion detection. Comput. Security 81 (2019). https://doi.org/10.1016/j.cose.2018.11.005

Chapter 6
Anomaly Detection Using Unsupervised Machine Learning Algorithms

Pavitra Kadiyala, K.V. Shanmukhasai, Sai Shashank Budem, and Praveen Kumar Reddy Maddikunta

6.1 Introduction

Anomalies are values that deviate from the expected ones. Depending on the deviation, the amount of loss or harm caused varies [1]. They are a risk to other machines or humans and also lead to loss of money [2]. If one machine stops due to any sensor anomaly, the other connected to it might be affected as well [3]. As a result, they pose a huge risk to the security of a company. Machine Learning is learning the data and predicting the future. Hence we are going to model some parameters and predict the possibility of anomalies [4].

Anomaly discovery is something like how our human minds are continually attempting to perceive something strange or out of the normal or ordinary or the standard stuff [5]. Anomaly detection is the distinguishing proof of information focuses, things, perceptions, or functions that don't adjust to the normal example of a given gathering. These anomalies happen rarely yet may signify an enormous and critical danger [6]. Anomaly recognition is vigorously utilized in conducting investigation and different types of examination to help in finding out about the discovery, distinguishing proof, and forecast of the event of these abnormalities.

In Machine Learning, Anomaly detection is any cycle that finds the exceptions of a dataset, those things that don't have a place with the dataset [7–9]. These peculiarities may highlight uncommon organization traffic, reveal a sensor acting up or not working, or distinguish information for cleaning before investigation [10–12]. Machine Learning is mainly of 3 types. Supervised and Unsupervised and Reinforcement Learning. Supervised learning is where we have the labeled data but in Unsupervised, the data is not labeled [13–15]. For anomaly detection, both methods

---

Vellore Institute of Technology and Engineering.

P. Kadiyala · K. V. Shanmukhasai · S. S. Budem · P. K. R. Maddikunta (✉)
Vellore Institute of Technology and Engineering, Vellore, Tamilnadu, India
e-mail: praveenkumarreddy@vit.ac.in

© The Author(s), under exclusive license to Springer Nature Singapore Pte Ltd. 2021   113
A. Makkar and N. Kumar, *Deep Learning for Security and Privacy Preservation in IoT*,
Signals and Communication Technology,
https://doi.org/10.1007/978-981-16-6186-0_6

can be used. We can use algorithms like SVM(Support Vector Machine) and KNN (K Nearest Neighbour Classifier) in Supervised and in Unsupervised we can use Statistical and Neural Network models [16–18].

An anomaly can be of different types. A few of them include Data cleaning, Intrusion detection, Fraud detection, Systems health monitoring, detection in sensor networks and machines, Ecosystem disturbances [16, 19, 20].

We mainly focus on anomaly detection in Machines. We use the unsupervised data methods to determine if there is an anomaly. This prediction mainly depends on three factors for a machine.

1. The number of cycles: This is the time/duration of usage of the machine engine. This tells us how old the machine is and the chances of the machine stopping might increase with time.
2. Setting Details: Basic Setting details of the engines of the machine.
3. Sensor details: The sensor details of all the sensors present in the machine are a very important factor for anomaly detection. Even if one value deviates from the ideal value, it is a threat to the machine.

A few of the existing methods for anomaly detection are:

1. Use of KVM(Kernel-based Virtual Machine): Multiple Virtual Machines can be run in this and the data can be analyzed. But the drawback here is that only 3 Virtual Machines can be run at a time and the power and money required are more.
2. Manual Checking and Detection: Checking the readings and comparing them with the actual values. This is very tedious and time-consuming.

Machine Learning helps us analyze large data easily and can be adjusted from time to time and hence helps in determining the anomaly in a faster way [21, 22]. We propose the use of Autoencoder Neural Network and Principal Component Analysis for anomaly detection and condition monitoring of the machines. We have the inputs as engine number, cycle number, setting details, and sensor details. We predict if there is any anomaly based on calculating the threshold and comparing the values with the threshold. The method of calculating the threshold varies from model to model. The rest of the paper is organized as follows, Sect. 6.2 covers Literature Survey, Sect. 6.3 presents Proposed architecture, Sect. 6.4 explains the results and discussion, followed by conclusion in Sect. 6.5.

6.2   Literature Survey

In [23], to move toward the difficulties securing the IoT devices, they proposed utilizing machine learning inside an IoT gateway to help secure the framework. They performed research utilizing Artificial Neural Networks as a gateway to recognizing anomalies in the information sent from the machines. They are persuaded that this methodology can improve the security of IoT frameworks. They trained the neural network based on the training dataset and then tested it on the test dataset. The model was able to predict if there is an anomaly or not.

In [24], summarizes the work of a decade in smart manufacturing to evaluate the measure of efforts being put towards propelling ML in manufacturing. As there is an increase in the use of IoT, a lot of data was generated. This work distinguishes both prominent areas of ML use and well-known algorithms. This additionally permitted them to feature any gaps or areas where ML could be used for a crucial job. They incorporated NLP techniques to sort the vast data of reports and key areas of research. The result of this paper is the introduction of current center areas and gaps in ML applications to the assembling business, with specific accentuation on cross-area information usage. A full enumerating of techniques and discoveries is introduced. They concluded that algorithms such as SVM's and Neural Networks will work efficiently with low investment.

In [25], they propose an algorithm for the security of IoT Devices. They have used Neural Network and EI Gamal for this algorithm. Their model mainly focuses on Neural Networks and the Encryption model. This is less time-consuming but has not been implemented.

In [26], a few machine learning models have been contrasted with anticipate anomalies on the IoT frameworks precisely. The machine learning (ML) calculations that have been utilized here are Logistic Regression (LR), Support Vector Machine (SVM), Decision Tree (DT), Random Forest (RF), and Artificial Neural Network (ANN). They compared the performances of these machines and the system had got the same accuracies for 3 models namely decision tree, random forest, and ann. But due to other features such as precision, recall, and the f1 score, they predicted that the random forest classifiers were better than the rest. But the dataset they used was supervised machine learning and hence the model would have been trained on the output beforehand.

In [27], they utilize stacked LSTM networks for anomaly identification in time arrangement. A network is prepared on non-anomalous information and utilized as an indicator over various time steps. The subsequent forecast mistakes are demonstrated as multivariate Gaussian dissemination, which is utilized to survey the probability of peculiar conduct. The viability of this methodology is shown on four datasets: ECG, space transport, power interest, and multi-sensor motor dataset.

In [28], the execution of programming modules and tuning formal models and rules to test situations of anomalies in physical conditions are given. This incorporates programming with profound learning limits and intelligent UIs. Then the transfer of modules into modern settings, first assessments, and business displaying has additionally been given and an overview of anomalies detection in different domains such as robots and steel has been given.

In [29], they efficiently audit the security prerequisites, attack vectors, and the current security answers for the IoT networks. They at that point shed light on the gaps in these security arrangements that call for ML and DL approaches. They likewise examine in detail the current ML and DL answers for tending to various security issues in IoT networks. Finally, keeping in view the current arrangements, they examine the future exploration bearings for ML-and DL-based IoT security. They examine multiple algorithms and their uses for IoT security.

Keeping in mind the advantages of the LSTM model [27] and Neural Networks we propose the use of LSTM-Autoencoder Neural Network and PCA for condition monitoring and anomaly detection prediction.

6.3 Preliminaries and Proposed Architecture

We have used two Machine Learning Algorithms for anomaly detection. They are Autoencoder Neural Network and Principal Component Analysis. The data set we used was from the NASA Turbofan Jet Engine dataset. The training data set consists of multiple multivariate time series with machine-cycle as the time unit, together with 21 sensor readings for each cycle and a few setting details for each. Each cycle is being generated by diff engines. In the dataset, it is assumed that at the initial stage the engine works properly and degrades over time. The degrading of the parts advances and increases in magnitude. At the point when a predefined limit is reached, at that point the motor is viewed as dangerous for additional activity. The last cycle in each time arrangement can be considered as the failure or the final point of the corresponding motor. The testing information has a similar information pattern as the training information. The solitary contrast is that the information doesn't show when the failure happens (at the end of the day, the last time doesn't address the failure or breaking point). It isn't shown the number of more cycles this motor can last before it falls flat. Hence this is Unsupervised data as the output is not known.

Figures 6.1 and 6.2 are the snippet of the dataset. The algorithms we used are Autoencoder Neural Network and Principal Component Algorithm. We first import the required libraries and preprocess the data. In preprocessing we understand the data and we normalize the data. Once we preprocess the data we can apply the required algorithm for anomaly detection.

Shape of Train dataset: (20631, 26)

	id	Machine_Cycle	setting1	setting2	setting3	s1	s2	s3	s4	s5	...	s12	s13	s14	s15	s16	s17	s18	s19
0	1	1	-0.0007	-0.0004	100.0	518.67	641.82	1589.70	1400.60	14.62	...	521.66	2388.02	8138.62	8.4195	0.03	392	2388	100.0
1	1	2	0.0019	-0.0003	100.0	518.67	642.15	1591.82	1403.14	14.62	...	522.28	2388.07	8131.49	8.4318	0.03	392	2388	100.0
2	1	3	-0.0043	0.0003	100.0	518.67	642.35	1587.99	1404.20	14.62	...	522.42	2388.03	8133.23	8.4178	0.03	390	2388	100.0
3	1	4	0.0007	0.0000	100.0	518.67	642.35	1582.79	1401.87	14.62	...	522.86	2388.08	8133.83	8.3682	0.03	392	2388	100.0
4	1	5	-0.0019	-0.0002	100.0	518.67	642.37	1582.85	1406.22	14.62	...	522.19	2388.04	8133.80	8.4294	0.03	393	2388	100.0

5 rows × 26 columns

Fig. 6.1 Snippet of train dataset

Shape of Test dataset: (13096, 26)

	0	1	2	3	4	5	6	7	8	9	...	16	17	18	19	20	21	22	23	24	25
0	1	1	0.0023	0.0003	100.0	518.67	643.02	1585.29	1398.21	14.62	...	521.72	2388.03	8125.55	8.4052	0.03	392	2388	100.0	38.86	23.3735
1	1	2	-0.0027	-0.0003	100.0	518.67	641.71	1588.45	1395.42	14.62	...	522.16	2388.06	8139.62	8.3803	0.03	393	2388	100.0	39.02	23.3916
2	1	3	0.0003	0.0001	100.0	518.67	642.46	1586.94	1401.34	14.62	...	521.97	2388.03	8130.10	8.4441	0.03	393	2388	100.0	39.08	23.4166
3	1	4	0.0042	0.0000	100.0	518.67	642.44	1584.12	1406.42	14.62	...	521.38	2388.05	8132.90	8.3917	0.03	391	2388	100.0	39.00	23.3737
4	1	5	0.0014	0.0000	100.0	518.67	642.51	1587.19	1401.92	14.62	...	522.15	2388.03	8129.54	8.4031	0.03	390	2388	100.0	38.99	23.4130

5 rows × 26 columns

Fig. 6.2 Snippet of test dataset

6.3.1 Autoencoder Neural Network

An autoencoder is a kind of artificial neural network(ANN) used to learn effective information codings in an unsupervised way(not knowing the output). The reason for an autoencoder is to get familiar with a portrayal (encoding) for a bunch of information, normally for dimensionality decrease, via preparing the network to disregard signal commotion. Hence it is very useful for a large unknown dataset.

Autoencoder tries to replicate the input data and get the output data and see the difference between them. We utilize the distribution or plot of reproduction loss (mean square error) as the model yield for the training information addressing the good equipment to recognize abnormalities. Using this, we would be able to define a threshold for what to think about an anomaly. The assessment of the strategy to identify the engine degradation currently comprises of figuring the recreation loss for all information focuses in the test data set and contrasting the misfortune with the characterized edge an incentive for hailing this as oddity gear to recognize anomalies. One important feature is that the hidden layer in the neural network ought to have a few restrictions forced on it to such an extent that it pulls out significant insights regarding the information from the training dataset, without really expecting to keep all the data that info gave, accordingly going about as such a lossy pressure, and it ought to do this consequently from the models which would be very helpful for unsupervised data. The amount of similarity in the input and output after encoding, better is the autoencoder.

Algorithm for Autoencoders:

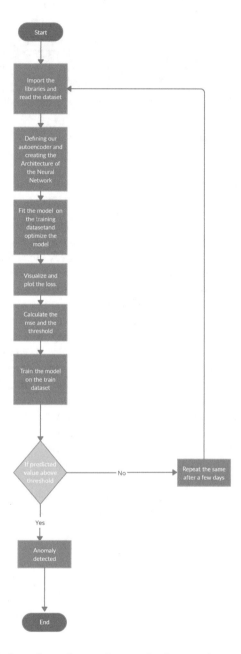

The encoding is done through neural networks. In neural networks, the model has mainly 3 layers: the input, hidden, and output layers. The hidden layer is used the encoding layer and the output is the decoding. It uses backpropogation for estimation of output for unsupervised data (Fig. 6.3).

Fig. 6.3 Neural network model

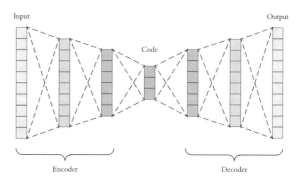

Fig. 6.4 Loss distribution

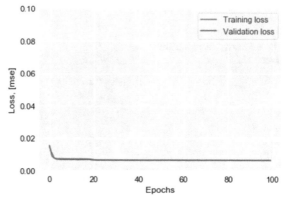

In our model, we use LSTM neural network cells. LSTM, long short term memory, can store the data for further use. Also, LSTM can include multivariate features. We use Mean Square Error for calculation and comparing the losses in our model. We can also use Mean Absolute error in place of mean square error for the same.

The following three figures tell us more about the autoencoder model. Figure 6.4 tells us about the distribution of the training/validation loss in the 100 epochs and the Fig. 6.5 tells us about the accuracy of the autoencoder neural network model and Fig. 6.6 tells us about the distribution of the calculated loss in the training set which helps us to get the threshold.

6.3.2 PCA

Principal Components Analysis (PCA) is a calculation to change the segments of a dataset into another arrangement of highlights called Principal Components. By doing this, a huge piece of the data across the full dataset is adequately packed into fewer component sections. This empowers dimensionality decrease and the capacity to envision the partition of classes or bunches assuming any. The procedure

Fig. 6.5 Accuracy of the
model

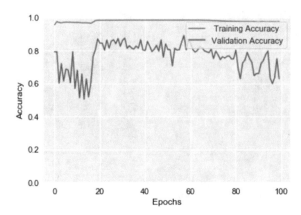

Fig. 6.6 Loss: mean square
error

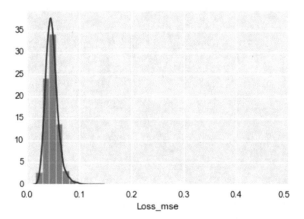

is broadly used to accentuate variety and catch solid examples in a data set. It changes
an enormous arrangement of variables into a more modest one that actually contains
the majority of the data in the huge set.

Algorithm for PCA:

1. Import the dataset
2. Preprocess the data
3. Define the PCA Model:

   (a) Co-Variance Matrix define
   (b) Mahalanobis define.
   (c) Detect the outliners and the threshold
   (d) Check if all eigen vectors in the matrix are definitely positive

4. Set up Model:

   (a) Co-varience Matrix calculate
   (b) Mahalanobis calculate

Fig. 6.7 Mahalanobis distance

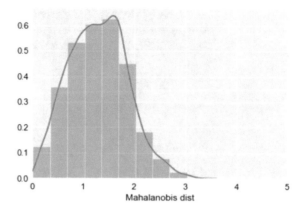

(c) Plot the distance for a threshold

5. Compare with threshold and detect anomaly

Figure 6.7, tells us about the Mahalanobis distance which helps us to get the threshold. Mahalanobis distance is widely used in cluster analysis and classification techniques.

6.4   Results and Discussion

Sensor Anomalies pose a huge risk to the system and the environment nearby. It is very important to predict it. We used two Unsupervised Machine Learning Algorithms namely Autoencoders and Principal Component Analysis to predict the percentage of anomalies present in the given input of sensor details. Both approaches give similar outcomes, where they can predict the breakdown well ahead of time of the actual failure. The fundamental contrast is how to characterize a reasonable threshold, to avoid wrong predictions. Autoencoders are more complex and expensive than PCA. These models reduce the complexity of the dataset and help in easier calculation.

1. Figs. 6.8 and 6.9 depict the outcome of the Autoencoder model. The threshold is taken from the observations in Fig. 6.6. The MSE Loss is then compared to the threshold and if the value of the loss is more than the threshold then there is an anomaly. Figure 6.8 gives us a tabular comparison whereas Fig. 6.9 depicts the graph. The red line depicts the threshold whereas the blue line depicts the use loss. If the mse loss line touches the threshold line then there is an anomaly present.
2. Figs. 6.10 and 6.11 depict the outcome of the PCA model. The threshold is taken from the observation in Fig. 6.7. If the Distance is less than the threshold then there is no anomaly else there is an anomaly. Figure 6.11 gives us a tabular comparison whereas Fig. 6.11 depicts the graph. The red line depicts the threshold whereas

	Loss_mse	Threshold	Anomaly
0	0.050477	0.125	False
1	0.055452	0.125	False
2	0.037016	0.125	False
3	0.043015	0.125	False
4	0.034332	0.125	False

Fig. 6.8 Autoencoder detection

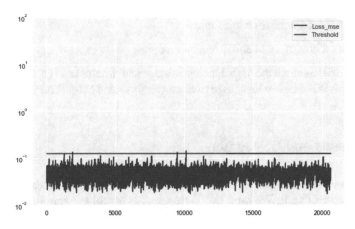

Fig. 6.9 Autoencoder detection graph

Fig. 6.10 PCA detection

	Mob dist	Thresh	Anomaly
0	1.957307	3.880702	False
1	2.124568	3.880702	False
2	1.933620	3.880702	False
3	1.982727	3.880702	False
4	2.077709	3.880702	False

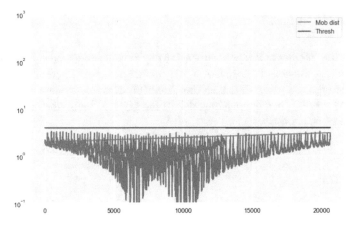

Fig. 6.11 PCA detection graph

the green line depicts the Mahalanobis distance. If the Mahalanobis line touches the threshold line then there is an anomaly present.

Autoencoders do not have tied weights, that is equal weights on encoder and decoder, and unit norm properties, that is each layer weights unit norm(this is useful to get efficient variance value). These are present in the PCA model and hence the incorporation of PCA in the autoencoder model can be a better model which is more efficient and optimized.

6.5 Future Scope

In future work, we intend to propose an algorithm for anomaly detection for various fields where sensor networks are used as the primary source and are complex to detect anomalies. This model can tell the number of days prior to which the engine fails as well. We also plan to extend the testbed to multiple APs to explore new aspects of anomalies that concern the industries. We will also look forward to make the proposed system more robust and effective. We will also test our model on other parameters. There are many interesting applications of autoencoders like in computer vision, image editing. They can be used to convert black and white photos to color photos. They are also used in removing noises from images. The autoencoder model can be combined with the PCA model and further trained for the unit norm and tied weight properties for better efficiency of the model. On a large scale, the model can be deployed on a website with a good interface for ease of use of the user. This can also be done for a large scale use to prevent machine deterioration, in any place around the world. The users just have to give the details of the engine and sensors to get the anomaly details.

6.6 Conclusion

The use of the Internet of things is increasing day by day and the need for security in IoT plays a very important role in it. Anomaly detection is very important. Anomalies can be predicted using Machine Learning Algorithms. Autoencoders and PCA help us to do the same. When the machine details are given as input, the model predicts the chance of an anomaly.

References

1. Venkatraman, S., Alazab, M., Vinayakumar, R.: A hybrid deep learning image-based analysis for effective malware detection. J. Information Security Appl. **47**, 377–389 (2019)
2. Pham, Q.-V., Mirjalili, S., Kumar, N., Alazab, M., Hwang, W.-J.: Whale optimization algorithm with applications to resource allocation in wireless networks. IEEE Trans. Vehicular Technol. **69**(4), 4285–4297 (2020)
3. Patel, K., Mehta, D., Mistry, C., Gupta, R., Tanwar, S., Kumar, N., Alazab, M.: Facial sentiment analysis using ai techniques: state-of-the-art, taxonomies, and challenges. IEEE Access **8**, 90 495–90 519 (2020)
4. MK, M., Srivastava, G., Somayaji, S.R.K., Gadekallu, T.R., Maddikunta, P.K.R., Bhattacharya, S.: *An incentive based approach for covid-19 using blockchain technology*. arXiv preprint arXiv:2011.01468 (2020)
5. Bodkhe, U., Tanwar, S., Parekh, K., Khanpara, P., Tyagi, S., Kumar, N., Alazab, M.: Blockchain for industry 4.0: a comprehensive review. IEEE Access **8**, 79 764–79 800 (2020)
6. Khan, R.U., Zhang, X., Kumar, R., Sharif, A., Golilarz, N.A., Alazab, M.: An adaptive multi-layer botnet detection technique using machine learning classifiers. Appl. Sci. **9**(11), 2375 (2019)
7. Reddy, G.T., Reddy, M.P.K., Lakshmanna, K., Kaluri, R., Rajput, D.S., Srivastava, G., Baker, T.: Analysis of dimensionality reduction techniques on big data. IEEE Access **8**, pp. 54 776–54 788 (2020)
8. Bhattacharya, S., Kaluri, R., Singh, S., Alazab, M., Tariq, U., et al.: A novel pca-firefly based xgboost classification model for intrusion detection in networks using gpu. Electronics **9**(2), 219 (2020)
9. RM, S.P., Maddikunta, P.K.R., Parimala, M., Koppu, S., Reddy, T., Chowdhary, C.L., Alazab, M.: An effective feature engineering for dnn using hybrid pca-gwo for intrusion detection in iomt architecture. In *Computer Communications* (2020)
10. Deepa, N., Khan, M.Z., Prabadevi, B., Vincent, P.D.R., Maddikunta, P.K.R., Gadekallu, T.R.: Multiclass model for agriculture development using multivariate statistical method. IEEE Access (2020)
11. Bhattacharya, S., Maddikunta, P.K.R., Pham, Q.-V., Gadekallu, T.R., Chowdhary, C.L., Alazab, M., Piran, M.J., et al.: Deep learning and medical image processing for coronavirus (covid-19) pandemic: a survey. In: *Sustainable Cities and Society*, p. 102589 (2020)
12. Gadekallu, T.R., Rajput, D.S., Reddy, M.P.K., Lakshmanna, K., Bhattacharya, S., Singh, S., Jolfaei, A., Alazab, M.: A novel pca—whale optimization-based deep neural network model for classification of tomato plant diseases using gpu. J Real-Time Image Process. 1–14 (2020)
13. Maddikunta, P.K.R., Srivastava, G., Gadekallu, T.R., Deepa, N., Boopathy, P.: Predictive model for battery life in iot networks. IET Intelligent Transp. Syst. **14**(11), 1388–1395 (2020)
14. Deepa, N., Prabadevi, B., Maddikunta, P.K., Gadekallu, T.R., Baker, T., Khan, M.A., Tariq, U.: An ai-based intelligent system for healthcare analysis using ridge-adaline stochastic gradient descent classifier. J. Supercomputing (2020)

15. Alazab, M., Khan, S., Krishnan, S.S.R., Pham, Q.-V., Reddy, M.P.K., Gadekallu, T.R.: A multidirectional lstm model for predicting the stability of a smart grid. IEEE Access **8**, 85 454–85 463 (2020)
16. Gadekallu, T.R., Kumar, N., Hakak, S., Bhattacharya, S., et al.: *Blockchain based attack detection on machine learning algorithms for iot based e-health applications*, arXiv preprint
17. Ch, R., Srivastava, G., Gadekallu, T.R., Maddikunta, P.K.R., Bhattacharya, S.: Security and privacy of uav data using blockchain technology. J. Information Security Appl. **55**, 102670 (2020)
18. Deepa, N., Pham, Q.-V., Nguyen, D.C., Bhattacharya, S., Gadekallu, T.R., Maddikunta, P.K.R., Fang, F., Pathirana, P.N., et al.: *A survey on blockchain for big data: Approaches, opportunities, and future directions*, arXiv preprint arXiv:2009.00858 (2020)
19. Rajadurai, S., Alazab, M., Kumar, N., Gadekallu, T.R.: Latency evaluation of sdfgs on heterogeneous processors using timed automata. IEEE Access **8**, 140 171–140 180 (2020)
20. Alazab, M., Layton, R., Broadhurst, R., Bouhours, B., Malicious spam emails developments and authorship attribution. In: *Fourth cybercrime and trustworthy computing workshop*. IEEE, pp. 58–68 (2013)
21. Gadekallu, T.R., Khare, N., Bhattacharya, S., Singh, S., Maddikunta, P.K.R., Srivastava, G.: Deep neural networks to predict diabetic retinopathy. J. Ambient Intell. Humaniz Comput (2020)
22. Gadekallu, T.R., Khare, N., Bhattacharya, S., Singh, S., Reddy Maddikunta, P.K., Ra, I.-H., Alazab, M.: Early detection of diabetic retinopathy using pca-firefly based deep learning model. Electronics **9**(2), 274 (2020)
23. Canedo, J., Skjellum, A.: Using machine learning to secure iot systems. In: *14th annual conference on privacy, security and trust (PST)*. IEEE, pp. 219–222 (2016)
24. Sharp, M., Ak, R., Hedberg, T., Jr.: A survey of the advancing use and development of machine learning in smart manufacturing. J. Manuf. Syst. **48**, 170–179 (2018)
25. Alam, M.S., Husain, D., Naqvi, S., Kumar, P.: Iot security through machine learning and homographic encryption technique. In *International Conference on New Trends in Engineering & Technology (ICNTET), Chennai* (2018)
26. Hasan, M., Islam, M.M., Zarif, M.I.I., Hashem, M.: Attack and anomaly detection in iot sensors in iot sites using machine learning approaches. Internet of Things **7**, 100059 (2019)
27. Malhotra, P., Vig, L., Shroff, G., Agarwal, P.: Long short term memory networks for anomaly detection in time series. In *Proceedings*, vol. 89. Presses universitaires de Louvain, pp. 89–94 (2015)
28. Sonntag, D., Zillner, S., van der Smagt, P., Lörincz, A.: Overview of the cps for smart factories project: Deep learning, knowledge acquisition, anomaly detection and intelligent user interfaces. In *Industrial internet of things*. Springer, Berlin, pp. 487–504 (2017)
29. Hussain, F., Hussain, R., Hassan, S.A., Hossain, E.: Machine learning in iot security: current solutions and future challenges. In *IEEE Communications Surveys & Tutorials* (2020)

Chapter 7
Game Theory Based Privacy Preserving Approach for Collaborative Deep Learning in IoT

Deepti Gupta, Smriti Bhatt, Paras Bhatt, Maanak Gupta, and Ali Saman Tosun

7.1 Introduction

In recent years, Internet of Things (IoT) is becoming a pervasive reality of our lives with billions of IoT devices which are continuously increasing in number. These smart devices are connected to or associated with users and generate huge amount of data, from user health information [7] to social networking [5] information of the users. This large amount of valuable data enables to utilize Deep Learning (DL) models for training and enhancing intelligence of various data-driven IoT applications. Generally, these devices are resource constraint and leverage the cloud computing services and platform for expanding their storage and analytics power [8, 10]. Thus, most of the IoT devices connect to a central cloud platform [6, 21, 25, 26] to use

D. Gupta (✉) · A. S. Tosun
Department of Computer Science, University of Texas at San Antonio, San Antonio,
TX 78249, USA
e-mail: deepti.mrt@gmail.com

A. S. Tosun
e-mail: ali.tosun@utsa.edu

S. Bhatt
Department of Computer and Information Technology, Purdue University,
West Lafayette, IN 47905, USA
e-mail: smbhatt@purdue.edu

P. Bhatt
Department of Information Systems and Cyber Security, University of Texas at San Antonio,
San Antonio, TX 78249, USA
e-mail: paras.bhatt@utsa.edu

M. Gupta
Department of Computer Science, Tennessee Technological University, Cookeville,
TN 38505, USA
e-mail: mgupta@tntech.edu

© The Author(s), under exclusive license to Springer Nature Singapore Pte Ltd. 2021
A. Makkar and N. Kumar, *Deep Learning for Security and Privacy Preservation in IoT*,
Signals and Communication Technology,
https://doi.org/10.1007/978-981-16-6186-0_8

remote services. These services are crucial for storage of the datasets and learning Machine Learning (ML) models. However, there is additional latency incurred while these smart devices interact with the cloud services. To overcome this issue, edge computing is shaping a new paradigm enabling low latency real-time communications between IoT devices and edge devices, such as gateways (e.g., smartphones). These edge devices, also known as edge cloudlets [9, 27], will then communicate with the cloud services. Edge devices are performed data training locally and are also be employed to preserve privacy of personal data. Unlike constrained IoT devices, these edge gateways have the capability to support ML models. A simple example would be a video enabled doorbell that performs training on its local datasets, and identifies person at the door.

DL models are often associated with the size of training dataset. While training a learning mechanism or model, large training data will enhance the accuracy and performance of a trained model. In today's connected world and new era of big data, data is often distributed across several smart devices, edge cloudlets, and cloud and it cannot be brought together due to user privacy constraints. Collaborative Deep Learning (CDL) allows multiple IoT devices to train their models, without exposing any associated sensitive and private data. CDL offers an attractive trade-off between user privacy and utility of data sets.

Recent research [13, 22, 24, 29] have discussed the privacy issues of local training devices and the impact of communication latency between edge gateways and Parameter Server (PS). However, the strategic behavior of the rational local training gateways have not been discussed in previous research, i.e., the authors have assumed that all IoT devices are altruistic. Altruistic devices are ones which always follow a suggested protocol as decided initially, regardless of whether they are benefiting or not by following the specific protocol. However, in a real-world scenario, devices are not altruistic, they are rational. Rational devices are the ones which will deviate from suggested protocol if they think that they will be benefited more by following a different protocol. In our proposed system model, we assume that all mobile edge devices or edge gateways are rational.

Generally, a mobile edge device that has a low quality data, always wants to be a part of CDL to increase accuracy of their local model. Whereas other mobile edge devices have high quality data, do not want to collaborate with low quality data holder mobile edge devices due to privacy concerns while sharing their local gradients. Therefore, there is a dilemma for mobile edge devices to be part or not of CDL. In this chapter, we address the problem of learner's dilemma by proposing a CDL game model and a novel fair collaboration strategy which enables each participant to cooperate in CDL based on the clusters formed to achieve overall benefit to itself in training the local ML model. We also evaluate our CDL game model and novel fair collaboration strategy in smart home deployment using ARAS dataset [2]. The main contributions of this work are summarized as follows.

1. We identify the problem of unfair cooperation of participants in CDL. In other words, a local training device, which has low quality data and builds its learning model to take advantage from other devices which has high quality data.

2. We propose a game-theoretic model for analyzing the behavior of mobile edge IoT devices, where each device aims at maximizing the accuracy of its local model with minimal cost of participation in CDL.
3. We propose a novel fair collaboration strategy for addressing the issue of unfair cooperation in CDL between rational IoT devices.
4. We also implement our fair collaboration strategy on ARAS dataset [2], and the results reflect that proposed solution elicit cooperation in CDL.

The rest of the chapter is organized as follows. Section 7.2 presents relevant work and related background. Section 7.3 presents different types of DL techniques applicable in IoT. The System model along with rational assumptions are discussed in Sect. 7.4. Game model and game analysis are explained in Sect. 7.5. Section 7.6 presents implementation of proposed system model on ARAS smart home data along with the analysis of results. Section 7.7 concludes this work with future research directions.

7.2 Background and Related Work

In this section, we describe related work on information leakage on deep learning models in IoT, and give a brief overview of privacy preserving techniques. Here, we also discuss game theoretical models, which have been used to secure user's personal data.

7.2.1 Information Leakage on Deep Learning Models in IoT

Information leakage of user's personal data has become a well known problem for deep learning models. It is a common problem of accidentally revealing the personal information of individuals. To avoid this, various data masking techniques such as *pseudonymize* and *anonymize* have been user to secure the data towards ensuring user privacy. It is critical to understand the difference between pseudonymized data and anonymized data. In pseudonymize, there is possibility to trace back data into its original state, whereas it becomes impossible to get back data into its original form in anonymize. However, data can trace back data into its original form indirectly. For instance, Netflix released a hundred million anonymized film ratings that included a unique subscriber ID, the movie title, year of release and the date on which the subscriber rated the movie. This anonymized Netflix dataset was matched with data crawled from the Internet Movie Database (IMDb). Even with a small sample of 50 IMDb users it was easy to identify the records of two users. Hence, pseudonymization and anonymization approaches are still vulnerable to some inference attacks that would compromise user data privacy.

Today, big Internet giants including Google and Amazon are already offering *Machine Learning as a service* and any customer with a specific dataset and a data classification task can upload this dataset to the service and pay it to construct a ML model. This model is then made available to the customer, typically as a black-box API, which is vulnerable to attacks where the adversary can observe the model prediction; however, they cannot access the model parameters, nor any computation. But there are still some possibility of data leakage at cloud platform. The membership inference attack on black-box API is discussed in [51, 57]. The attacker queries the target model with a data record and obtains the modelÃ¢â¬â„¢s prediction on that record. An adversary can also build an algorithm to trace the modelÃ¢â¬â„¢s training dataset of data holders. Rahman et al. [48] show that differential private deep model could also fail against membership inference attack. Similarly, a novel white-box membership inference attack was proposed by Nasr et al. [42]. This attack measures their training datasets membership leakage against deep learning algorithms. In the white-box attack, the adversary has access to the full model including model prediction, model parameters, and intermediate computation at all different layers. Melis et al. [37] demonstrate that the updated parameter leaks unintended information about data holders' training datasets; thus, develops passive and active inference attacks to exploit this leakage.

7.2.2 Privacy Preserving Deep Learning

In a collaborative model, each participant has its own sensitive datasets and various privacy mechanisms have been proposed to preserve privacy and protect against exchanging parameters such as Secure Multi-party Communication (SMC) [31], Homomorphic Encryption (HE) [49], and Differential Privacy [15]. SMC helps to protect intermediate steps of the computation when multiple parties perform collaborative ML on their proprietary inputs. Mohassel et al. [40] adopt a two-server model for privacy-preserving training, commonly used by previous work on privacy-preserving deep learning via SMC [18, 43, 44]. In this model, during the setup phase, the data holders process and encrypt their data among two non-colluding servers, and during the computation phase, the two servers can train various models on the data holders' joint data without learning any information beyond the trained model. However, Aono et al. [3, 4] showed that the local data information may be actually leaked to an honest-but-curious server. To obscure an individual's identity, Differential Privacy (DP) adds mathematical noise to a small sample of the individual's usage pattern. Prior work [1, 29, 50, 53] have employed DP on privacy-preserving collaborative deep learning system to protect privacy of training data. However, Hitaj et al. [28] pointed out that the above mentioned work failed to protect data privacy and demonstrated that a curious parameter server can learn private data through Generative Adversarial Networks (GAN) learning.

With the deep learning approaches, a dominant technique to optimize the loss function is Stochastic Gradient Descent (SGD). SGD is a method to find the optimal parameter configuration for a ML algorithm. It iteratively makes small adjustments to a ML network configuration to decrease the error of the network. It has been applied in various privacy-preserving DL models in the literature [1, 37, 40, 42]. Moreover, a distributed selective SGD [50] assumes two or more data holders training independently and concurrently. After each round of local training, data holders share their gradients asynchronously. On the other hand, downpour SGD [3] is a variant of asynchronous SGD, where a global vector for neural network is initialized randomly. At each iteration, replicas of neural networks are run over local datasets, and the corresponding local gradient vector is sent to the server. A subset or gradient of the local model is shared with a server. The server receives the gradients from data holders by using different approaches like round robin, random order [50], cosine distance [12], time based [53]. The server then aggregates these received parameters using FederatedAveraging algorithm [36], and weighted aggregation strategy [12]. One of the other challenges in CDL is to reduce the client-server communication. A temporally weighted aggregation strategy is introduced for less communication cost and high model accuracy. While a number of privacy-preserving solutions exist for collaborating organizations to securely aggregate the parameters in the process of training the models, a rational framework for the participants is discussed in [54] that balances privacy loss and accuracy gain in their collaboration.

While most of the prior research focus on designing the optimal privacy mechanisms, there is a major requirement to choose a particular privacy mechanism for a particular dataset, such as non-IID dataset, high-quality dataset, and low-quality dataset. Zhao et al. [58] proposed a solution to reduce the impact of low quality data holders. Although there have been a number of privacy mechanisms focusing on data protection, these studies are limited to specific scenarios, for example privacy of exchanging parameters, which makes it difficult to apply these techniques to protect and ensure privacy for the whole training dataset.

7.2.3 Game Theory

Game theory has been applied to data privacy game for analyzing privacy and accuracy. Pejo et al. [46] defined two player game, where one player is privacy concerned and other player is not. Esposito et al. [16] proposed a game model to analyze the interaction between a provider (global ML model) and a requester (local ML model) within a CDL model. Gupta et al. [20, 23] presented CDL for rational players in their prior work. In this chapter, we construct a game model for rational mobile edge devices cooperation in CDL and present an analysis of the game.

7.3 Deep Learning in IoT

IoT architecture, by design, is associated with the generation of multifaceted data. From sensors to automated responses, IoT devices output a swarm of data points that are particularly well suited for ML tasks. Within the domain of ML, the advancing field of DL has of late started using a variety of techniques for harnessing the power of these millions of data points available from IoT sensors and devices. With reference to DL, we discuss some of the most popular techniques as follow.

7.3.1 Convolutional Neural Network (CNN)

In its basic form, a CNN DL algorithm differentiates among a set of input images to output a desired category of images as specified by a user. A CNN model derives its efficiency from the ability to learn filters and features in data, that would otherwise have to be hand engineered. With enough training, a CNN model can do that on its own. Using hand engineered features by a programmer to curate learning that is aimed at solving a specific problem cannot to be generalized to solve other similar problems. A powerful general-purpose learning procedure, that replaces the programmer with a set of predefined algorithms which can then be used to obtain effective solutions for a much wider problem domain. This is where the true power of CNN lies. With sufficient data and computing power, learning trumps programming by a long shot [32].

Figure 7.1 a) represents a generic view of the layers in a CNN model which correspond to - 1) Convolutional layer which is responsible for extracting high level features from a set of input images; 2) Pooling Layer which is aimed at reducing the computational power needed for processing the data; and, 3) Fully Connected Layer that is appended for classifying the desired set of images with the help of a softmax function. Recently, CNN has been widely used in the IoT domain. A classic example is of drones which have cameras mounted that can collect images of crops, traffic on road, or even land use. These images can then be collated to form a large dataset that can be then used to predict crop diseases, traffic congestion, or drought conditions as per specific application domains. It has become a popular deep learning tool with its various instantiations being used across different IoT domains including precision agriculture [38], smart traffic management [45], and medical diagnosis [33].

7.3.2 Recurrent Neural Network (RNN)

A Recurrent Neural Network (RNN) can be understood as a learning model that has an internal memory. As the name suggests, an RNN model is recurrent by design where it performs the same function for every input. Here, whilst producing an output,

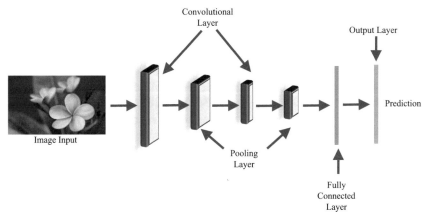

a) Convolutional Neural Network (CNN)

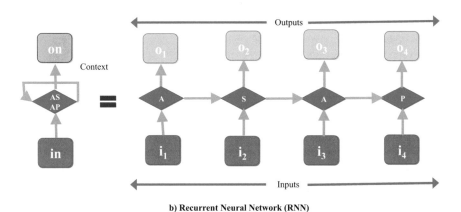

b) Recurrent Neural Network (RNN)

Fig. 7.1 A diagrammatic view of CNN and RNN

the model maintains a copy of that output in the internal memory and then during prediction it uses both the current input as well as the past output to make a decision. There are certain variants of this model which expand on this internal memory concepts primarily Long Short Term Memory (LSTM) models [30]. Figure 7.1 b) presents a RNN model architecture. In the first step as shown in the figure, the model receives an initial input, then it produces a corresponding output based on it. Then subsequently for the next step the model uses the output obtained in the first step plus a new input for the next step. In this manner the model keeps in mind the context of the training process.

RNN has been applied in several IoT domains including IoT security. More specifically, it has been used to detect attacks against IoT-connected smart home environments [17]. In the context of Industrial IoT, RNN has been used to predict maintenance needs of industrial and commercial plants [47]. RNNs have also been deployed for data analytics in order to learn from the time series data that is typical form of the data generated by IoT and smart city deployments [55].

7.3.3 Generative Adversarial Networks (GAN)

Generative Adversarial Networks (GAN) are mainly composed of two networks that work in conjunction to produce synthetic and high-quality data. A generative network produces data and the discriminative network distinguishes the generated data from real input data [19]. The generator tries to trick the discriminator into accepting the generated data as if it were coming from a legitimate source. The two networks are thus pitted as adversaries in a GAN model. The objective function in such a model corresponds to the existence of two networks where one tries to maximize the value function and the other tries to minimize it. If the discriminator accurately classifies the data produced by generator as being fake, then it is considered to be functioning well. Similarly, for the generator it is said to be performing well if it produces data that tricks the discriminator into accepting it as being true [39].

GANs have been used in novel pursuits to generate descriptive texts from a given image [14], which is especially relevant for aiding visually impaired persons. They have also been used for optimizing energy consumption in IoT devices [34]. In addition, they have been used in healthcare domain for obtaining reliable data, which in turn support model training, and thus enable clinical decision making [56].

7.3.4 Federated Deep Learning (FDL)

A new privacy preserving collaborative paradigm is Federated Deep Learning (FDL). DL requires labeled data for training accurate models, that can perform highly structured tasks, such as classification and prediction. However, labeling a dataset has an additional cost in terms of privacy. The identification of data points can have serious implications for the generating source of such data, which are the users. Using such labeled data, it is possible to identify the source which poses a security and privacy risk. To preserve privacy in such settings, FDL has emerged as a reliable solution.

The proliferation of smartphones and the increasing popularity of mobile computing has led to the creation of application domains which are useful, but at the same time, vulnerable too. With the adoption of the smartphone, the potential for privacy violations to occur has no doubt shot up, especially since the past couple of years. A lot of the IoT devices such as wearables and medical devices collect users' personal data and store it on users' smartphone. Users are in general wary of sharing personal data, so is the case for other such sensitive data that may exist on the phones. Researchers have proposed that users should be able to define privacy-based policies for securing their data using novel models and mechanisms, such as attribute-based communication control (ABCC) [11]. However, using such data can have significant benefits in terms of getting personalized models that are trained on a variety of people. FDL provides a solution in such contexts where people may not want to share their data. By training a model locally on a user's smartphone and then transferring just the model to a central server can help to reduce the privacy risk. Since only the

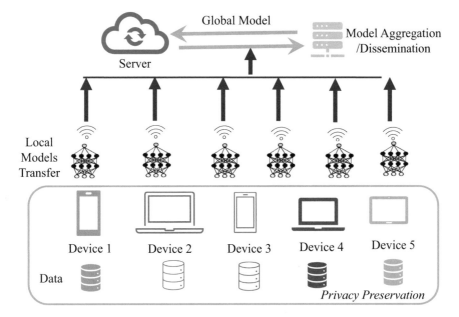

Fig. 7.2 An overview of federated deep learning

model is communicated with the external server, it does not have any personal information about the user. By aggregating over a range of such local users' model, an efficient global model can be trained which does not contain personal information. The implications of FDL are huge for mobile devices as they are the primary surface where individual model training takes place. Fig. 7.2 depicts how a FDL framework can deployed in IoT settings.

FDL can help to solve hitherto difficult problems in the IoT field. By using mobile devices and training learning models directly on them, user privacy is effectively preserved. Also there are benefits in terms of communication latency, cost and speed. FDL has been successfully used in Industrial IoT for enhancing quality of service by ensuring privacy preserving data sharing [35]. Further FDL can result in resource optimization in edge computing systems by reducing the need to share data over the network. In its place, only the model parameters can be shared. This would result in obtaining comparable model performance, which is on par with models trained using traditional ML techniques [52].

7.4 System Model

Here, we present comprehensive details of CDL model, where mobile edge devices or edge gateways perform training in a collaborative manner. We assume that all the mobile edge devices are altruistic in CDL model. Further, we analyze the issue of the rationality of mobile edge devices in CDL model (Table 7.1).

Table 7.1 List of symbols

Symbol	Definition
N	Number of mobile edge devices
n	Total number of IoT devices
K	Batch size
H	Numbers of local epoch
D_i	Generated data from IoT device i
Δw_i	Local gradient of participant i
w^{global}	Global parameter
α	Learning rate
M	Privacy mechanism
θ_i	Loss value of participant i, train individually
ϕ_i	Loss value of participant i, train collaboratively
τ_i	Loss value of participant i, train individually on auxiliary dataset
B	coefficient
c^{plocal}	Computation cost to build a local model
$c^{pglobal}$	Computation cost to build a global model
c^m	Communication cost to upload the parameters to PS
$c^{m'}$	Communication cost to download the parameters from PS
c_i^t	Total cost for build a ML model
C_i	Number of cooperative participants
$N - C_i$	Number of defective participants

7.4.1 Collaborative Deep Learning Model in IoT

The system model allows multiple participants to build their ML model collaboratively. Figure 7.3 presents our CDL model, which illustrates major modules of the system model. In this model, we consider that N number of mobile edge devices or edge gateways are connected with multiple IoT devices. These IoT devices generate tremendous amount of data, which help to enhance the intelligence of their local ML model. The CDL model improves privacy of training data by exchanging local gradients instead of raw data without compromising data privacy. Each mobile edge device preserves a local vector w^i of ML model, and PS also preserves another separate parameter vector w^{global}. After becoming a part of CDL, each edge gateway start to initialize parameters (weights) w^i, where i=1,2,3,...N, randomly. To improve the efficiency of local ML model, these initialize parameters (weights) w^i are also update by downloading their updated parameters w^{global} from PS.

The mobile edge devices or edge gateways participate in CDL to build their local ML model to learn a common goal. In this system model, SGD approach is used to optimize the loss value. The weight sample is selected randomly and this optimization process runs continuously until SGD reaches to a local optimum. The

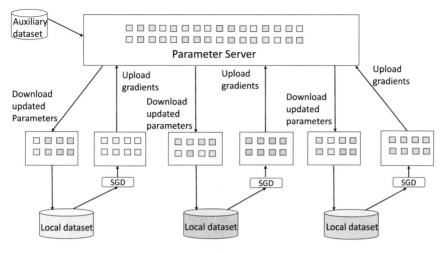

Fig. 7.3 A collaborative deep learning system model

loss value E, which is the difference between the true value of the objective function and the computed output of the network, this value is calculated by L^2 norm or cross entropy. The back-propagation algorithm computes the partial derivative of E with respect to each parameter in w^k and updates the parameter so as to reduce its gradient. All mobile edge devices or edge gateways build their local ML model simultaneously.

Algorithm 1: Pseudo Code for Mobile Edge Device i

1: Define initial parameters w^i, learning rate α and number of local epochs H.

2: Repeat all the steps until minimum error is obtained:

3: Download parameters w^{global} from PS to learn a common learning objective.

4: LocalTraining (i, w^i): Train local data on each device to build own ML model

5: Split local dataset D_i to minibatches of size K which are included into the set K_i.

6: **for** for each local epoch j from 1 to H **do**

7:   **for** for each $k \in K_i$ **do**

8:

$$\Delta w^i = \Delta w^i - \alpha \frac{\partial E_i}{\partial w^i}$$

9:   **end for**

10: **end for**

11: Each participant uploads local gradients Δw^i to PS

12: Each participant downloads updated parameters w^{global} and loss value τ_i of each participant.

The CDL system model does not allow any one to one communication among participating mobile edge devices, however they can influence each other's training indirectly through PS. When each edge gateway receives updated parameters Δw^{global} from PS. There are many ways to exchange the parameters from PS to mobile edge device. In this model, PS does not hold the process of aggregation until receiving all local gradients from all edge devices, and it works in asynchronous manner. This training and exchanging parameter process continue until the model achieves the goal.

Algorithm 2: Pseudo Code of Parameter Server

1: Set initial global parameters w^{global}
2: PS runs these local gradients Δw^i on auxiliary dataset and
   calculate loss values τ_i of each participant
3: PS also aggregates these local gradients Δw^i asynchronously

$$w^{\text{global}} = w^{\text{global}} + \Delta w^i$$

7.4.2 Training Cost on Edge Gateways

We define two major costs including computation and communication borne by mobile edge devices or edge gateways for participation in the CDL system model. There are two different phases including training and participating in this system model. Each mobile edge device or edge gateway builds a local model in the time of training and initialize their weights/parameters to train its local ML model. Then, each mobile edge device or edge gateways upload its calculated local gradients on PS in the time of participating. PS receives all the local gradients and aggregates all of them, and sends back to each mobile edge device or edge gateway. This training process continues until loss value becomes negligible.

In an epoch, the total cost of a mobile edge device to build ML model in collaborative manner based on execution of both phases. A mobile edge device pays costs c^{plocal} and c^{pglobal}, which are computation costs to build a local ML model and builds a local model using updated global parameters respectively in training phase. In participating phase, a mobile edge device pays another costs c^m and $c^{m'}$, which are communication costs to upload its parameters to PS and download the updated parameters from PS respectively. The average per mobile edge devices cost c_i^t for participation in each epoch of CDL system is defined as

$$c_i^t = c^{\text{plocal}} + c^{\text{pglobal}} + c^m + c^{m'} \tag{7.1}$$

In a particular case, a participant may not participate in CDL, and avoids to pay some specific costs c^m, $c^{m'}$, and c^{pglobal}. In the next section, we present rationality assumption, which provides details to avoid the pay some specific costs based on choice of strategy.

7.4.3   Rationality Assumption

Most of research has done in distributed DL, this study [12] shows that mobile edge devices or edge gateways are controlled by an adversary. If mobile edge devices or edge gateways are behave as malicious participant, they could arbitrarily deviate from suggested protocol in CDL and they can arbitrarily drop communication between mobile edge device and PS. In our research, we assume that mobile edge devices or edge gateways and IoT devices are honest, but they behave selfish and making own benefit at minimum cost. The notion of *rationality* means that a rational mobile edge device or edge gateway decide to participate or not to participate for maximizing its profit in CDL.

7.5   The Collaborative Deep Learning Game

A key contribution of this work is to show how training issue of IoT devices and mobile edge devices or edge gateways through game model. We describe the Collaborative Deep Learning game which controls the actions of multiple mobile edge devices or edge gateways and enforce them for collaboration to train their data under privacy preserving mechanism. This CDL game G is introduced with N-players, and these players communicate to PS simultaneously. To learn a common objective without compromising the privacy of data, each mobile edge device send local gradients to PS. PS aggregates all the gradients and sends them back, which helps to increase the accuracy of local model. However, some of edge gateways are still lacking to receive benefit from other IoT devices via gateways.

7.5.1   Game Theoretic Model

Game theory is a theoretical framework for modeling conflict situations among competing players and for analyzing the behavior of various players. In the CDL game G, mobile edge devices or edge gateways, which are connected with multiple IoT devices, are participants where these gateways do not have any awareness about others and communicates to PS simultaneously. This game G is a static game, because all participants must choose their strategy simultaneously. The Game G is a tuple (P, S, U), where P is the set of players, S is the set of strategies and U is the set of payoff values.

- **Players** (P): The set of players $P = \sum_{i=1}^{N} P_i$ corresponds to the set of mobile edge devices or edge gateways, where each device receives a goal from PS to build its own local model in CDL game G.
- **Strategy** (S): The CDL game G has two different strategies S_i (i) Cooperative (CP) or (ii) Defective (DF), each player P_i has choice between these two strategies. We

refer a set of strategy as $S = \{CP, DF\}$. These strategies determine that player P_i either participates or does not participate in CDL to build the model. If a player P_i chooses CP strategy, it allows to send its local gradients to PS and also downloads updated parameters from PS to update its local model. There is a need to pay for various costs including communication costs $(c^m, c^{m'})$ and computation costs $(c^{pglobal}, c^{plocal})$, according to CP strategy. In contrast, if a player P_i chooses DF strategy to play, it neither uploads its local gradients to PS nor downloads the updated global parameters from PS. According to this strategy, the player pays only local computation cost c^{plocal}. It implies that this player is not a part of CDL and trains its local model individually on its gateway device only.

- **Payoff** (U): In CDL game G, each player's goal is to maximize their payoff, which is a function of the loss value and its various costs. Our work does not present any malicious side of players. In this game, each player receives benefit in terms of accuracy of the model and pays various costs to train the local model.

In our CDL game G, the payoff value is depend on the loss value of the model and various costs. However, the loss value and cost value are not on the same scale. To make them similar, we introduce a coefficient B, which is multiplied by loss value.

Now, we compute the payoff of each mobile edge device P_i in this game. If we assume that the participant P_i is cooperative, i.e. $P_i \in CP$. Similarly, if P_i is defective, i.e. $P_i \in DF$, and the payoff u_i of each mobile edge device is defined as follows.

$$u_i(CP) = B\left(\frac{1}{\phi_i}\right) - (c^{plocal} + c^m + c^{m'} + c^{pglobal}) \tag{7.2}$$

$$u_i(DF) = B\left(\frac{1}{\theta_i}\right) - (c^{plocal}) \tag{7.3}$$

Where ϕ_i is the loss value of the trained model using CDL and θ_i is the loss value of the trained model individually. Based on the above defined equations, we analyze our CDL game G.

7.5.2 Game Analysis

We apply the most fundamental game-theoretic concept, known as Nash Equilibrium, introduced by John Nash [41] to understand the behavior of players.

Definition 1 A Nash Equilibrium is a concept of game theory where none of the players can unilaterally deviate from their strategy to increase their payoff.

In a nutshell, if both strategies present mutual best responses to each other, then no player has any motivation to deviate unilaterally from the given strategy, one Nash Equilibrium strategy profile. For instance, prisonersÃ¢â‚¬â„¢ dilemma game shows that individual players always have an incentive to choose in a way that creates a less than optimal outcome for the individuals as a group. If both players play cooperative-CP strategy, it produces the best outcome for both players. In contrast, if both players decide not to cooperate with each other, they choose defective-DF strategy to achieve benefit from other players. In prisoners' dilemma defective strategy strictly dominates the cooperation strategy. Hence, the only Nash Equilibrium in prisoners' dilemma, is a mutual defection.

Based on the cost and benefit of mobile edge devices to learn a neural-network model, we build a one-shot CDL game model G. In the following theorems, we show that the game G is a public good game.

Theorem 1 *In an iteration of collaborative deep learning game G with N mobile edge devices or edge gateways, if aggregated parameters are equally shared among all participants to build its local ML model, then this game G reduces to a public good game.*

Proof We assume that all N number of players follow defective-DF strategy, and neither send their local gradients to PS nor download updated global parameters from PS. In this case, each edge gateway prefers to build local ML model individually and saves various costs including communication costs c^m, $c^{m'}$, and global computation cost $c^{pglobal}$. Each participant P_i aims to minimize its loss value θ_i to achieves high accuracy of its ML model. None of participants cannot change his strategy profile unilaterally. Now we consider that if a participant deviates from defective-DF strategy to cooperative-CP strategy unilaterally, then that participant pays various costs $(c^m + c^{m'} + c^{pglobal} + c^{plocal})$. The total payoff of cooperate-CP strategy is less than defect-DF strategy, so All-DF is a Nash equilibrium profile and G is a public good game. □

Theorem 2 presents that we can never enforce an all cooperative-CP strategy in CDL game G, and therefore, a Nash Equilibrium cannot establish when all players choose cooperative-CP strategy.

Theorem 2 *In an iteration of collaborative deep learning game G with N mobile edge devices or edge gateways, if aggregated parameters are equally shared among all participants to build its local ML model, then we cannot establish All-Cooperation strategy profile as a Nash Equilibrium.*

Proof We assume that N number of players choose cooperative-CP strategy, and ready to cooperate in collaborative deep learning. In this case, the player pays various costs including communication costs $(c^m, c^{m'})$ and computation costs $(c^{pglobal} + c^{plocal})$. The total payoff of each player P_i is calculated by Eq. 7.1. Now, if a player deviates from the cooperative-CP to defective-DF unilaterally, then that player pays only local computation cost, which is defined in Eq. 7.2, this payoff is always greater than cooperative payoffs at Eq. 7.1. Hence, each participant has incentive to deviate unilaterally and increases its payoff. Then, the All cooperate-CP strategy profile is never a Nash Equilibrium. □

7.5.3 Fair Collaboration Strategy

Each mobile edge device or edge gateway sends their local gradients to PS and these local gradients run on auxiliary dataset to calculate loss value of each dataset. Each mobile edge device downloads updated global parameters and matrix of loss values from PS. Before begin the CDL game G, each mobile edge device, which is participant has to choose its strategy to play this game G. However, in the beginning of the game, the participant is not sure about his strategy, which will depend on other participant's strategy. Therefore, all the participants are in dilemma to choose a strategy between CP and DF. This problem is solved by proposing a novel fair collaboration strategy. K-means clustering is an unsupervised ML technique, whose purpose is to segment a data set into K clusters. Each participant applies k-means cluster algorithm on all loss values (one-dimensional data).

Algorithm 3: Cluster-Based Fair Strategy

1: Apply k-means clustering algorithm on loss values of each
   participant i.
2: Make the clusters
3: **if** participant i belongs a cluster with at least one other
   participant j **then**
4:     P_i , $P_j \in CP$
5: **else**
6:     $P_i \in DF$
7: **end if**

7.6 Implementation and Analysis

We implemented our novel fair collaboration strategy on real-world IoT based smart home datasets for analyzing the results.

7.6.1 Data Collection

For this experiment, we select publicly available ARAS datasets [2] to build smart home interaction model. ARAS dataset is real-world IoT dataset, where various

IoT devices setup to capture users' activities. In this smart home, the living residents did not follow any specific rules. This dataset contains two real smart home data with multiple residents for one month. It contains 3000 daily life activities captured by 26 million sensor readings in smart homes. The various sensors capture resident's various activities including washing dishes, sleeping, studying, talking on phone, and other activities. The most common sensors such as photocell, contact sensor, sonar distance, temperature sensors are attached at these smart homes. This dataset also has ground truth labels for activities, which enables to develop a new sophisticated ML smart home interaction model.

7.6.2   Data Analysis

We present an absolute set of numerical simulations to verify our proposed fair collaborative strategy. In this experiment, we simulate the proposed system model along with mobile edge devices based on our proposed fair collaboration strategy. We performed two different experiments based on participants. First experiment of CDL is setup among 10 smart home participants, and second experiment of CDL is setup among 30 smart home participant. On the demand of our system model, we partitioned ARAS dataset unevenly into different number of participants (e.g., 10, 30 participants). Each participant (e.g., mobile edge gateway device) is connected with multiple IoT devices. Some mobile edge devices or edge gateways are connected with high number of IoT devices; however, some edge gateways are connected with low number of IoT devices. The number of IoT devices connected with edge gateway represent the quantity of dataset, while the loss value of each edge gateway represent the quality of dataset. For unbalanced datasets setting, the data is sorted by class and divided into two cases: (a) low quality dataset, where the participant receives data partition from a single class, and (b) high quality, where participant receives data partition from 27 classes. Figure 7.4 shows unbalanced partitioning of the dataset, which is our first experiment. Smart home-1 generates high quality data where a high number of IoT devices are attached to the gateway device, while smart home-10 generates low quality dataset where only less number of IoT devices are attached. The following parameters are used for Algorithm 1 and 2: batch size $K = 10$ or 100, $H = 1$ or 3, $\alpha = 0.01$.

7.6.3   Experimental Results

In this work, we develop a novel strategy for enforcing the participants to cooperate in CDL. This proposed fair collaboration strategy brings together those participants who has similar kind of data in CDL. The game theory approach proves that participants start to leave the game if they are not getting benefit from each other. The proofs of defection is presented in Sect. 7.5. To validate the fair collaboration strategy, which is

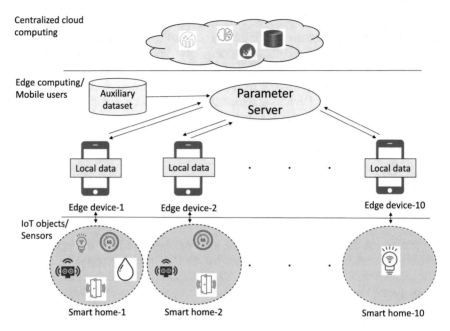

Fig. 7.4 Experimental setup of proposed game model

based on k-means cluster, these smart-home based clusters are shown in Figs. 7.5 and 7.6. The range of clusters depends on loss values of each participants. Figure 7.5

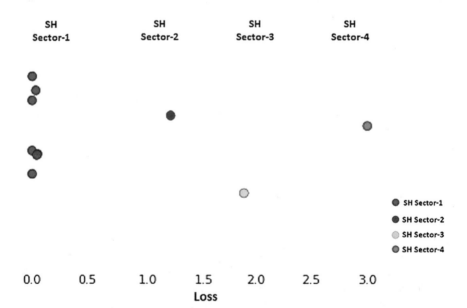

Fig. 7.5 Clustering visualization of 10 participants in one dimensional loss value

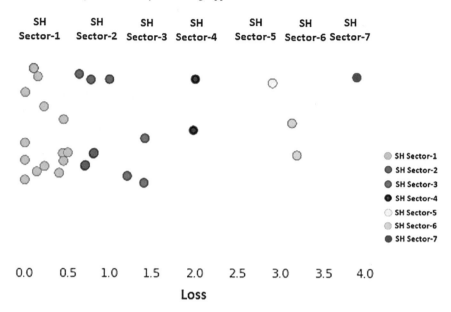

Fig. 7.6 Clustering visualization of 30 participants in one dimensional loss value

shows the collaboration among 10 participants using our fair collaboration strategy, and similar participants join cluster. There are 4 different clusters among 10 participants, which is referred as SH (Smart Home) Sectors. The set of each SH Sector: SH Sector-1 = {SH1, SH2, SH4, SH5, SH7, SH8, SH9}, SH Sector-2 = {SH3}, SH Sector-3 = {SH6}, and SH Sector-4 = {SH10}. The above defined set indicates that smart home-1 collaborates with smart home-2, smart home-4, smart home-5, smart home-7, smart home-8, and smart home-9, while rest of the smart homes learn their local ML models individually.

Figure 7.6 also shows the cluster form of participants, and the set of each SH Sector: SH Sector-1 = {SH1, SH2, SH3, SH4, SH5, SH6, SH7, SH8, SH9, SH11, SH17, SH18, SH19, SH20, SH26, SH27}, SH Sector-2 = {SH10, SH16, SH21, SH22, SH28}, SH Sector-3 = {SH12, SH13, SH25}, SH Sector-4 = {SH24, SH30}, SH Sector-5 = {SH14}, SH Sector-6 = { SH15, SH23}, and SH Sector-7 = {SH29}. Some loss values for the smart homes could be same and may overlap in the evaluation figures. These graphs show that more number of participants collaborates with other participants, while individual participants are less. The overall results also show that most of participants collaborates with other participants using our proposed fair collaboration strategy in CDL.

7.7 Conclusion and Future Work

In this chapter, we present a system model of CDL and introduce the issue of participant rational behavior of mobile edge devices in a CDL system. We evaluate rationality of mobile edge devices in CDL using game theory model. We establish the Nash Equilibrium (NE) strategy profile for each scenario, where the learning mobile edge devices are enforced to cooperate using our novel fair collaboration strategy in CDL. This is a first step towards a deeper understanding of the effect of irrational participant behaviour and resulting non-cooperative behavior in CDL. As a part of the future work, we plan to propose new and revised fair collaboration strategy that can handle overlapping clusters issue by applying more efficient clustering algorithms. We also plan to calculate the accuracy of each local ML model and apply our proposed model with other IoT domain datasets.

References

1. Abadi, M., Chu, A., Goodfellow, I., McMahan, H.B., Mironov, I., Talwar, K., Zhang, L.: Deep learning with differential privacy. In: Proceedings of the 2016 ACM SIGSAC Conference on Computer and Communications Security, pp. 308–318. ACM (2016)
2. Alemdar, H., Ertan, H., Incel, O.D., Ersoy, C.: Aras human activity datasets in multiple homes with multiple residents. In: 2013 7th International Conference on Pervasive Computing Technologies for Healthcare and Workshops, pp. 232–235. IEEE (2013)
3. Aono, Y., Hayashi, T., Wang, L., Moriai, S., et al.: Privacy-preserving deep learning: revisited and enhanced. In: International Conference on Applications and Techniques in Information Security, pp. 100–110. Springer (2017)
4. Aono, Y., Hayashi, T., Wang, L., Moriai, S., et al.: Privacy-preserving deep learning via additively homomorphic encryption. IEEE Trans. Inf. Forens. Secu. **13**(5), 1333–1345 (2018)
5. Atzori, L., Iera, A., Morabito, G., Nitti, M.: The social internet of things (siot)-when social networks meet the internet of things: concept, architecture and network characterization. Comput. Netw. **56**(16), 3594–3608 (2012)
6. Awaysheh, F.M., Alazab, M., Gupta, M., Pena, T.F., Cabaleiro, J.C.: Next-generation big data federation access control: a reference model. Fut. Generat. Comput. Syst. **108**, 726–741 (2020)
7. Baker, S.B., Xiang, W., Atkinson, I.: Internet of things for smart healthcare: Technologies, challenges, and opportunities. IEEE Access **5**, 26521–26544 (2017)
8. Bhatt, S., Lo'ai, A.T., Chhetri, P., Bhatt, P.: Authorizations in cloud-based internet of things: current trends and use cases. In: 2019 Fourth International Conference on Fog and Mobile Edge Computing (FMEC), pp. 241–246. IEEE (2019)
9. Bhatt, S., Patwa, F., Sandhu, R.: An access control framework for cloud-enabled wearable internet of things. In: 2017 IEEE 3rd International Conference on Collaboration and Internet Computing (CIC), pp. 328–338. IEEE (2017)
10. Bhatt, S., Patwa, F., Sandhu, R.: Access control model for aws internet of things. In: International Conference on Network and System Security, pp. 721–736. Springer (2017)
11. Bhatt, S., Sandhu, R.: Abac-cc: attribute-based access control and communication control for internet of things. In: Proceedings of the 25th ACM Symposium on Access Control Models and Technologies, pp. 203–212 (2020)
12. Chen, X., Ji, J., Luo, C., Liao, W., Li, P.: When machine learning meets blockchain: a decentralized, privacy-preserving and secure design. In: 2018 IEEE International Conference on Big Data (Big Data), pp. 1178–1187. IEEE (2018)

13. Chen, Y., Sun, X., Jin, Y.: Communication-efficient federated deep learning with asynchronous model update and temporally weighted aggregation. arXiv preprint arXiv:1903.07424 (2019)
14. Dai, B., Fidler, S., Urtasun, R., Lin, D.: Towards diverse and natural image descriptions via a conditional gan. In: Proceedings of the IEEE International Conference on Computer Vision, pp. 2970–2979 (2017)
15. Dwork, C., Roth, A., et al. The algorithmic foundations of differential privacy. Foundat. Trends® in Theoret. Comput. Sci. **9**(3–4), 211–407 (2014)
16. Esposito, C., Su, X., Aljawarneh, S.A., Choi, C.: Securing collaborative deep learning in industrial applications within adversarial scenarios. IEEE Trans. Ind. Inf. **14**(11), 4972–4981 (2018)
17. Farsi, M.: Application of ensemble rnn deep neural network to the fall detection through iot environment. Alexandria Eng. J. (2020)
18. Gascón, A., Schoppmann, P., Balle, B., Raykova, M., Doerner, J., Zahur, S., Evans, D.: Secure linear regression on vertically partitioned datasets. IACR Cryptology ePrint Archive **2016**, 892 (2016)
19. Goodfellow, I., Pouget-Abadie, J., Mirza, M., Xu, B., Warde-Farley, D., Ozair, S., Courville, A. Bengio, Y.: Generative adversarial nets. In: Advances in Neural Information Processing Systems, pp. 2672–2680 (2014)
20. Gupta, D., Bhatt, P., Bhatt, S.: A game theoretic analysis for cooperative smart farming. arXiv preprint arXiv:2011.11098 (2020)
21. Gupta, D., Bhatt, S., Gupta, M., Kayode, O., Tosun, A.S.: Access control model for google cloud iot. In: 2020 IEEE 6th International Conference on Big Data Security on Cloud (BigDataSecurity), IEEE Intl Conference on High Performance and Smart Computing, (HPSC) and IEEE Intl Conference on Intelligent Data and Security (IDS), pp. 198–208. IEEE (2020)
22. Gupta, D., Bhatt, S., Gupta, M., Tosun, A.S.: Future smart connected communities to fight covid-19 outbreak. Internet of Things **13**, 100342 (2021)
23. Gupta, D., Kayode, O., Bhatt, S., Gupta, M., Tosun, A.S.: Learner's dilemma: iot devices training strategies in collaborative deep learning. In: 2020 IEEE 6th World Forum on Internet of Things (WF-IoT), pp. 1–6. IEEE (2020)
24. Gupta, M., Abdelsalam, M., Khorsandroo, S., Mittal, S.: Security and privacy in smart farming: challenges and opportunities. IEEE Access **8**, 34564–34584 (2020)
25. Gupta, M., Awaysheh, F.M., Benson, J., Azab, M.A., Patwa, F., Sandhu, R.: An attribute-based access control for cloud-enabled industrial smart vehicles. IEEE Trans. Ind. Inf. https://doi.org/10.1109/TII.2020.3022759 (2020)
26. Gupta, M., Benson, J., Patwa, F., Sandhu, R.: Dynamic groups and attribute-based access control for next-generation smart cars. In: Proceedings of the Ninth ACM Conference on Data and Application Security and Privacy, pp. 61–72 (2019)
27. Gupta, M., Benson, J., Patwa, F., Sandhu, R.: Secure V2V and V2I communication in intelligent transportation using cloudlets. IEEE Trans. Serv, Comput (2020)
28. Hitaj, B., Ateniese, G., Pérez-Cruz, F.: Deep models under the gan: information leakage from collaborative deep learning. In: Proceedings of the 2017 ACM SIGSAC Conference on Computer and Communications Security, pp. 603–618. ACM (2017)
29. Jiang, L., Tan, R., Lou, X., Lin, G.: On lightweight privacy-preserving collaborative learning for iot objects. arXiv preprint arXiv:1902.05197 (2019)
30. Kayode, O., Gupta, D., Tosun, A.S.: Towards a distributed estimator in smart home environment. In 2020 IEEE 6th World Forum on Internet of Things (WF-IoT), pp. 1–6. IEEE (2020)
31. Kerschbaum, F., et al.: On the practical importance of communication complexity for secure multi-party computation protocols. In: Proceedings of the 2009 ACM symposium on Applied Computing, pp. 2008–2015. ACM (2009)
32. Krizhevsky, A., Sutskever, I., Hinton, G.E.: Imagenet classification with deep convolutional neural networks. Commun. ACM **60**(6), 84–90 (2017)
33. Liu, C., Cao, Y., Alcantara, M., Liu, B., Brunette, M., Peinado, J., Curioso, W.: Tx-cnn: setecting tuberculosis in chest x-ray images using convolutional neural network. In: 2017 IEEE International Conference on Image Processing (ICIP), pp. 2314–2318. IEEE (2017)

34. Liu, S., Li, M.: Multimodal gan for energy efficiency and cloud classification in internet of things. IEEE Internet of Things J. **6**(4), 6034–6041 (2018)
35. Yunlong, L., Huang, X., Dai, Y., Maharjan, S., Zhang, Y.: Blockchain and federated learning for privacy-preserved data sharing in industrial iot. IEEE Trans. Ind. Inf. **16**(6), 4177–4186 (2019)
36. McMahan, H.B., et al.: Communication-efficient learning of deep networks from decentralized data. arXiv preprint arXiv:1602.05629 (2016)
37. Melis, L., Song, C., De Cristofaro, E., Shmatikov, V.: Exploiting unintended feature leakage in collaborative learning. IEEE (2019)
38. Milioto, A., et al.: Real-time semantic segmentation of crop and weed for precision agriculture robots leveraging background knowledge in cnns. In: 2018 IEEE international conference on robotics and automation (ICRA), pp. 2229–2235. IEEE (2018)
39. Mohammadi, M., Al-Fuqaha, A., Sorour, S., Guizani, M.: Deep learning for iot big data and streaming analytics: a survey. IEEE Commun. Surv. Tutor. **20**(4), 2923–2960 (2018)
40. Mohassel, P., Zhang, Y.: Secureml: a system for scalable privacy-preserving machine learning. 2017 IEEE Symposium on Security and Privacy (SP), pp. 19–38. IEEE (2017)
41. Nash, J.: Non-cooperative games. Ann. Math. 286–295 (1951)
42. Nasr, M., Shokri, R., Houmansadr, A.: Comprehensive privacy analysis of deep learning: stand-alone and federated learning under passive and active white-box inference attacks. arXiv preprint arXiv:1812.00910 (2018)
43. Nikolaenko, V., Ioannidis, S., Weinsberg, U., Joye, M., Taft, N., Boneh, D.: Privacy-preserving matrix factorization. In: Proceedings of the 2013 ACM SIGSAC Conference on Computer and Communications Security, pp. 801–812. ACM (2013)
44. Nikolaenko, V., Weinsberg, U., Ioannidis, S., Joye, M., Boneh, D., Taft, N.: Privacy-preserving ridge regression on hundreds of millions of records. In: 2013 IEEE Symposium on Security and Privacy, pp. 334–348. IEEE (2013)
45. Pan, X., Shi, J., Luo, P., Wang, X., Tang, X.: Spatial as deep: spatial cnn for traffic scene understanding. arXiv preprint arXiv:1712.06080 (2017)
46. Pejó, B., Tang, Q., Biczók, G.: The price of privacy in collaborative learning. In: Proceedings of the 2018 ACM SIGSAC Conference on Computer and Communications Security, pp. 2261–2263. ACM (2018)
47. Rahhal, J.S., Abualnadi, D.: Iot based predictive maintenance using lstm rnn estimator. In: 2020 International Conference on Electrical, Communication, and Computer Engineering (ICECCE), pp. 1–5. IEEE (2020)
48. Rahman, M.A., Rahman, T., Laganiere, R., Mohammed, N., Wang, Y.: Membership inference attack against differentially private deep learning model. Trans. Data Privacy **11**(1), 61–79 (2018)
49. Rivest, R.L., Adleman, L., Dertouzos, M.L., et al.: On data banks and privacy homomorphisms. Found. Sec. Comput. **4**(11), 169–180 (1978)
50. Shokri, R., Shmatikov, V.: Privacy-preserving deep learning. In: Proceedings of the 22nd ACM SIGSAC Conference on Computer and Communications Security, pp. 1310–1321. ACM (2015)
51. Shokri, R., Stronati, M., Song, C., Shmatikov, V.: Membership inference attacks against machine learning models. In: 2017 IEEE Symposium on Security and Privacy (SP), pp. 3–18. IEEE (2017)
52. Wang, S., Tuor, T., Salonidis, T., Leung, K.K., Makaya, C., He, T., Chan, K.: Adaptive federated learning in resource constrained edge computing systems. IEEE J. Select. Areas in Commun. **37**(6), 1205–1221 (2019)
53. Weng, J., et al. Deepchain: auditable and privacy-preserving deep learning with blockchain-based incentive. Cryptology ePrint Archive, Report 2018/679 (2018)
54. Wu, X., Wu, T., Khan, M., Ni, Q., Dou, W.: Game theory based correlated privacy preserving analysis in big data. IEEE Trans, Big Data (2017)
55. Xie, X., Wu, D., Liu, S., Li, R.: Iot data analytics using deep learning. arXiv preprint arXiv:1708.03854 (2017)

56. Yang, Y., Nan, F., Yang, P., Meng, Q., Xie, Y., Zhang, D., Muhammad, K.: Gan-based semi-supervised learning approach for clinical decision support in health-iot platform. IEEE Access **7**, 8048–8057 (2019)
57. Yeom, S., Giacomelli, I., Fredrikson, M., Jha, S.: Privacy risk in machine learning: analyzing the connection to overfitting. In: 2018 IEEE 31st Computer Security Foundations Symposium (CSF), pp. 268–282. IEEE (2018)
58. Zhao, L., Zhang, Y., Wang, Q., Chen, Y., Wang, C., Zou, Q.: Privacy-preserving collaborative deep learning with irregular participants. arXiv preprint arXiv:1812.10113 (2018)

Chapter 8
Deep Learning Based Security Preservation of IoT: An Industrial Machine Health Monitoring Scenario

Aneesh G. Nath and Sanjay Kumar Singh

8.1 Introduction

The internet of things (IoT) is the collection of devices or objects connected to each other and to the internet, which can automatically transfer or receive data through different communication systems like Wi-Fi, RFID, Bluetooth, cellular, satellite, Ethernet, etc. Studies reveal that 127 new IoT devices are connecting to the internet every second. According to Statista [1], approximately 75.44 billion devices will be connected to the internet, and the connected devices generate 79 zettabytes of data by 2025. This creates real-time big data processing issues and security vulnerabilities to the connected devices [2, 3]. Moreover, there is another dimension in viewing the data sensing issues, which can be better described by 'risks' rather than security. Some of such risks are sensor failures, irregular triggering of sensors, noisy or abnormal data issues, etc.

Among the IoT applications in various fields, like health, traffic monitoring, agriculture, smart grid, and energy-saving, the IoT application in industry is of greater importance. As a slight increase in industrial productivity will improve the worldwide GDP on the scale of trillions of dollars, the application of IoT in industry invites a lot of research attention. At the same time, the primary moto of Industrial IoT (IIoT) lies in increasing efficiency and improving health/safety of industrial production while IoT tries to provide one more objective, i.e., the 'better experience' to the end-user. Other than that, IIoT takes favor of IoT technology to enhance the intelligence of the network and its security options for the automation of industrial

A. G. Nath · S. K. Singh (✉)
Department of Computer Science and Engineering, Indian Institute of Technology (BHU),
Varanasi, Uttar Pradesh 221005, India
e-mail: sks.cse@itbhu.ac.in

A. G. Nath
e-mail: aneeshgnath.rs.cse18@itbhu.ac.in

© The Author(s), under exclusive license to Springer Nature Singapore Pte Ltd. 2021   151
A. Makkar and N. Kumar, *Deep Learning for Security and Privacy Preservation in IoT*,
Signals and Communication Technology,
https://doi.org/10.1007/978-981-16-6186-0_9

processes and its optimization. The physical processes are managed and controlled by the programmable logic controller. They collect the sensed data and send commands to the actuators as the sensor-actuator direct communication is not possible. Finally, the overall network is configured with servers, computers, and other devices with internet services on top of it.

8.1.1 Deep Learning and IIoT

The ideology of 'right information and data at the right time for decision making' is the driving force of data-driven failure detection and predictive maintenance and manufacturing, through which organizations are transforming into the revolutionary Industry 4.0. Failure detection and predictive maintenance play a vital role in automation in the manufacturing industry. It ensures optimum cost, safety, availability, and reliability by monitoring different machinery components employing various sensors and other equipment. The availability of low-cost sensors and big data made data-driven approaches more popular as opposed to model-driven techniques nowadays. Since 2006, deep learning (DL) started to refine all the state-of-the-art models and has ever since becoming a rapidly growing research covering a wide range of areas. DL becomes popular in a short span of time of its automatic feature engineering, unsupervised pre-training, and high abstraction capabilities. Even in resource-constrained networks, DL becomes more employable well with these features.

Furthermore, DL has been implemented extensively potential to provide more accurate results and faster processing time. The internet-connected low-cost sensors have given popularity to modern manufacturing systems, which generate big data of machinery. Big data demands deep learning processing and analyzing capabilities, and hence DL plays a vital role in decision making [4, 5] of big machinery data. Compared to the traditional physics-based models [6], data-driven machine health monitoring systems offers a bottom-up paradigm for solutions. The detection of faults after the occurrence of certain failures are called diagnosis, and the predictions of the future working conditions and the remaining useful life is called prognosis.

8.1.2 Security and Risks

The security in terms of an IoT requires to satisfy integrity, confidentiality, authentication, availability, and access control. Among these, integrity and availability are the most critical features that an IIoT system required. The security service providers most often develop refined IoT systems that prevent IoT-based attacks, confidentiality, authentication, etc. These security requirements have been considered by big data technologies, and DL algorithms excel in security attack detection. In this context, this study investigates deep learning and big data technologies in the security of IIoT in view of SRF diagnosis.

IoT has been proven to be vulnerable to security breaches. IIoT devices tend to generate large volumes of data, with a large variety and veracity. This forces it to incorporating big data technologies to get better data handling and enhanced performance. Similarly, environmental factors, noise, and missing data issues are prevalent with IIoT data acquisition. They are categorized into the risk category rather than security in this study. When data is uploaded to the cloud to decision making, the security challenges become more complicated. The significant cybersecurity challenges and opportunities for cybersecurity with IoT and artificial intelligence (AI) has been discussed by Pan et al. [7].

8.1.3 Security and Integrity Issues of Rotating Machinery: A Background

Approximately 40% of all machinery in the daily production process is constituted by Rotating machinery, and it is prevalent in any industry [8]. Almost all manufacturing processes involve correlated rotating machines. All these machines have its limits, and when it goes beyond its particular limits, faults may occur, which affects the machine component's structural integrity. It leads to a detrimental impact on product quality and the performance of the equipment. Unfortunately, in most cases, these faults may also aggregate secondary faults. In one of such claims, high vibrations and wear of the bearings resulted from misaligned machines, leading to leaking shaft seals or hot couplings. Similar to misalignment, unbalance and looseness also creates several such impacts. These are called 'structural faults' [8], which is very common in rotating machinery. This study focus on the IIoT security issues and DL in view of rotating machinery fault diagnosis. In this, the primarily used IoT device is the sensor, which is used for data acquisition. In the rotor faults diagnosis scenario, the integrity and data sensing issues can be primarily reflected with vibration data, and a giant portion of works use vibration as the data source; our discussion mainly focuses on vibration based fault categorization and analysis. The unbalance, misalignment, and looseness are the primary causes of vibration in rotating machinery [9].

Around 40% of rotor related problems are due to unbalance, 30% by misalignment, 20% by resonance, and the remaining 10% are due to other reasons [10]. According to the fault categorization that we are considering, SRF is followed by the faults affecting the shaft, which are the secondary cause of vibration. Also, the broken rotor bar (BRB) fault has also been included in the fault category list. The most common. Bent shaft (BS), shaft crack (SC), rub impact fault (RIF), and corrosion and wear (Cr&Wr) are the faults that affect the shafts. They are frequently associated with SRF and are considered to fall within the shaft fault category. This categorization is shown in Fig. 8.1. Shaft faults are the crucial rotor faults considered a secondary phenomenon resulting from structural rotor faults. Usually, the vibration that affects the rotor is highly non-linear and complicated vibration motion such as periodic, quasi-periodic, and chaotic vibrations. The rotor-bearing system is a multi fault system that can have

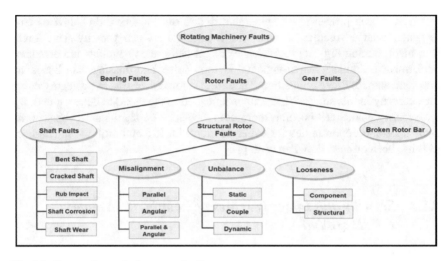

Fig. 8.1 Structural rotor faults categorization

a varying degree of nonlinearity. But the remaining discussion uses the assumption of a single fault rotor system, which often an idealistic situation.

8.1.4 Structural Rotor Faults for Case Analysis

When the distribution of mass in the rotor is not even then, it results in rotor unbalance, and it causes the inertia axis of the rotor misaligned with the geometric axis. The causes of misalignment are improper aligned couplings and bearings, thermal distortion, asymmetrical load, etc., which induce vibration in the rotor. The effect of misalignment is that the bearings have to bear a higher load than they are particularly designed for. Long-term running of machinery or improper assembly causes looseness of machinery; it is of two types, structural looseness and component looseness. The looseness effect is similar to unbalance, while component looseness causes detachments and secondary damage. The rub fault is caused by the contact between stationary parts and the rotor under tighter clearances. Thermal and mechanical stresses create cracks, which makes the shaft non-withstandable for normal operating forces. A broken rotor bar fault is typical induction motor rotors due to uneven current flow that create thermal and bending issues. The environmental factors intensify the electrochemical reaction, which causes corrosion-based faults on the shaft's surface.

8.2   Framework Description

Figure 8.2 shows an ideal framework which deals with an industrial system with IIoT based fault diagnosis and prognosis. The industrial manufacturing system uses equipment and production processes to create products, which is being controlled by the manufacturing and operating control module. This manufacturing process has to be monitored for the prediction of faults and so that it can be protected from unexpected shutdowns. Hence a module called a data acquisition module is connected to it. There are six main modules in the framework: (1) Data (3) Decision-Making Module, (4) Performance Checking module, and (5) Maintenance planning and corrective decision module.

8.2.1   Data Acquisition Module

This is step gathers the data for machinery diagnostics and prognostics. The sensor module selection and sensor strategy developments are the two primary functions associated with this module. The communication technology, especially wireless communication, helps in transferring the data to other modules. The data acquisition process transforms the raw data into different formats convert it into proper representations suitable for further processing.

The main parameters of data acquisition systems are sampling rate, number of channels, and resolution, etc. The wireless transmission of data is done by means of a Wireless Sensor Network (WSN), which comprises other wireless sensing

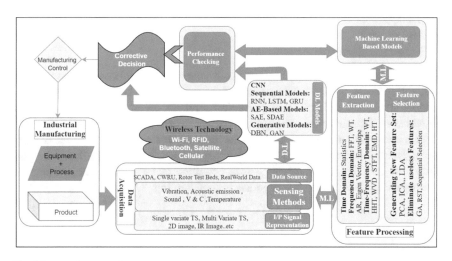

Fig. 8.2 IIoT framework

units. WSN is composed of different stages such as data acquisition communication, processing, and fusion. The mainly used transmission protocols are Modbus, BACnet, DNP3, MQTT etc. These have their security vulnerabilities as follows:

Modbus fails to provide authentication, integrity or confidentiality. As Modbus communicate without encryption, it lacks confidentiality. Authentication not provided since it does not have public/private key management. Lack of security check leads to compromise on the integrity of the data. Availability can be limited by flooding attacks.

BACnet contains no proper mechanisms for maintaining the confidentiality of data, resulting in a reconnaissance attack. Data Encryption Standard (DES) and Advanced Encryption Standard (AES) encryption mechanisms are used, but no procedure for providing authentication. It is prone to denial of service (DoS) attacks.

DNP3 is comparatively reliable but lacks sufficient security mechanisms, so that it fails to provide authentication, encryption, and access control. The non-availability of message authentication causes data integrity issues, and lack of encryptions results in eavesdropping and spoofing. DoS attacks are also common. The public key infrastructure (PKI) in IIoT devices is not feasible also.

MQTT has no encryption method implemented. By accessing the identity of a single client, all the client information is exposed to the intruder. Data integrity is provided by message authentication code like hash-based message authentication code (HMAC), which uses a lightweight cryptographic hash function. The commonly used sensors in IIoT are:

- Accelerometers
- Velocity transducers
- Displacement or Distance transducers: (Infrared sensors, LVDT or Hall-effect sensors, etc.)
- Piezo-electric sensors.

As described before, vibration sensors are most commonly used. From the data availability point of view, it has got certain drawbacks. The effectiveness of the reading affects the sensor mount position. Moreover, its contacting nature creates a number of disturbances to the sensor readings. There are three kinds of vibration signals are collected: displacement, velocity, and acceleration. The other sensing methods are acoustic emission [11], sound [12], voltage and current [13], and temperature [14] are more and more applied in condition classification. The statistics of sensing methods in rotor fault diagnosis is shown in Fig. 8.3.

8.2.2   Feature Processing

Feature processing extracts the information buried in a raw signal and suppresses the noise, and identify the most specific features of a particular fault, and presents

Fig. 8.3 Sensing methods in RFD

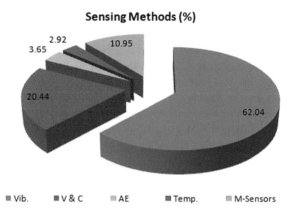

Sensing Methods (%)

2.92
3.65
10.95
20.44
62.04

■ Vib.   ■ V & C   ■ AE   ■ Temp.   ■ M-Sensors

the essential features of an incipient failure or fault for decision making. It uses a variety of signal processing techniques in two phases, known as feature extraction and feature selection. The signal processing techniques such as filtering, data compression, amplification, data validation, and de-noising are the most commonly used in feature processing. In feature selection, meant for selecting prominent features with techniques, eliminates unwanted and non-sensitive features using specific criteria. [15].

The signal processing technique uses various algorithms to preprocess the raw data and extract specific characteristic features of different faults. The significant methods under this are categorized into three domains: frequency domain, time domain, and time–frequency domain. Time–frequency distributions, wavelet and wavelet packet methods, empirical mode decomposition (EMD), spectral kurtosis (SK), envelope analysis, and minimum entropy deconvolution are some subcategories of these three rotating machinery fault diagnosis methods. These methods include Fourier transform, statistical moments, autoregressive, Walsh transform, power spectral density, and entropy. The popular dimensionality reduction techniques like principal component analysis (PCA), linear discriminant analysis (LDA), independent component analysis (ICA), etc. come under the first category, and people use Rough Set Theory (RST), genetic algorithm (GA) and sequential selection in second category methods [15].

8.2.3 Decision-Making Module

The decision-making module can be divided into four categories, that are (i) physical model, (ii) statistical model, (iii) data-driven model, and (iv) hybrid model. Data-driven and hybrid models are the most common models in today's fault diagnostics system. As the large amount of data generated from sensors and the historical data is available at any time, data-driven methods have proven to be ideal in identifying the fault and evaluate the machine health condition. Hybrid models are used when there is no sufficient data available for data-driven models. Semi-supervised techniques are also used in such scenarios. Diagnostics and prognostics are the two strategies in maintenance decision-making. Fault diagnostics take actions such as fault detection, isolation, and identification only when the fault has been occurred, while prognostics predict the fault before they occur.

The data-driven models are nowadays classified mainly into shallow learning (or simple machine learning) and deep learning. Based on architecture, design philosophy, underlying principle, and type of input, these models are further divided into subcategories. The ML models work with the features that are extracted from the feature processing phase, while DL-based models process the raw data directly. This feature processing demands extensive domain expertise and time. The most widely used ML classifiers for SRF are support vector machines (SVM) and artificial neural networks (ANN). SVMs are tried with different kernels, while various learning algorithms and activations are used with ANN. Under the instance-based category of algorithms, the k-Nearest Neighbor (k-NN) is popular, and the probability-based Bayesian methods are also demonstrated in RFD. Then the decision tree (DT), random forest (RF) algorithms are also used at large in RFD. Along with these models, simple classifiers like linear discriminant analysis (LDA), logistic regression (LR), etc., can also be found in the literature. The ensemble classification algorithms AdaBoost (AB) are experimented with by some researchers by combining the hypothesis of well-known models.

The deep learning algorithms are not constrained with the limitation of learning the non-linear relation of features. It learns higher levels of abstraction of input data with deeper layers, limits the time needed for feature processing, and avoids the need for specialized expertise in the domain. By multiple-layer deep architectures enables DL to find multiple complex features on their own. CNN's are the most accepted model compared to any other DL models in RFD. CNN's are influential with temporal data adequate solution for images, where the user has to provide appropriate input representation. Stacked autoencoder (SAE), stacked denoise autoencoder (SDAE), etc., are the autoencoder-based models commonly IIoT based RFD framework. From the generative hybrid graphical model category, multiple RBMs or AEs are stacked together to generate deep belief networks (DBN) has been widely used in this context. To deal with the temporal data, sequential DL models such as a recurrent neural network (RNN), long short-term memory (LSTM), gated recurrent unit (GRU), etc., have been explored [16]. Generative adversarial network (GAN) is widely used from the deep generative model category.

8.2.4 Performance Checking Module

This module visualizes and analyses the performance of the manufacturing process with the help of some key performance indicators. The primary tools used in this module are diagrams, charts, graphs, alarms, etc. It can either directly make visualizations from raw data collected through sensors or processed data which is delivered by the previous steps. These indicators help the operators to evaluate the performance and take decisions by visual inspection of the performance indicators.

8.2.5 Maintenance Planning and Corrective Decision Module

Based on the output of the performance indicators, maintenance planning and corrective decision are taken by scheduling optimization and other algorithm-based techniques [17] by this module. Certain optimization algorithms such as Genetic Algorithm (GA), Particle Swarm Optimization (PSO), Ant Colony Optimization (ACO), and Bee Colony Algorithm (BCA) are utilized in this module. The maintenance scheduling or other corrective measures are are the outcome of this module. Finally, the corrective measure is performed through the manufacturing control module, which gives necessary instructions to the manufacturing unit and sensors through IIoT protocols. The feedback control based on the decision from the maintenance decision-making module and other previous modules is the triggering source of this module.

8.3 IIoT Security Issues and Attacks

The data that IIoT deal with possessing different characteristics compared to the general big data. To better understand the demands for IIoT data analytics and security issues, it is needed to explore the properties of IIoT data. It is essential to address the fact that IIoT data is streaming data of large-scale. The IIoT sensors are distributed widely among the different applications, and they stream data continuously. This leads to generating data with temporal relation and at a huge volume. In connection to this, the property of heterogeneity of data due to the veracity of data acquisition devices has to be considered. Then in order to correlate with time and location information, timestamps must be included with IIoT data. The sensing frequency and other resolution information are also important. The data gathered from the industry is highly noisy. Irregular triggering of sensors and hard-working environments results in generating irregular and noisy data. All these issues will affect the security-related operations performed on data as discussed in Table 8.1.

Table 8.1 Attacks and security issues

Layer affected	Attack category	Description	Effect
Perception layer	Botnets	A malware that infects the misconfigured device or attacks the server	Attack the physical objects and affect the infrastructure
	Sleep deprivation attack	Disturb the sleep routine of battery-powered devices, and extend the wakeup period	Battery drains and shutdowns
	Node tampering and jamming	The node is wholly or partially undergoes physical replacement or wireless sensor nodes' radio frequencies being interfered with	It jams the node, and the service is denied
	Eavesdropping	The attacker overhears information that is passed via a private communication channel	Affects the confidentiality of the message. RFID is most affected
Network layer attacks	Man-in-the-middle (MIM.)	The attacker captures the total control of the communication channel	Attacker reads, changes, erases and inserts the message
	ARP cache poisoning	counterfeiting ARP packets of another host on the network	Enables impersonation for the attacker
	DNS Spoofing	Malicious mapping information forges the response of a recursive DNS query	Malicious mapping information has been stored in DNS resolver
	Session Hijacking	Attacker secure the user's session identifier	Attacker's session transferred instead of user's
	Denial of Service (DoS)/DDoS: U.D.P. Flood, SYN Flood, ICMP Flood, Ping of Death, Slowloris, N.T.P. Amplification	Malicious attack that aims in consuming resources or bandwidth of genuine users. Multiple UDP datagrams, continuous ICMP Echo-Request packets, TCP SYN Packets, large ping packets, TCP) SYN Packets, multiple HTTP requests are used by the attacker	Genuine users will not get service at the right time

(continued)

Table 8.1 (continued)

Layer affected	Attack category	Description	Effect
	Routing Attacks: Sybil Attack, Selective Forwarding Attack, Sinkhole Attack, Hello Flood, Wormhole Attack	Disrupt routing operation. Nodes are selected to break the network, absorb the traffic, selectively forward, tunnel the messages, etc	Wrong routing and message delivery
	Middleware Attacks: Cloud-Based- Cloud Malware Injection, Cloud Flooding Authentication Attacks- Brute Force, Dictionary Attack, Replay Attack Signature Wrapping Attack-	Information theft, flooding attack, etc., happens over the middleware components like a cloud by malicious activities. A malicious copy of the victim's service instance will be uploaded. Authentication attacks exploit the authentication process by finding the login credentials by a number of methods	Use users information to masquerade as that person
Application layer attacks	Malware	The devices are disrupted through firmware flaws using executable codes by the attackers	Disrupting the entire IoT architecture
	Phishing Attack: Spear Phishing, Clone phishing, Whaling,	Appearing to be a trustworthy entity, attackers extract critical information such as username and password from individual users, organizations, important officials, etc	Security breaches of IoT applications
	Code Injection Attack: SQL Injection, Script Injection, Shell Injection	Malicious executable codes are deployed into the address space of the victim's process. It injects SQL database statements, scripts, and commands	IoT application failure

8.3.1 The Way DL Deal with IIoT Security

DL effectively finds the security issues by a mechanism such as rule-based, signature-based, flow-based, and traffic-based. Traditional data flow and working conditions are predefined; it can successfully detect abnormal activities. But the frequent network updates and topological changes and to encounter intelligently planned attacks, the detection system should also be smart. Sensor network traffic flow is one of the main indications of the DL methods to identify security issues. From the anomaly detection perspective, DL considers the anomalies in a system as patterns that are different from a standard pattern. Any security issues mentioned in the previous section, as well as the fault conditions, creates abnormal patterns. For instance, the intruder's intervention in the connections of the victim creates abnormal traffic with the unusual data flow. These anomalies are categorized into three, namely, point anomalies, contextual anomalies, and collective anomalies.

A point anomaly is indicated by a data instance different from a normal pattern in the dataset, but the anomalous behavior of a data instance in a particular context is called a contextual anomaly. The anomalous behavior of a group of similar data instances compared with the entire dataset is called a collective anomaly. The abnormal activities of a host in a network are monitored with the Host Intrusion Detection System (HIDS) [18]. In remote devices also, these monitoring systems are deployed. Similarly, different network layers are analyzed to detect any possible security threats by Intrusion Detection System (NIDS) [19]. DL can analyze or detect Malware either statically or dynamically. In static, it is done in binary form, and in dynamic, the activities are monitored by executing binary files. DL can identify ransomware attacks where Malware encrypts the victim's computer for demanding a ransom for decryption. Similarly, the three types of intruders are detected by DL, named Masquerader, Misfeasor, and Clandestine user. A masquerader is a person who tries to get unauthorized access while the misfeasor tries to access privileged features that a user was not supposed to access. Clandestine user tries to achieve supervisory control of a system to avoid auditing and access control. IoT Botnet Attack Detection [20] is done by DL to avoid remotely controlling a device connected to a common protocol infrastructure by the attacker. By turning the device into a bot, a variety of attacks, including DDoS, is possible.

The situation becomes difficult to detect when there is no direct contact of the intruder with the elements of the network. As DL is capable of detecting small anomalies, it can identify the anomaly patterns that are difficult for humans to discover. In the case of Integrity, DL is a very effective tool to detect data integrity issues. A DL based system is trained using normal working conditions and sensor data flow. In the case of faults or attacks like command injection, the pattern difference is identified by DL models. The node that is compromising the integrity of the data is identified by the DL algorithm and can block it to maintain trustworthiness. So for the attacks targeting the security elements, DL is a very effective tool. The denial of service attack is very critical in sensor networks, which affects the availability of data to a great extent. DL methods are instrumental in detecting the broadcasting nodes, sources with unfamiliar addresses, an unreasonable amount of traffic making nodes, etc., which are easily found out by DL algorithms. It can perform the operation of a simple network analyzer to detect the DoS attacks, as well as analyzing the network logs as a human operator do.

In the case of attacks affecting the confidentiality of data, it can be used to find the intruder. If the intruder merely eavesdrops on the network traffic, it is very hard to detect using DL. The attacker has to change the network flow to detect his presence by the DL algorithm. But once the intruder engages with an activity that changes the network flow, DL will be able to recognize the abnormal behavior. Normally the malicious activities severe than eavesdrop attacks and are classified under other attack categories. When the security elements are targeted, authentication of the network will be challenged. The is a security control technique more essential when the attacks are targeting the security element. The 'prevention is better than cure' policy is most appropriate for these kinds of attacks. Encryption, good password management, frequently changing passwords, key management, etc., are important in this scenario. Even though these techniques have their weaknesses, they improve the system's robustness against unauthenticated access. Authorization issues are indicated by the change in the normal pattern of traffic from the verified user can be one of the indications of authorization issues. Such activities include executing abnormal commands, manipulating the sensors and actuators, or sending random traffic on the network. The intruder attacks will eventually be exposed by a DL if the sensitivity of the learning technique is high. The normal conditions of the system learned to find the abusive commands, unauthorized users, or intruders. There are chances of identifying normal traffics as attacks if the DL method is not trained carefully. But IIoT security matters demands this overcautious because an undetected attack could results in a higher cost than false positives.

8.3.2 Challenges of IIoT Security Implementation

(1) Data safety and privacy

Safety of data that comes from a large number of IIoT devices of different types that are being passed from device to device is very challenging. So the security rules should be in compliance with these components. Avoiding unnecessary and irrelevant data is also crucial in IIoT. When the data has to deal with mobile and cloud platforms, the data must be in compliance with its regulatory structures.

(2) IoT software related issues

There are chances that IoT software disrupts access to the computer system. As the number of IIoT devices is increasing day by day, this kind of threat is also increasing at the same pace. So, we have to reduce such issues and deal with the challenges created by IoT ransomware.

(3) Lack of upgradation

The IoT devices and software are not updated from time to time to deal with the newly araising security threats. The enormous number of IIoT devices are being manufactured every day to meet the demands of the market without concern over security. But even after the implementation also, the devices are not checked or updated for security attacks that are faced by IIoT devices.

(4)   Network issues

A properly configured networking system is essential for the smooth functioning of IoT devices. A number of factors in networking affect IIoT security. Hence the organizations must plan security policies to protect IIoT devices too. The attackers are able to achieve access to the network through open ports, buffer overflows, and DoS attacks. Moreover, proper care must be given to configure the gadgets to protect them from the attackers.

(5)   Data consolidation and conversion

Data consolidation and transportation must consider security concerns. In IIoT, the privacy of data involves a variety of processes such as data segregation, avoiding tactful information. Also, in order to avoid unauthorized access to the device, the data is encoded. But there is a chance of Malware if a large number of smart IoT devices are unable to encrypt the user data. Proper encryption of data that does not lead to any threat by hackers. Weak encryptions are not recommended as it causes the intruders to gain access to data during data exchange.

(6)   Strong password usage

Password security can be effective only if it uses strong passwords and keep it changing frequently. The IIoT must not use the default password and other credentials to enhance its security. Smart gadgets with weak passwords are most prone to hacker attacks. When the default passwords are inadequate, issues related to session management and lockout are present, and chances are there for the exposure of credentials, then the user interface with IIoT devices will become a failure.

(7)   IoT hardware

IIoT hardware has to be undergone critical examination of the chip manufacturers to make it up to date with the security issues. The battery backup issue is a connection problem that the manufacturers must take care of for a long-running backup.

8.3.3 Industrial IoT Security Solutions

It is observed that more than 40% of security issues are due to brute force attacks or Malware, even though a number of intrusions have been there. There are four tiers assumed for security called device, communication, cloud, and lifecycle management. But the speed of growth of the industry makes it difficult for the security solutions to cope up so that no end-to-end security solution is available. Segmenting the network is one solution in which those things that control the devices and equipment are kept as a separate network. A second method is to ensure basic structure, i.e., the credentials should be locked out after a few wrong tries and a change of default credentials upon activation. Imposing strong rules for multi-level password authentication can also control unauthorized access. It must make sure that buffer overflow doesn't affect the services, and it should not keep the ports open when it is used. Such practices will limit the chances for the intrusion of attackers. The firmware development and upgradation in a well-disciplined manner will help to solve the security issues to a great extent. Keeping up with industry standards and protocols, involvement, and collaboration in their development, etc., will help the industry to come out from a number of small security issues. Keeping a base architecture that addresses these issues, its standardization and inclusion will make the service providers be free from certain simple issues and concentrate on intensive security issues. This basic architecture provides a base security surety so that both purchasers and service providers have to least bother about the deploying platform security. So the services must include security as a part of the platform can only survive in the future.

8.3.4 SRF Case Study for IIoT Security with DL

We have done a literature review on SRF diagnosis works that have dealt with security issues of IIoT. But a very few researchers have attempted to address the data related issue that can handle the data security of IIoT with DL. One of such works was done by Yao et al. [21]. The raw data converted to color and polar images so that a number of security issues on data were overcome. Similar way, the raw input data converted to a symmetrized dot pattern (SDP) by Zhu et al. [22]. The signal's power spectral function was converted to a 2-D image form and was applied to a batch regularized CNN with VGG16 architecture by Yu et al. [23]. To handle multi-sensor data, a multi-stream CNN was proposed by Yuan et al. [24]. Some works attempted data fusion and/or future fusion methods. There were several attempts to make CNN suitable for multi-sensor data through data fusion or feature fusion methods along with structure alteration. Similarly, we can find 1-D convolution, multi-channel CNN, etc. Likewise, analyzing the DL works in SRF in terms of IIoT security perspective [25], there were no papers that strictly deal with IIoT security issues.

8.4 Conclusion

Rather than providing a general scenario of IoT security challenges and the role of deep learning in it, we have discussed the IIoT related security challenges in view of rotor fault diagnosis. A general description of the rotating machinery fault categorization, security and integrity issues, risks, etc., are given. Most importantly, an IIoT framework which deals with the different phases of rotor faults with deep learning security provision is explained. The layer-wise categorization of the security attacks and their effects is also demonstrated to understand the types of security attacks better. Further, the DL approach in IIoT security issues has been discussed, and the challenges were analyzed. The market situation of IIoT security solutions is described briefly. Finally, we have investigated the literature of IIoT security challenges in RFD scenario, which revealed the fact that, so far, there have been no serious studies that happened in this regard. Hence, we suggest more works in IIoT security research to provide a more reliable fault diagnosis environment.

References

1. https://www.statista.com/statistics/1101442/iot-number-of-connecteddevicesworldwide/#:~:text=Internet%20of%20Things%20%2D%20active%20connections%20worldwide%202015%2D2025&text=The%20total%20installed%20base%20of,billion%20units%20worldwide%20by%202025
2. Mohan, N., Kangasharju, J.: Edge-fog cloud: a distributed cloud for internet of things computations. In: Proceedings of Cloudification of the Internet of Things (CIoT), 2016, pp. 1–6. https://doi.org/10.1109/CIOT.2016.7872914
3. Habeeb, R.A.A., Nasaruddin, F., Gani, A., Hashem, I.A.T., Ahmed, E., Imran, M.: Real-time big data processing for anomaly detection: a survey. Int. J. Inf. Manage. 45, 289–307 (2019)
4. Yin, S., Li, X., Gao, H., Kaynak, O.: Data-based techniques focused on the modern industry: an overview. IEEE Trans. Industr. Electron. 62(1), 657–667 (2015)
5. Jeschke, S., Brecher, C., Song, H., Rawat, D.B.: Industrial internet of things
6. Li, Y., Kurfess, T., Liang, S.: Stochastic prognostics for rolling element bearings. Mech. Syst. Signal Process. 14(5), 747–762 (2000)
7. Pan, J., Yang, Z.: Cybersecurity challenges and opportunities in the new edge computing+ iot world. In: Proceedings of the 2018 ACM International Workshop on Security in Software Defined Networks and Network Function Virtualization, ACM, 2018, pp. 29–32
8. Chen, P.: Foundation and Application of Condition Diagnosis Technology for Rotating Machinery. Sankeisha Press, Japan (2009)
9. Patel, T., Darpe, A.: Vibration response in misaligned rotors. J. Sound Vib. 325, 609–628 (2009)
10. Fahy, F., Thompson, D.: Fundamentals of sound and vibration. CRC Press, Boca Raton (2016). https://doi.org/10.1201/b1834 8
11. Caesarendra, W., Kosasih, B., Tieu, A.K., Zhu, H., Moodie, C.A., Zhu, Q.: Acoustic emission-based condition monitoring methods: review and application for low speed slew bearing. Mech. Syst. Signal Process. 72, 134–159 (2016)
12. Lu, S., He, Q., Zhao, J.: Bearing fault diagnosis of a permanent magnet synchronous motor via a fast and online order analysis method in an embedded system. Mech. Syst. Signal Process. 113, 36–49 (2018)
13. Oumaamar, M.E.K., Maouche, Y., Boucherma, M., Khezzar, A.: Static air-gap eccentricity fault diagnosis using rotor slot harmonics in line neutral voltage of three-phase squirrel cage induction motor. Mech. Syst. Signal Process. 84, 584–597 (2017)
14. Lu, Y., Wang, F., Jia, M., Qi, Y.: Centrifugal compressor fault diagnosis based on qualitative simulation and thermal parameters. Mech. Syst. Signal Process. 81, 259–273 (2016)
15. I. Guyon, A.E.: An introduction to variable and feature selection, J. Mach. Learn. Res. 3, 1157–1182 (2003)
16. Nath, A.G., Sharma, A., Udmale, S.S., Singh, S.K.: An early classification approach for improving structural rotor fault diagnosis. IEEE Trans. Instrum. Meas. 70, 1–13 (2020)

17. Konar, P., Sil, J., Chattopadhyay, P.: Knowledge extraction using data mining for multi-class fault diagnosis of induction motor. Neurocomputing **166**, 14–25 (2015). https://doi.org/10.1016/j.neucom.2015.04.040
18. Cox, K., Gerg, C.: Managing security with Snort and IDS tools. O'Reilly Series. O'Reilly Media, Inc. p. 3 (2004). ISBN 978-0-596-00661-7
19. Mazini, M., Shirazi, B., Mahdavi, I.: Anomaly network-based intrusion detection system using a reliable hybrid artificial bee colony and AdaBoost algorithms. J. King Saud Univ. Comput. Inf. Sci. **31**(4), 541–553 (2019)
20. Soe, Y.N., et al.: Machine learning-based IoT-Botnet attack detection with sequential architecture. Sensors **20**(16), 4372 (2020)
21. Yao, Y., Li, Y., Zhang, P., Xie, B., Xia, L.: Data fusion methods for convolutional neural network based on self-sensing motor drive system. In: Proceedings: IECON 2018—44th Annual Conference of the IEEE Industrial Electronics Society vol. 1, pp. 5371–5376 (2018)
22. Zhu, X., Hou, D., Zhou, P., Han, Z., Yuan, Y., Zhou, W., Yin, Q.: Rotor fault diagnosis using a convolutional neural network with symmetrized dot pattern images. Meas J Int Meas Conf **138**, 526–535 (2019)
23. Yu, W., Huang, S., Xiao, W.: Fault diagnosis based on an approach combining a spectrogram and a convolutional neural network with application to a wind turbine system. Energies (2018)
24. Yuan, Z., Zhang, L., Duan, L.: Multi-sourced monitoring fusion diagnosis for rotating machinery faults. In: Proceedings—Annual Reliability and Maintainability Symposium 2019, vol. 1, pp. 1–7 (2019). https://doi.org/10.1109/RAMS.2019.8769018
25. Nath, A.G., Udmale, S.S., Kumar Singh, S. (2020) Role of artificial intelligence in rotor fault diagnosis: a comprehensive review. Artif. Intell. Rev. 2020. (Online). Available: https://doi.org/10.1007/s10462-020-09910-w

Chapter 9
Deep Learning Models: An Understandable Interpretable Approach

Reenu Batra and Manish Mahajan

9.1 Introduction

New inventions in machine learning and deep learning results in intense reverberations on low level quest like identification of objects and behavior tracking. In present scenario, many of researchers are prospecting how these techniques can also be useful in high level quest like healthcare, stock marketing, military and other decision making applications. As many of decision aided applications with machine learning are implemented in a significant way, users need to be weight their assistance. For any of the designed model most important artefact is interpretability. Interpretability defines that user must be able to understand and rationalize the output of model. In recent years many of researches has been done so far based on interpretability. For instance, multilayer neural networks gained an immense achievement in classification and prediction work by achieving near human accuracy. But they were not able to explain why certain features are selected over other features in training of model. They also provided a little to no information about why a certain route is selected over other routes. Nero-Scientific evolution was the main drive for deep learning models because of grasp in human brain working that was further able to differentiate between human and neutral networks [1]. Humans have capability of thinking which can help a human to predict, justify and rationalize through a series of choices. The justification characteristic of human helps to associate a measure of confidence for a decision making process. We can define interpretability as the human thinking capability in deep learning models. Human justifications must be relevant to low level parameters and their updates because of machine learning algorithms. In close inspection of human thinking process it is find that our brain working is not interpreted on basis of low level parameters. It is difficult to justify the predictions based

R. Batra (✉) · M. Mahajan
Faculty of Engineering and Technology, SGT University, Gurugram, India
e-mail: reenubatra88@gmail.com

© The Author(s), under exclusive license to Springer Nature Singapore Pte Ltd. 2021
A. Makkar and N. Kumar, *Deep Learning for Security and Privacy Preservation in IoT*,
Signals and Communication Technology,
https://doi.org/10.1007/978-981-16-6186-0_10

on learning model. Using the prior information based on model it is very typical to provide the justification. Interpretability concept is not confined to just low level parameters but it also can be defined at functional operation of model, learning algorithms and also at the combination of models and algorithms. Interpretability can be described in context of many dimensions that can be summarized as:

9.1.1 Transparency of Model Used

Transparency of model can be defined based on three variables:

(a) Simulatability: In order to produce every calculation step used in prediction model is processed on some input data. By making use of training data model parameters can be changed and that will help a human to understand the model.
(b) Decomposability: All model parameters can be described by the inherent explanation.
(c) Transparency of Algorithms: It is an ability to explain the working of an algorithm. For example, in Support Vector Machine (SVM) learning algorithm two variables named marginal point and decision boundary can be used to make choice for hyper-plane. In case of deep neural networks, at each and every layer non linearity added up in to features [2]. It makes hard to understand or know which features are being used in output.

9.1.2 Functionality of Model Used

Functionality of a model can be described using three factors:

9.1.2.1 Documentary Description

Output of a model can be described by textual semantic description which can be created by combining two models i.e. one can be used for prediction purpose and other one can be used for generating textual description of model output.

9.1.2.2 Visualization

Functionality of model can be understood by explaining the working of model. This can be done by proper visualization of parameters used in model. Although, many approaches can be used for visualization. For example, t-SME is one of mechanism used for visualizing high dimensional data.

9.1.2.3 Local Changes Description

Some times for a model used it is only requirement to describe or define only local changes incurred by a specific input vector for a given output class rather than explaining whole mapping of parameters involved [3]. In case of neural networks, all changes that are influenced by an input vector and to know specific weights it only needs gradient of output.

This chapter mainly emphasize on machine interpretability on basis of above said dimensions and also identifies all challenges while training interpretable deep neural network model.

9.2 Work Done so Far

In the introduction part of this chapter some dimensions has been introduced related to interpretability. Much work has been done on all dimensions to better understand the concept of deep neural network interpretability. Recent work done on deep learning interpretability mainly relies to understand the algorithm's transparency i.e. what a particular network learnt and why only this network.

9.3 Deep Learning Methods

Deep learning is basically a part of machine learning techniques. It mainly make use of many layers for feature extraction, prediction and transformation etc. In deep learning models information is mainly processed in non- linear manner and low level information used to process the high level data or information [4]. Deep learning mainly used in many of applications like speech recognition, information retrieval, image processing etc. For all tasks like prediction, recognition and classification many of deep learning methods can be used.

There are some examples of deep learning methods like convolutional neural network (CNN), Recurrent neural network (RNN),de-noising auto-encoders(DAE), deep belief networks(DBF), long short term memory (LSTM).Let us we discuss all these examples of deep learning methods.

9.3.1 Convolutional Neural Networks (CNN)

Convolutional neural network (CNN) is the most familiar framework of deep learning methods. CNN is best suitable for the applications related to image processing. CNN mainly consist of three types of layers. All these layers are fully connected to each other. Training part in CNN also accomplished by two phases named feed forward

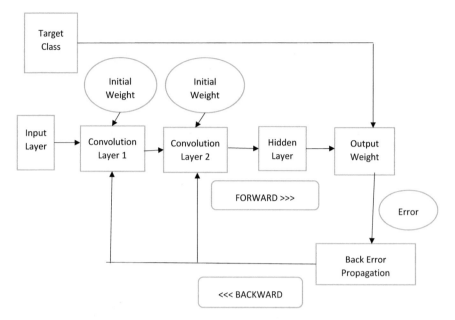

Fig. 9.1 CNN architecture

phase and back propagation phase. Google NET, VGG NET, Alex Net are some common examples of CNN frameworks used.

CNN architectures can also be used in crop yield prediction, monitoring of energy resources e.g. wind turbines, medical image processing. CNN mainly works by collecting small pieces of information and then process them collectively deeper in the network [5]. CNN model works by considering first layer of network (Fig. 9.1) for edge detection and further subsequent layers transform the detected edges in to different shapes and templates of different scale. CNN architectures can be framed in to energy computations systems, computational mechanics and remote sensing etc.

9.3.2 Recurrent Neural Networks (RNN)

Recurrent neural networks are mainly used in applications involving speech recognition, image recognition, text recognition and pattern recognition etc. In RNN architecture inputs and outputs are related to each other and there is a sequence of vectors of inputs and outputs. Connection between units forms a cyclic structure that employ the recurrent computations.

In RNN every layer works on the standard parameters (Fig. 9.2) and the model can be trained by using back propagation method. Many of applications follows a variant of RNN named bidirectional recurrent neural networks [6].

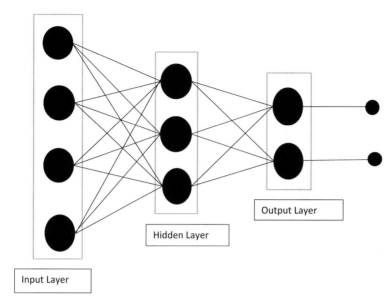

Fig. 9.2 RNN architecture

Bidirectional recurrent neural networks works on both previous output and expected future output. In both bidirectional and straightforward recurrent neural networks introduction of hidden layers may lead to concept of deep learning. RNN model can be used in applications like wind speed prediction, recognition of music genre, prediction of stock price.

9.3.3 DE Noising Auto-Encoder (DAE)

DE noising Auto-Encoder can be considered as extension of auto-encoder (AE). It is mainly an asymmetrical neural network model that mainly learns features from noisy data. DAE architecture mainly consist of three layers: input layer, encoding layer and decoding layer.

The model learns by using feed forward algorithm (Fig. 9.3). The concept of deep learning can be introduced by including multiple hidden layers in network. The applications where DAE can be implemented are electric load prediction, fraud detection, forecasting, and classification of images [7]. Many of cyber security applications may use the concept of DAE algorithm. DAE can be considered as best efficient algorithm used in deep learning modelling.

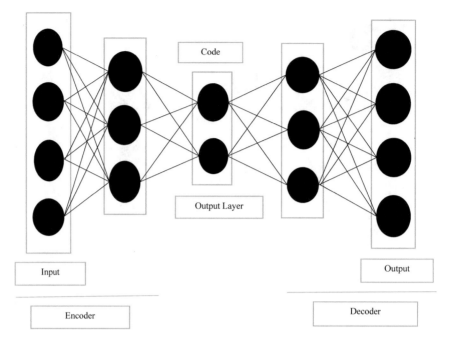

Fig. 9.3 DAE architecture

9.3.4 Deep Belief Network (DBN)

High dimensional data can be learned with help of Deep Belief Networks (DBNs). DBN consist of a number of layers. All layers are connected to each other except the units within each layer. The connections between layers may be of directed type or it may be undirected [8]. DBN networks are mainly implemented with help of Restricted Boltzmann Machines (RBM).DBN networks can be considered as a network of multiple RBM layers. Each RBM layer has connection with its previous layer as well as its next layer. There are a number of RBM layers in a DBN network.

In a DBN network RBM can be considered as feature extractor. RBM layers can be a hidden layer (Fig. 9.4) or it can be considered as a visible layer [9]. The applications of DBN network relies in time series prediction, recognition of human emotions, breast cancer diagnosis and recognition of wind speed. The main benefit of using DBN in deep learning is its high accuracy and high computational efficiency. A number of engineering and scientific problems can be solved with help of DBN networks [10].

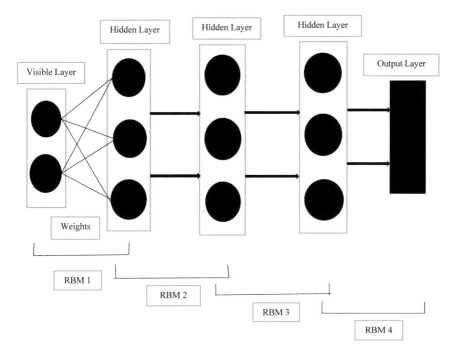

Fig. 9.4 DBN architecture

9.3.5 Long Short Term Memory (LSTM)

Long Short Term Memory (LSTM) is a type of artificial recurrent neural network (RNN) used in modelling with deep learning. The point to be noted with LSTM is that it mainly consist of feedback connections and it can process a sequence of data at once rather than processing single data point. The applications of LSTM mainly includes handwriting recognition, speech recognition, prediction of air quality and atmosphere and earthquake prediction [11].

LSTM architecture mainly made up of cells and gates. Gates may be of type input gate, output gate and forget gate. The values are just remembered with help of cells over arbitrary interval of time (Fig. 9.5) and the flow of information into and out of cell can be regulated with help of input gate, output gate or forget gate. In other words we can say that working of a cell can be managed with help of these three type of gates. LSTM can be used time series applications like prediction of data applications, classifying data applications and so on. An optimization algorithm can be used in training RNN using LSTM. This can be done in supervised manner with help of training sequence [12]. In LSTM, an error generally propagates backward from output gate but it remains in LSTM unit's cell. If we compare the LSTM network with conventional RNN network it proved to be more effective than that of RNN.

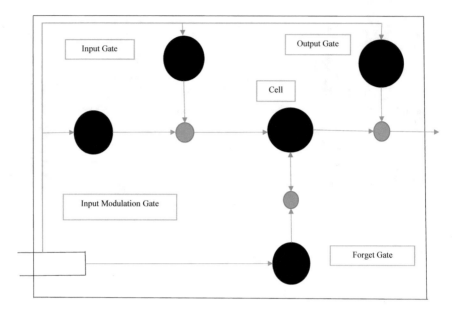

Fig. 9.5 LSTM architecture

9.4 Importance of Deep Learning

Deep Learning is basically a technique of Machine Learning (ML) that helps to learn computers by example. It is the concept of deep learning behind the driverless car so that the car itself can recognize sign of move, sign of stop or can find the mismatch between pedestrian and lamppost [13]. Deep Learning (DL) is basically a type of neural network with a number of parameters and layers. It can follow any of four fundamental architectures: Unsupervised Pre-trained Neural Networks, Convolutional Neural Networks, Recurrent Neural Network and Recursive Neural Networks.

With help of deep learning, a model can be trained to perform classification based on images, text and sound. With help of deep learning a high level of accuracy or recognition can be achieved [14]. As many advancements have been done in the field of deep learning that further achieving state of art results in many difficult problem domain. Many of applications including automatic colorization of black and white images, adding sound to silent movies, classification and detection of objects in photographs etc. Deep learning mainly works on large amount of labelled data. Deep learning can be combined with other technologies like cloud computing, big data that results in reduction in training time for development team members [15].

In the last five years there is a rapid increase in DL models in various application domains. Figure 9.6 illustrates in year 2018 there was a great applicability of DL models as compared to past years. Deep learning can be included in domains like

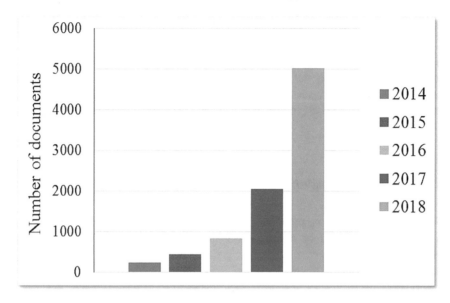

Fig. 9.6 DL models in five years

speech and text translation, aerospace and defense etc. Deep learning mainly follows the concept of neural network architectures. Sometimes deep learning model is also known as deep neural networks [16]. Deep learning model mainly consist of a number of hidden layers. On the other hand traditional neural networks consists of only 2 to 3 hidden layers.

9.5   The Future of Deep Learning

Deep Learning (DL) is mainly a technology revolving around an algorithm named Neural Network (NN).New methods and new technologies are going to be developed day by day. In modern technological environment, deep learning can be divided into three learning paradigms [14]. Each of these paradigm benefits in increasing the scope of deep learning.

9.5.1   Hybrid Learning

Hybrid learning paradigm consist of learning from supervised as well as unsupervised methods. In this learning a large amount of unused unlabeled data can be processed using deep learning methods. Hybrid learning can be used in many of business applications where large amount of data is mainly unlabeled.

9.5.2 Composite Learning

In composite learning a number of methods or models are combined which further results in a composite model. This composite model is more than that of individual model in efficient data processing and productivity [15]. Composite learning helps in processing data on basis of knowledge gained from various models rather than a single one model.

9.5.3 Reduced Learning

For the purpose of getting more performance the size and information flow of deep learning models need to be reduced. This may lead to perform with same or more predictive power.

9.6 Machine Learning Versus Deep Learning

Deep Learning is basically a part of machine learning. Whenever there is a need to process small data set for working it is always preferable to use machine learning for more accuracy [16]. On the other hand large data sets are processed on basis of deep learning.

The problem solving behind machine learning is to divide the problem task in to many sub tasks and then solve each sub task individually. At last result can be calculated by combining result of various sub tasks. In case of deep learning problem can be solved by taking problem as a whole and find the result. Machine learning takes less time in training of the model instead of deep learning. Deep learning technique is mainly dependent on high end machine. On the other hand low end machines are required for machine learning.

9.7 Conclusion

Deep learning concept is totally based on artificial neural network concept. Much of unstructured data can be handled with help of deep learning. It also make use of many mathematical algorithms that can work on data and further analyze data. This chapter mainly describes various deep learning methods used in processing data in various applications. Beside of deep learning methods this chapter also elaborates importance of deep learning in various applications. Deep learning concept can be combined with big data and cloud computing concept to enhance its capability in various applications.

References

1. Diamant, A., et al.: Deep learning in head and neck cancer outcome prediction. Sci. Rep. (2019)
2. Liu, Y.: Novel volatility forecasting using deep learning–Long short term memory recurrent neural networks. Expert Syst. Appl. **132**, 99–109 (2019)
3. Ludwiczak, J., et al.: PiPred—a deep-learning method for prediction of π-helices in protein sequences. Sci. Rep. 2019 (2019)
4. Matin, R., Hansen, C., Mølgaard, P.: Predicting distresses using deep learning of text segments in annual reports. Expert Syst. Appl. **132**, 199–208 (2019)
5. Nguyen, D., et al.: A feasibility study for predicting optimal radiation therapy dose distributions of prostate cancer patients from patient anatomy using deep learning. Sci. Rep. (2019)
6. Shickel, B., et al.: DeepSOFA: a continuous acuity score for critically ill patients using clinically interpretable deep learning. Sci. Rep. (2019)
7. Wang, K., Qi, X., Liu, H.: A comparison of day-ahead photovoltaic power forecasting models based on deep learning neural network. Appl. Energy (2019)
8. Aram, F., et al.: Design and validation of a computational program for analysing mental maps: aram mental map analyzer. Sustainability (Switzerland) (2019)
9. Asadi, E., et al.: Groundwater quality assessment for drinking and agricultural purposes in Tabriz Aquifer, Iran (2019)
10. Bemani, A., Baghban, A., Shamshirband, S., Mosavi, A., Csiba, P., Várkonyi-Kóczy, A.R.: Applying ANN, ANFIS, and LSSVM models for estimation of acid sol-vent solubility in supercritical $CO2$. Preprints, 2019060055 (2019). doi:https://doi.org/10.20944/preprints201906.0055.v2
11. Choubin, B., et al.: Snow avalanche hazard prediction using machine learning methods. J. Hydrol. (2019)
12. Choubin, B., et al.: an ensemble prediction of flood susceptibility using multivariate discriminant analysis, classification and regression trees, and support vector machines. Sci. Total Environ. **651**, 2087–2096 (2019)
13. Dehghani, M., et al.: Prediction of hydropower generation using Grey wolf optimization adaptive neuro-fuzzy inference system. Energies (2019)
14. Dineva, A., et al.: Review of soft computing models in design and control of rotating electrical machines. Energies (2019)
15. Dineva, A., et al.: Multi-label classification for fault diagnosis of rotating electrical machines (2019)
16. Farzaneh-Gord, M., et al.: Numerical simulation of pressure pulsation effects of a snubber in a CNG station for increasing measurement accuracy. Eng. Appl. Comput. Fluid Mech. 642–663 (2019)

Printed in the United States
by Baker & Taylor Publisher Services